"A wonderful tale of a woman's search for a good Icelandic horse that leads directly to self-discovery. Nancy Marie Brown has woven memoir, adventure, Icelandic Sagas, and travelogue into a book that will delight even those who don't find joy on horseback."
–Mark Derr, author of *Dog's Best Friend*

"The best journeys go two ways: out, into the unknown, and in, to what we might have known all along. Nancy Marie Brown's absorbing tale of looking for horses in Iceland is that kind of odyssey. Like the ancient legends she recounts, hers is rich and transporting, a true saga."
–Melissa Holbrook Pierson, author of *Dark Horses and Black Beauties*

"An enchanting, lyrical book about her search for the perfect Icelandic horse, her symbol of freedom and courage. You don't need to like horses to enjoy this book. ... It is terrific."
–Pat Shipman, author of *The Animal Connection*

"Nancy Brown's fascinating book reminds us that the pursuit of happiness often leads down strange paths.... A can't-put-down read about loss and healing, joy and discovery."
–Jeanne Mackin, author of *The Sweet By and By*

"A fascinating on-the-ground investigation of how a very different, very ancient culture understands, lives with, and trains its vital animals. Brown's book is unique. I know of no other book remotely like it."
–Donald McCaig, author of *Nop's Trials*

A GOOD HORSE HAS NO COLOR

Also by Nancy Marie Brown

Song of the Vikings: Snorri and the Making of Norse Myths

The Abacus and the Cross:
The Story of the Pope Who Brought the Light of Science
to the Dark Ages

The Far Traveler: Voyages of a Viking Woman

Mendel in the Kitchen:
A Scientist's View of Genetically Modified Food
(with Nina V. Fedoroff)

A GOOD HORSE HAS NO COLOR

Searching Iceland for the Perfect Horse

NANCY MARIE BROWN

For Chuck and Will

Copyright 2001 by Nancy Marie Brown

First published 2001 by Stackpole Books, Mechanicsburg, PA

Electronic edition published by the author in 2011

Paperback edition published by the author in 2013

All rights reserved, including the right to reproduce this book or portions thereof in any form or by any means, electronic or mechanical, including photocopying, recording, or by any information storage and retrieval system, without permission in writing from the author.

Nancymariebrown.com

Map by Jeffery Mathison

CONTENTS

PROLOGUE: Carried Away xi

CHAPTER ONE: Saga Land 1

CHAPTER TWO: Used to Horses 19

CHAPTER THREE: A Horse Like Elfa 37

CHAPTER FOUR: An Eye for Horses 55

CHAPTER FIVE: Travelers' Tales 71

CHAPTER SIX: The Business of Horse Breeding 89

CHAPTER SEVEN: Willingness Is All That Matters 109

CHAPTER EIGHT: The Dapple Gray 131

CHAPTER NINE: The Perfect Mare 149

CHAPTER TEN: Ghosts 163

CHAPTER ELEVEN: Well Mounted 183

CHAPTER TWELVE: Give and Take 205

EPILOGUE: Getting Under the Horse 221

ACKNOWLEDGMENTS 223

BIBLIOGRAPHY 225

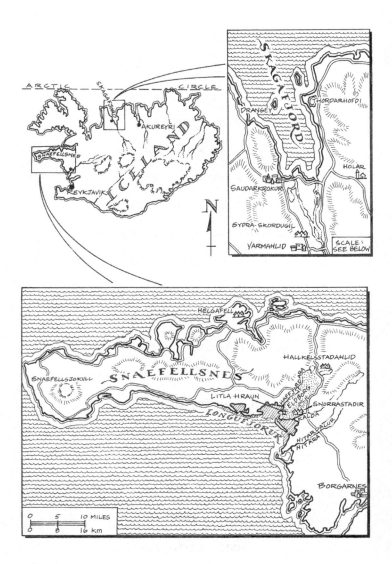

AUTHOR'S NOTE

Since an Icelander's last name is generally his or her father's name plus "son" or "daughter" (spelled *dóttir*) and not a "family name," I follow Icelandic style in this book, using first names for all Icelanders.

I have anglicized the spellings of most Icelandic words and names, changing the letters "eth" to "d," "thorn" to "th," and "ash" to "ae," and omitting all accents, but, unlike many translators, I have retained most nominative endings. Icelandic words in italics in the text are correctly spelled.

When trying to pronounce Icelandic words or names, it helps to know that the stress is always on the first syllable and that lengthy words are usually compounds. The letter "j" is soft, making a "y" sound in "Bjorn" or "fjord." The "sh" sound is not common in the language; thus the Icelandic word *keppnishestur* should be read "keppnis hestur," a show horse. *Hestur* is Icelandic for "horse"; the plural is *hestar*.

Many of the conversations in this book were conducted in Icelandic, although my notes were taken in English. Such quotations, therefore, are both translations and reconstructions. I apologize to any Icelanders whose words I might have misunderstood.

PROLOGUE

CARRIED AWAY

I could hear the horses before I saw them, their hoofbeats the high slap of cupped hands clapping, beating the punctuated four-beat rhythm of the *tölt*, the breed's distinctive running-walk gait. From our summerhouse, I watched them through binoculars. Pinpricks on the silvery wet sand, they shimmered like a vision out of the Icelandic Sagas, the medieval literature that had brought me to Iceland in the first place.

Briefly the horses took shape as they cut across the tide flats—necks arced high, manes rippling, long tails floating behind. Their short legs curved and struck, curved and struck. I would watch them until they disappeared beyond the black headland and wonder who their riders were, where they went on their rapid journey.

I wanted to go with them.

Icelandic folktales warn of the gray horse that comes out of the water, submits briefly to bridle and saddle, and at dusk carries its rider into the sea. For me, it was the watcher who was carried away.

CHAPTER ONE

SAGA LAND

Our summerhouse sat on the edge of the sand, in a patch of tall grass fenced round by lava fields. It was called Litla Hraun—in English, Little Lava. My husband, Chuck, and I, both writers, had rented it for the solitude. It had seemed a grand place to sit tight and write books when I'd first found it, on a visit to Iceland four years before; yet when we finally arrived, in June of 1996, we were fleeing far more than the common distractions of twentieth-century life.

Litla Hraun was a singular place of retreat. To the west its windows opened onto a long line of mountains, with names like Horse and Buckets and Old Troll Wife, that marched down to Snaefellsjokull, the Snow Mountain Glacier, a stratovolcano at the tip of the peninsula, whose cone seemed to float above the sea, coming closer on cloudless days. To the east, inland, we saw Eldborg, the Fire Fortress, a spatter-ring crater that on hazy, rainy days faded eerily into the mist. Between the two mountains, between ice and fire, were wet pastures cut by swift rivers and old volcanic flows. The rock was black rubble or red heaps of stones, coated with golden moss or broken up by thickets of waist-high birch. Where the hot lava had long ago rushed into the sea now stood brittle headlands; on their cliffs and ledges kittiwakes and other gulls nested in swarms. Elsewhere the green pastures stretched down to beaches, golden or black, shell-sand or volcanic ash, littered with wrack. Sheep and cows grazed above the tide line, and bands of horses roamed along the shore.

The house had the amenities of a tent. Abandoned in the 1940s, before electricity made it out to the coast, the three-room concrete box had no lights or running water. No road led to it: The gravel track petered out just past the garbage dump at Stora Hraun (Big Lava), where Kristjan and Margret and their three children, and Kristjan's twin sisters, and one sister's daughter kept two hundred sheep, fifteen milk cows, four dogs, and three horses—half wild, too old to ride. Between their garbage dump, where we parked the car, and our summerhouse lay a maze of tussocky pasture, salt marsh, bog, and tide flats, the mud of the flats grading into firmer sand cut here and there by tidal streams. A large rock in the middle of the flats acted as our tide gauge. When it was fully exposed, we could walk across it in just under twenty minutes, if we avoided what our eight-year-old son, William, named the "sucky mud." When the rock was half underwater, we had to hike for an hour around the rim of the tidal zone, as the sand and mud—and sometimes even the marsh, bog, and pasture—would soon be reclaimed by the rising sea. At dead low tide we could barely see from our windows where the ocean splashed white onto the beaches to westward. When the tide was high, we looked out onto a lagoon. At the full moon, the sea came in so close that for half the day we were cut off completely from our neighbors, with their telephone and washing machine, and from our car.

Yet those tidal flats between us and the apparent end of the road were themselves a highway. Nearly twice a day—more often on weekends—I would look up from my books or chores to see a string of horses, three to fifty in a group, purposefully crossing the sands. Bays, chestnuts, sorrels, duns, pintos, palominos, blacks, whites, and grays. Horses as blue-black as ash or the dusty gray of the lava chunks. Reds and browns like dry earth, stream banks, shell sand, or clay. Light grays and yellows and whites in shades from pumice to sulfur to chalk. And piebalds and skewbalds and paints, like snow lying haphazardly on broken ground. All were the stocky, stout-legged Icelandic breed, the only horse allowed in Iceland since the 1100s.

A man named Haukur Sveinbjornsson, I soon learned, often led the riders over the sands, conspicuous on his cream-colored gelding, Bjartur, whose name means Bright. Haukur lived at Snorrastadir (Snorri's Homestead), the farm to the south of the lava field that was our backyard. His holdings included the lava and the crater of the volcano, Eldborg. He owned the mouth of the River Kalda, the Cold River, and the tidal islands on which sea eagles nested and seals sunned themselves. He had marshy hayfields and scrubby pastures, a barn full of milk cows, a flock of sheep, and a stable of some seventy horses.

I had walked through his farmyard once four years ago, while hiking with my friend Anna, whose mother was born at Litla Hraun, and Anna's then-partner, Petur. Both Petur and Anna were artists. They prized the little hut for its simplicity, for its elemental setting, for the way it focused the mind. The tide marsh and the lava seemed to cut the place off, not just from the highway, but from clock time itself, and to all of us it had seemed a rough jolt when the faint track we'd been following that day dumped us abruptly into the midst of Haukur's farmyard. We snuck past the two houses, hoping not to be seen. "They might invite us in for coffee," Anna said. My spirits picked up at that; Anna frowned and walked faster. When we'd regained the wilderness, she elaborated: Haukur was related to her in some distant way, but the two sides of the family were at odds. She couldn't pretend to be polite. Not even for coffee.

Fortunately the family breach had been mended by the time my husband and I rented Litla Hraun from Anna and her mother. Haukur was delighted that an American family would be summering next door. He'd help us in any way he could, Anna had told me. Now I wondered, would he rent me a horse for the summer?

It was a week before I could ask him. We had first to fix the hut's leaky roof, clear out years of detritus (burning the worst), repair chairs and cabinets (there were crates of nails and odd chair parts in one of the rooms), and stock the cleaned kitchen with flea-market dishes and imperishable food. Then we drove round to Snorrastadir to see about a horse.

We found Haukur at the newer of the two houses, a modern concrete ranch. The three-gabled farmhouse, where he had been born and where Anna's mother had gone to school, was now home to his daughter Branddis and her family. That week it was getting a new red tin roof. Mingling with the work crew were the men who took care of the cows and helped to make hay, a pack of boys spending a few weeks on the farm in the traditional Icelandic version of summer camp, and a riding instructor up from the city to give the boys lessons and school the young horses. The four new summerhouses on the hill behind the barn were filled with tourists. Some of them had come by horseback—theirs was the small herd lounging in the sandy paddock. Others would rent mounts from Haukur and take a ride along the seashore each day of their stay. In front of the barn was parked a tour bus; its daytrippers had disappeared down the trail to Eldborg. Shaped like a crown three hundred feet high, the volcano rose up from the brushy woods beyond the pastures, blackened and ancient. The trail slanted up its side, over its thin crest, and down into the crater, two hundred feet down, from the bottom of which, wrote a traveler in 1814, "we had a most august view of the clouds."

From Haukur's kitchen the view held to the south, where the horse pastures rolled into marshes and met the blue sea. Ingibjorg, Haukur's wife, had of course offered us "coffee," which in rural Iceland means a smorgasbord laden with a variety of cakes and breads, cheeses, jam, smoked lamb and paté, slices of small hard tomatoes and wrinkled cucumbers, pickled herring or dried cod, perhaps some crepe-like pancakes stuffed with whipped cream or dainty crullers fried in horse fat or even some soft-boiled seabirds' eggs—all served up with strong coffee in sturdy cups and milk straight from the cow.

Ingibjorg hovered at the counter watching us eat. A blade-thin and fine-boned woman, bowed by the years, her blue eyes shielded by thick lenses but still with a snap to them, she seemed filled with nervous energy. We were keeping her from some kind of work, clearly, but I couldn't come up with those simple words one woman offers to another—*Can I give you a hand? Don't let us keep you!*—that allow the visit and the chores to go on together. My Icelandic was too rudimentary for that. It's a difficult language, with an excess of grammar. Though I'd visited Iceland five times in ten years and had studied its literature for seven years more, to converse on anything more substantial than the weather I was forced to resort to hand-waving and meaningful looks. Yet since neither she nor Haukur spoke English, while Chuck and William had no Icelandic, conversation of any kind at all depended on my translating. It took a great deal of time. William was soon bored and, after the cake was gone, Ingibjorg took him outside and shooed him toward a pack of boys picking rhubarb in the tiny garden, while she, profiting by the distraction, began hanging wash on the line.

Haukur was more patient. At sixty-four, he was ruddy-faced, with a short white beard accentuating his jaw, and sky-blue eyes that darted and probed. He was keen and alert, a wiry, small man, sudden in his movements. His large hands were gnarled and grimed from hard work. He tamped his pipe with his thumb and wiped his eyeglasses on the window curtain. He spoke slowly and enunciated well, staring into my eyes as if to lodge the meaning in my head by sheer force of will. From my letter of introduction, sent a few months before, he knew that Chuck would be writing a book about our summer, a book about nature along a volcanic coastline, and he knew that I had studied Icelandic literature. Haukur assumed it was this, natural history and literature—not horses—that we had come to talk about. He spread out a map and showed us where we could fish for salmon or sea trout, and where the sea eagles nested. It was against the law to go within five hundred meters of them during the nesting season, he said, and repeated carefully: *against the law*.

"Have you found *Gvendarbrunnur*?" He stabbed a thick finger at the spring where we fetched our drinking water. "It was blessed by Gudmundur the Good. It hasn't failed since."

Gudmundur the Good, I knew, was a bishop in Iceland in the thirteenth century.

"And Eldborg, do you know the story? About Seal-Thorir?"

I nodded. At least, I knew a story about Seal-Thorir. There was one in the earliest Icelandic history book, the *Landnámabók*, or *Book of Settlements*, a more-or-less factual account of more than four hundred people who came to Iceland between 870 and 930 from Scandinavia and the British Isles. One of these settlers was Grimur, the nephew of a Norwegian chieftain and the father of a boy named Seal-Thorir. According to the story, Grimur sailed to Iceland in an open boat with his wife, his infant son, his household servants, and all the wealth he could carry, including a sturdy mare named Skalm. He set up camp in the north, intending to look around a bit before he made a formal land claim, in the usual fashion, by riding around his proposed acres with a flaming torch in his hand. One day he went fishing, taking along his young son tucked into a waterproof sealskin bag tied tight under his chin.

The boy must have looked like one of the seal people, who can cast off their sealskins and dance on the shore in human form on certain days of the year, for a merman came up to see what was going on. Grimur hooked him with his gaff and hauled him into the boat.

"What can you tell us about the future?" he asked, for mermen were known to be seers.

"There's no point in making prophecies about you," said the merman, "but that boy in the sealskin bag will settle and claim land where your mare Skalm lies down under her load."

Grimur drowned on his next fishing trip. His widow, Bergdis, took the merman's words to heart and loaded up Skalm (whose name comes from the Icelandic verb *skálma*, "to stride with a long pace"). Bergdis and her son, Seal-Thorir, followed the mare's path. They traveled southwest to the edge of a broad fjord, a distance of some seventy-five miles, and, as the story says, *Skalm went ahead of them but never lay down*. When they next set out, after a winter's rest, the mare turned south again, going around the fjord and over the high mountains of the peninsula until *just as they reached two red-colored sand dunes, Skalm lay down under her load*. She had covered a hundred more miles. Bergdis and Seal-Thorir claimed the land from one river south to the next, and from the mountains down to the sea. They lived at Western Raudamelur (Red Sands), where an "ale spring" of mineral water bubbles to the surface.

From our kitchen window at Litla Hraun, we could see the red sand dunes where the mare lay down under her load. Once we drove the rutted road up to them, past a small sharp-gabled church and a cluster of abandoned farm buildings. We found "sand dunes" to be quite a misnomer. The hills were scoria cones: smooth heaps of red lava scrap spewed out at the tail end of an eruption. The bits ranged from flecks to fist-sized chunks. Gravity barely held them into hills. Climbing one, our feet slid back a foot for every two we advanced, and sent little landslides tinkling down far below us. From the hilltop we could see all of Seal-Thorir's land claim: large placid lakes, marshes drained into pasture and hay meadow, the vast jumbled black "sea" of the lava field, and far away the real sea, crashing on a long golden sandbar on the edge of sight.

Now with Haukur nodding encouragement, I summarized the story of Seal-Thorir and Skalm briefly in English.

"But where," I asked Haukur, switching back to Icelandic, "does Eldborg come in?"

Haukur smiled, pleased to complete the tale. "One night when he was old and blind," he began, dropping his voice to a mysterious sing-song, "Seal-Thorir saw a huge man row up to the mouth of the River Kalda in a great iron boat. He walked over to the sheep pen and dug a hole at the gate. That night the eruption started. Lava came shooting out of the hole. Where the farm was then," Haukur concluded, "Eldborg stands now."

It was queer to be sharing tales a thousand years old, an American tourist and an Icelandic farmer, as if I and a neighbor in central Pennsylvania had discussed over coffee the mere-hall scene in *Beowulf* or the Old English riddles of the Exeter Book. Queer and delightful—and why I'd come back to Iceland again and again since the first time ten years before: I shared a culture with the Icelanders, even if I could hardly be said to share their language.

In 1986 I was studying at Penn State toward a doctorate in medieval literature and in love with the Icelandic sagas. I'd been introduced to them in my second year of college by a professor of folklore, Sam Bayard, an impish man, small, bald, rotund, and hunched like a wise turtle walking upright. He had an impressive nose, which he periodically aroused with snuff taken from one of the half-dozen boxes secreted in his pockets. He would courteously offer me some, smile when I declined, then, snuffling up a liberal pinch, *harrumph* into a large handkerchief which he subsequently used to brush the dust off his breast. His snuff boxes were antiques, portable works of art carved of horn, cast in silver or brass with ancient scenes of hunts or warfare, shaped of handsome woods. Another pocket held a tin whistle, which he'd occasionally demonstrate. A fiddle hid in his filing cabinet. A narrow bookshelf along one wall was crammed with Icelandic Sagas, which he loaned to me, one after the next.

Medieval Iceland, a kingless land with long winter nights—and, historians pointed out, a ready supply of lambskins for writing upon, given its sheep-herding economy—had produced a set of texts that were "the envy of most world literatures," as the scholar William Ian Miller has written. About forty tales, some as quick as a short story, others stretching to several volumes in today's paperback translations, make up the corpus, along with companion works like the *Book of Settlements*. They tell of Iceland's Golden Age, the Saga Age, four hundred years of a free republic before the island succumbed to Norwegian rule in 1262. And they tell it beautifully: "This is not only the stuff of art," said Miller, "it is the stuff of a confident art that needs no instruction in sophistication."

In the thirteenth century, when verse was the norm in Europe, Icelanders were writing a vernacular prose that "achieved a height of excellence which can only be paralleled in modern times," declared E. V. Gordon, author of the standard Old Icelandic grammar book. Peter Hallberg, who wrote a college text on the sagas, compared their style to Hemingway's, with its simple, lucid sentence structure and finely calculated artistic effects. And there was none of that "metaphysical brooding," in Hallberg's words, that made medieval works like Dante's *Divine Comedy*, for example, so tedious.

From France and England, at the same time, came the tales of King Arthur: black knights who hove at the fords challenging all passersby, splendid queens in white samite who wandered the woods with their attendant dwarves. The Icelanders instead told of Gunnar of Hlidarendi, a handsome farmer outlawed for his part in a feud that broke out when a neighbor wouldn't sell him any hay. According to *Njal's Saga*, Gunnar had set off for the ship that would take him away from Iceland forever, when his horse stumbled. As he leaped from the saddle, he chanced to look back. "How lovely the hillsides look," he said, "more lovely than they have ever seemed to me before." He would not leave his home, he decided, but would stay and face the certain attack of his enemies.

Another saga tells of Thormod, who, fighting for his life on a cliff by the sea, finds himself suddenly grappling in deep water. Thinking quickly, he cuts his opponent's belt, pulls his pants down around his ankles, and leaves him to drown. "In an artificial heroic world, as among Arthurian knights, heroes would not have fought like this," wrote Gordon. "But Thormod was of the real world, where men fight with desperation and not always with dignity."

"The medieval Icelanders wrote the sagas about themselves and for themselves," concluded historian Jesse Byock, "thus opening an extraordinary window through which we can observe the operation of a medieval society."

It was a window I stepped through completely—not like Alice into Wonderland, where she was baffled and ill-at-ease, but like Lucy slipping through the magic wardrobe into Narnia: In no other books had I felt so at home.

I read the sagas first in English and then, when the translations proved stilted or old-fashioned or, worse, non-existent, in the original Old Norse. The professor who taught me the language, Ernst Ebbinghaus, was an icon of his occupation—high forehead, aquiline nose, a halo of silky white hair. He wore French cuffs and ascots. Rumor whispered of a mistress. I found him inordinately distant and stiff, traits I linked to his European training. He was

Old School, German-educated. He even knew Sanskrit. We translated bits of sagas into our notebooks, puzzling over the three genders and four cases, singular and plural, into which the grammar slotted the words, memorizing the twenty-four different forms of such essentials as "the" or "this" or "who." Ebbinghaus stood above us and explicated such words as *ójafnaðarmaðr*: the unjust, overbearing man, the man who upsets the balance of the world. He refused to hazard pronunciation. No one knew how to pronounce Old Norse, he said. The language was dead. Like Latin. I found that vastly disappointing. It would be a worthy life's work, I thought (people think that way at twenty-three), to keep the stories, at least, alive.

I passed my first set of exams and went to ask Ebbinghaus to head my doctoral committee. I sat across from him at the small oak table in his narrow office, stacks of manila-bound journals and papers and books thrown about, the one window backlighting him, his hands pressed together, the heavy gold ring prominent. I had been his best student for more than two years. But no, he said, I was not cut out for a doctorate. Nor, for what I wanted to do, did I need one. I did not want to teach literature, that was true. I had a job already, as an editor for a magazine the university published. I thought I'd like to write books about the sagas. Perhaps translate a few? *You don't need a doctorate to be a translator*, he said. Only scholars need doctorates, only linguists. And for them a translation is superfluous. In fact, he forbade any of his students to include translations in their dissertations, he said. *Forbade them*.

That created rather a dilemma. I was registered in Comparative Literature and the program required that all foreign citations be translated. Ebbinghaus knew that. His home department was German, and though he taught in Comparative Literature he didn't truck with their rules. He smiled and gave the little wheeze that was the closest he ever came to a laugh.

I told no one what he had said. I wondered: Was he right that I didn't need a doctorate? Did he really have my best interests at heart? Or was I merely a pawn in some game of academic politics, a way to make Comparative Literature waive its new rules? Could I do without him—though he alone on campus taught Old Norse? Should I give up my job and go elsewhere? (Could I pry my husband loose from his hand-built house and thirty acres of woods?) Perhaps Ebbinghaus would change his mind.

In the meantime I'd plumb my own. I'd make a pilgrimage to Iceland, as William Morris and Jorge Luis Borges and W. H. Auden and many lesser writers had done before. I'd see the saga sites, the landscapes I'd long imagined. I'd look for an idea for a dissertation—or a book.

I stopped in to see Ebbinghaus before I left. "Can I bring you anything back?" I asked.

"Two of those shaggy horses," he said, without hesitation. "They're like big dogs."

He would be dead, of a brain tumor, as it turned out, before I did bring home two of those shaggy Icelandic horses, eleven years later. And I would still be missing a doctorate. I didn't petition him again after I returned from my trip. I didn't ask if he'd reconsider. I didn't need to. I had found in the Icelandic countryside what I'd sought among scholars: a community.

My husband was with me on that first trip, though afterwards I often went to Iceland alone. One day we took a bus to a small fishing village on the west coast. We shouldered our backpacks and hiked four miles out to Helgafell, an egg-shaped hill that marked the ancestral holdings of the saga chieftain Snorri Godi, who died in 1031. Of all the saga heroes, he was my favorite, a crafty, pragmatical man and a bit of a trickster. His farm at Helgafell was still a working farm: sheep, cows, horses, a barking dog. I knocked on one door of the low modern duplex. The old man who answered, dressed formally in coat and tie, could not make out my first attempts at Icelandic. He called his son out of the milk house.

"*Snorri Goði— Búa hér?*" I asked tentatively. "Living here?"

The son, a lanky man in his early forties, in orange coveralls and a stocking cap, beamed. "*Já, já, já, já, já,*" he exclaimed, in the Icelander's long-repeated yes. Snorri Godi had indeed lived here—a thousand years ago, he said. He took off his cap and shook our hands.

He led us around to his half of the house and, as his wife and five children and her old crippled mother all gathered around the too-small table, and the coffee and cakes and cheeses and cucumbers appeared and then disappeared, he began to tell stories of Helgafell from the sagas.

One night a shepherd saw the whole north face of Helgafell swing open like doors. The god Thor was holding a feast inside the hill.

Occasionally he would take a sip of coffee, straining it through a sugar cube clamped between his teeth. He would look at me and nod, and I would nod back as if to say, "Yes, that's how I learned it." My Icelandic was so poor I understood only a tenth of what he was saying, yet it was enough to recognize the tale.

And enough to know that Old Norse wasn't "dead" after all. It had just shifted into Icelandic, changing about as much as English has since Shakespeare's day. Neither were the sagas of only antiquarian interest, the property of linguists who *forbade* translation. They were alive here, part of—and preserved by—the landscape. Icelandic schoolchildren study the sagas in history class, I discovered. Modern Icelanders trace their family trees to heroes in the old tales. Geographically, Iceland has changed little in a thousand years. The farmstead of Ingolfur Arnarson, the first settler, has grown into the capital city of Reykjavik, home to more than half of Iceland's tiny population of 280,000. But many other Saga Age farms, like Helgafell, are still being worked. The medieval past is remembered in the name of every hill and farmstead. There is a saga everywhere you turn. And, as I was soon to learn, there are horses in every saga.

A short drive from our summerhouse at Litla Hraun, down a red-graveled road that cut weirdly through black lava, lay the grassy Hitardalur (Hot River Valley), named for a river warmed by underwater hot springs that shoot up in hidden jets amidstream. This was the country of *Bjarnarsaga Hitdoelakappi*, "The Saga of Bjorn the Hitardal-Champion." I had bought a cheap copy in modern Icelandic at The Owl, a used book store on a side street in Reykjavik. The bespectacled old man behind the counter, whom I thought of as the Owl himself (there was something feathery about him, though in body type he was more an elongated heron than a compact owl), offered me "biscuits" and chatted happily in a patois of English and Icelandic about his son in Chicago. He was impressed that I was learning Icelandic. I neglected to tell him that I had been learning it now for more than fifteen years and still couldn't converse on much of anything except the weather. I replied, merely, that I enjoyed reading the sagas. He nodded, as if to say, *there's nothing unusual in that.*

I read Bjorn's saga at Litla Hraun, sitting in the sun on the grassy floor of an old sheep pen, the lava-stone walls too rough to lean against but good for blocking the wind. Across the dark expanse of the lava field, I could see the gray-blue mountains at the mouth of Hitardalur, where the action takes place. William, who sat lounging beside me, was reading *The Never-Ending Story*. My husband was off somewhere on his own, as he usually was that summer, the solitude he sought so extreme it excluded even his own wife and son.

Bjorn, the saga said, was a tall youth, freckle-faced, with curly hair, a red beard, and handsome features, a good fighter even though his eyesight was weak. He was in love with the beautiful Oddny Island-Candle, and with the consent of her father they were betrothed. Bjorn then went off to Norway to seek his fortune, as did many young Icelanders in the Saga Age, with the promise that Oddny would wait for him for three years. In Norway Bjorn fell in with another Icelander, Thordur. He was a good poet, although his verses tended to be mocking and spiteful. He was about fifteen years older than Bjorn. One night just before Thordur left for Iceland, he and Bjorn sat up late drinking, and the subject of Oddny Island-Candle came up.

Two years passed. Thordur, in Iceland, learned that Bjorn had been wounded in a duel. He paid some Norwegian merchants to spread the news that Bjorn had been killed, then he went to ask for Oddny's hand himself. Her father, a wealthy man, put him off. But when Bjorn didn't arrive at the appointed time for the wedding, Oddny and her father assumed he must truly be dead. Saddened but practical, Oddny married Thordur instead. She was content with her choice until Bjorn turned up, a year too late, having recovered from his wounds. "I thought you were a good man," she said to her husband, "but you are full of lying and falsehoods."

Bjorn's joyful father gave him a stallion called Hvitingur (White One) and his two white colts—a great treasure, the saga said—to take his mind off the loss of his beloved Oddny. Bjorn pastured one colt with a herd of black mares and the other with all chestnuts to see what mix of colors might result. But horse breeding couldn't keep him away from Oddny. Year by year, the insults and attacks escalated between the two men.

At the height of the feud, Thordur invited Thorsteinn Kuggason, a rich and well-respected man from northern Iceland, to a midwinter feast. On his way, Thorsteinn was caught in a blizzard and forced to take refuge at Bjorn's house. By the time the weather broke, he had agreed to try to make peace between Bjorn and Thordur. To seal this agreement, Bjorn gave Thorsteinn a magnificent gift of four horses: a white stallion (one of Hvitingur's colts) and three chestnut mares. Thorsteinn asked Bjorn to keep the horses for him until he saw how the peacemaking went. Ironically, it was in the springtime, as he was trimming the white stallion's mane to present him to Thorsteinn Kuggason, that Bjorn was set upon by Thordur and killed.

Bjorn's was a classic saga, spun of honor and friendship, love and betrayal, all set against the harsh reality of medieval life. I felt particularly moved by Oddny's role: When she learned of Bjorn's death, she fell down in a faint. From then on, though she lived many years, she was out of her wits. She was only happy on horseback, the saga said, with her husband leading her about.

I closed the book and looked out at the gray-blue mountains that gated Hitardalur. I understood Oddny's predicament, caught between duty and desire. Although the summer at Litla Hraun had been my idea all along, it hadn't turned out as I'd planned. I was used to being in Iceland alone. Chuck found the language daunting. He didn't know the stories latched to every rock. He preferred to be away from people, to vacation out in nature. The logistics and expense made it best to leave him home—especially after William was born. (Someone had to babysit.)

But those were mostly excuses. I *preferred* being in Iceland alone. As the years passed, Iceland became my place of escape, of refuge, of freedom from marriage and family and professional duties, a world elsewhere, outside of the routine, where I could redefine myself—as a novelist, as a medieval scholar—where I could do as I pleased without negotiation. For me, as for the poet W. H. Audun, Iceland was "holy earth." Auden told an Icelandic newspaperman, "This memory is background for everything I do. Iceland is the sun which colours the mountains without being there." And yet, on what became my biennial pilgrimages, I was often achingly lonely. The thought of my family, so far away, could bring me to tears.

Then on one of my excursions my artist friends, Petur and Anna, took me to a little house in the lava, within sight (and a muddy hike) of civilization, but secluded enough for any naturalist. After three years of scheming and persuading, I convinced my family it was our perfect summerhouse. Chuck could write a book of natural history. (And the advance from his publisher would pay the rent.) William, then seven, could play outlaw in the lava caves, and I would show him the secret way, by ducking and squirming through a deep cleft in the rocks, to sneak up on the seals on their sunning grounds. And I would have both freedom and family: I would use the house as home base, taking the car—a luxury also underwritten by Chuck's book (I'd rarely rented a car in Iceland, they were so expensive)—and poke about in valleys impossible to reach by bus. There were some saga sites I wanted to find, tied to an early settler who intrigued me, a strong woman who was a chieftain in her own right, having brought twenty-five free-born men from the Outer Hebrides to Iceland in the late 800s. I intended to write a book about her. I called her Unna Djup.

As soon as Chuck sold the idea of the nature book, *Summer at Little Lava*, to a New York publisher, I set off for Scotland to find Unna Djup's homesite and begin to trace her life. While I was away, Chuck found his beloved seventy-three-year-old mother stabbed to death in the back bedroom of his childhood home in our quiet college town.

I flew home from the Outer Hebrides and put Unna Djup in a drawer.

Our summer at Little Lava became, not an adventure, but a time of quiet healing. Compared to a brutal murder, nothing

Iceland could throw at us—no rocks, no rain, no wild sea—could be frightening. The vast Icelandic sky showed no evil for miles. Even the crater and the glacier, our two compass points, seemed benevolent, while the people who lived around us—whom we had not told about the murder—were all as inviting and helpful as if we were old friends.

Yet as I sat reading companionably with my son, waiting for the return of my husband, whose best therapy seemed to be long walks in the lava or on the sands, alone, I often felt trapped, fenced in, hobbled by responsibility, and I'd think of what the murder, in its harsh voice, had hissed to me: *Hurry. Death may come sooner than you think. If there's something you've been dreaming of, make it happen. Do it now.*

CHAPTER TWO

USED TO HORSES

The summer we lived at Litla Hraun was sunnier than any of our neighbors could remember, and the number of horse-trekkers was high. Yet I'd sing out every time I saw them, and stop, and watch. I lived in a state of longing. They were Iceland now, those people riding by. Adventure, escape, a break from the confines of my life, a declaration that I was more than the duties I'd taken on. I had to go with them. I needed a horse.

The muddy hike between our summerhouse and our car, I'd learned from Haukur the day we introduced ourselves at Snorrastadir, was only a small part of the Longufjorur, or Long Beaches, a forty-mile riding trail uncovered only at low tide. The route had been in use since the Saga Age. The saga chieftain Snorri Godi himself had taken it at least once, when he rode down from Helgafell to fetch the corpse of his father-in-law, Killer-Styr, murdered at Jorfi, the next farm to the south of Snorrastadir.

Haukur had grown up riding the Longufjorur, and often he hired out now as a guide to tour groups. He had several trips scheduled for the summer, he told us.

"I'm used to horses," I said. "Can you rent me one? To keep at Litla Hraun?"

Haukur frowned.

"What did you ask him?" my husband whispered, alarmed at the abrupt stop in the conversation.

I shrugged at him, smiled ingenuously at Haukur. On earlier trips to Iceland I had taken two six-day treks by horseback into the rugged highlands, riding between the glaciers to a valley of hot-springs—although I'd had very little previous riding experience (I began taking lessons only after surviving the second trek). *Are you used to horses?* the horse trekkers would ask, and I had always answered yes. There was no one to rebut me. The same technique made up for my poor language skills. I would nod and smile and snatch at every word I understood, hoping that my pat answer, *I'd like to try it*, wouldn't be too out of place. (Only once did my method seriously fail, landing me in a two-hour demonstration of an institutional-strength vacuum cleaner when my hosts invited me to go see the *ryksuga*. I thought it was some kind of bird.)

Much later I would learn that the Icelandic phrase "used to horses" meant a proficiency that could take a lifetime to perfect. Haukur considered himself only ninety percent "used to horses" and he had been riding all his life. But Haukur was a gentleman. He did not call my bluff. He pulled the map toward him and with the stem of his unlit pipe traced a long wavy line down the coast. "It's a dangerous path," he warned, wagging his pipe, "if you don't know the tides."

The Longufjorur cut the mouths of several rivers, some of them deep-channeled salmon streams, others edged with quicksand. The safe paths shift from storm to storm, while the force of the wind and its direction, and the fullness of the moon, decide how fast a rider must cross. Ebenezer Henderson, a Scottish churchman who traveled throughout Iceland in 1814, described the crossing well:

"We advanced at a noble rate, it being necessary to keep our horses every now and then at the gallop, in order to escape being overtaken by the tide before we reached the land. At one time we were nearly two miles from the shore; and I must confess I felt rather uneasy, while my companion was relating the number of travelers who had lost their lives in consequence of having been unexpectedly surrounded by the sea."

"I'd like to try it," I persevered. "May I ride with you some day?"

Now Haukur looked pleased. He leaned over and with a devilish twinkle in his eye, took my hand between both of his. "You will take a horse across the Longufjorur with me some day," he declared.

I thanked him and slipped my hand out, with the excuse of folding up the map. Suddenly a hot blush crept up my neck. Had I used the verb *ríða* instead of the standard phrase, *að fara á hestbaki*, "to go by horseback"? *Ríða*, which sounded so much like our verb "to ride," but which colloquially meant "to have sexual intercourse"? I glanced up to see Haukur trying to subdue his bright smile. He winked. I ducked my head.

But from then on, as I watched the horses and riders cross the sands, I was hoping to see Haukur leading a horse with an empty saddle.

One morning when I hiked across the flats with a sack of dirty laundry on my back (which Margret of Stora Hraun would kindly wash for us), I saw a note in a plastic bag stuck under the windshield wiper of our car.

"Haukur called," it said, in carefully printed Icelandic. "You can ride with him tomorrow."

I hurried on to Stora Hraun to call him back.

Come by an hour before low tide, he had said. But the tide falls faster in Litla Hraun's shallow lagoon than by Snorrastadir, where the River Kalda meets the sea. Chuck and William and I, leaving Litla Hraun as soon as the water let us cross to our car, got to Haukur's house quite early. Ingibjorg set out coffee, but conversation was even more difficult than before: I was too excited to concentrate; Haukur, watching out the window, mumbled distractedly into the curtains. It was unclear even how many days I'd be gone. "You'll see us coming," Haukur said to my husband, in a tongue that was gibberish to him.

Across the river the paddock was full of horses. Haukur was keeping an eye out for their riders, a group of ten from the city of Reykjavik who'd slept in the summerhouses on the hill behind the barn. They were riding down the Longufjorur half way, he said, then turning inland, going up and over the mountains to meet a ferry that would take them over the fjord to ride again to land's end, to a tall cliff that Icelanders consider the westernmost point of Europe. They had hired Haukur to guide them across the sands to the farm of Stakkhamar, where he'd be picking up another tour group to guide back.

"And how long will that take," I asked, retranslating my husband's question.

Haukur chewed the stem of his unlit pipe and winked at me. He understood more English than he'd admit. "You'll see us coming," he told my husband again.

How do you find Haukur? one of our neighbors at Stora Hraun had once asked me in her high-school English. The horseman, guiding a party of tourists past their house, had stopped to give me a bearhug and deliver an off-color joke. I shrugged. By then I had met Haukur several times on the sands. I knew what she meant, but I also remembered the grace with which he'd covered over my grammatical faux pas. *He's very good with horses*, I said, and we both grinned. When the tourists later had trouble catching their mounts—and had riled up one black so much he broke through a barbed-wire fence and cut himself—Haukur proved my point. Crooning a deep slow tune way down in his throat, he soothed the startled black until it accepted being caught. For him, horses were no anachronism. Horses were part of his life, a knot in the net of work and ritual, duty and affection, that bound him to the land. I'd seen him touch a horse the way he handled his infant granddaughter, sing to it, speak with the same wonderment and bemusement. On horseback he was transformed; from a hardscrabble farmer he became, as the Icelandic poet Einar Benediktsson wrote, "king for a while."

Now Haukur saw the city riders gathering down by the barn. He filled his coat pockets with sandwiches and small cartons of juice, and told me to come out and saddle up. I said goodbye to my family, and grabbed my raincoat and riding helmet out of the car.

"You are used to horses?" he asked, eyeing my helmet suspiciously. None of the other riders, I noticed, had a helmet.

"Oh yes," I answered, as I always had before. By now there was at least some truth to it. Since the last time I had ridden in Iceland, two years ago, I had been taking lessons in English hunter-jumper technique—although I hadn't yet advanced enough to dare a jump. I could put on a bridle, pick out a hoof, adjust my stirrups. I knew enough not to startle a horse or walk up on one from behind. I was used to them.

The horses Haukur had picked for me to ride, a chestnut and a dun, were two of his best "family horses," he said, willing and spunky, but "soft" and eager to please. They would give me a smooth tolt on loose reins with little encouragement. Elfa ("Elf"), in addition, was five-gaited. She possessed not only walk, trot, and canter, but both of the special gaits Icelandics are known for: tolt and pace—though only "a little pace," Haukur said.

She jumped and danced about until Haukur slipped the bit into her mouth. Then she stood quietly, relaxed, chewing the bit.

Haukur dropped the reins and left her untied while he brushed the dust off her back with the flat of his hand. Her withers were level with his breast. He is not a tall man, and I guessed her height at under fourteen hands, technically classifying her as a pony—a word that to an Icelander is an insult. A pony is a child's pet. Polo ponies and cow ponies notwithstanding, bilingual Icelanders scowl at the word. American owners of Icelandic horses can be even more rigid. "I always tell people we don't say the P-word around here," an Icelandic horse owner from Texas told *Horse Illustrated* in 1994. Yet in looks, Haukur's horses seemed more like graduated ponies than the spider-legged, camel-high Thoroughbreds I was used to riding. Elfa was shaggy even in her summer coat, with a bushy mane and hairy fetlocks and a tail that touched the ground. Thick-necked, barrel-round, with a broad chest, long back, sturdy legs, and dainty feet, she had the powerful, prehistoric frame of a Przewalski's horse, or the ancient steeds depicted in the cave paintings at Lascaux. She was the archetypal, all-purpose horse—if a little plainer than I'd like, her dun color a dull tan without the zebra-striped hocks and tri-colored manes of some Icelandic duns I'd seen.

Pony was an acceptable word in the Icelandic horse world, I soon learned, if used as a verb in describing a common way to travel. When Haukur had saddled Elfa and handed me her rein, he unsnapped the chestnut mare's rein and threaded it through both rings on her bridle, leaving one end of it loose. I was to pony her, he said—leading her along, bridled but not saddled. The city riders intended to let their spare horses run free in a herd beside us, a plan that made Haukur shake his head and mutter. When we came to a rest stop and needed a fresh mount, he explained, he and I could switch saddles from one horse to another and then relax; they would be running around cutting their new mounts out of the herd and trying to catch them in an unfenced field. That each of us would bring more than one horse on a day's ride was never questioned: In this way, Icelanders can keep up a fast pace without flagging their mounts. Nor did Haukur ask if I knew how to pony a horse. I did not disappoint him with the truth.

At last the tide was low. We opened the paddock gate and let the swirl of color resolve itself into free-running horses. First after them went Haukur on Bjartur, the cream-colored gelding he always rode. His hand horse, a black, he led at his knee, and I did my best to mimic him, though I kept losing my right stirrup: with her every step the chestnut mare banged into my heel.

We rode beside the River Kalda on a path so deep our feet brushed the rim of the ruts and grass swished against our boot tops. The ponying got easier when the deep path emptied out onto a black-pebbled beach. I relaxed, took great drafts of the salty air, and settled in to enjoy the ride: *This* was Iceland.

We crossed over mudflats pocked with airholes and headed for several grass-topped islands abandoned by the tide like a pod of stranded whales. A sea eagle lifted off one of the islands as we approached and scolded us with a high-pitched cackle. Geese flew over, banking, startled. We rode north onto the sandbar, across some grassy flats, back out through the sucky mud to the hard wet sand, whose color ranged from black to coffee-colored to tawny to gold. Tide pools, I knew, held tiny shrimp and sea lettuce; their bottoms were mosaics of shells. The horses got spattered with muck and splashed water as high as our faces—icy, but delightful in the sunshine, since everyone wore rubber boots and rainpants or chaps. These were practiced riders, and they kept up a fast pace. The woman next to me occasionally rode at a trot, balancing above her saddle to spell her mount, yet Elfa and I matched her speed easily, tolting all the time. Later I overheard her remark to Haukur that I rode a tolt well for an American. He, knowing I understood her Icelandic, grinned at me. "It's the horse," he said.

Elfa was an *eðlistöltari*, a natural tolter. Although five-gaited, she would not trot or pace when asked to speed up from a walk, as some Icelandics do; she preferred to tolt. Automatically, she lifted her head high and drew her hindquarters deep. I leaned back, imagining an easy chair. The saddle, which looked like an English saddle with long flaps, was very flat, letting me position my weight far back. My stirrups were long, my hips and legs loose, my feet in my red rubber boots wiggling to the motion of the horse. The result was a sinuous dancing step without any bump or jolt, as Elfa lifted one foot then another in an incremental quickening of her walk. The snappy four-beat rhythm was fixed in my head by an American friend's insistent mnemonic: *Black-and-Decker-Black-and-Decker-Black-and-Decker-Black-and-Decker.*

It was a gait as old as the earliest hoofprints: When anthropologist Mary Leakey uncovered the tracks of three 3.5-million-year-old equids called Hipparions in East Africa, she found their footfalls to match those of a tolting Icelandic traveling at ten miles an hour. The rack of today's Tennessee Walkers is close to the Icelandic gait, only the tolt is faster. Tolting, I'd read, an Icelandic horse can cover five miles in fifty minutes under saddle; if rested ten minutes and spelled by another mount, it will keep up that pace for a ten-hour day. And I had no doubt I could ride Elfa that long: She was the most comfortable horse I had ever sat.

We rested and changed mounts in a grassy cove on the edge of the Stora Hraun lands. To the south and east across the sands the lava fields stretched unbroken, stark and undulant, Eldborg *sitting like a queen*, as Haukur put it, in the center of the rubble. Behind her, the horizon was gated by the gray-blue mountains guarding the entrance to Hitardalur Valley. My little summerhouse, close in on the edge of the sands, seemed on the edge of the world. America—and its murders—seemed barely conceivable. Then we turned the corner into the Stora Hraun fields, swept past the farmhouse and the cowsheds, and down the long lane with the dogs barking after us to the ford at the mouth of the Haffjardara (Goat-fjord River), a famous salmon river whose widened waters swirled cold above our stirrups even at dead low tide.

Our way turned west, past a scatter of low grassy islands. One of these had held the chief farm of the district, the priest's seat, and the church throughout the Middle Ages, from about the year 1000, when Iceland became Christian, until 1562. In that year, a boatload of churchgoers drowned coming home from Christmas mass; subsequently the church was moved inland. The graveyard remained on the island, eaten at by storms, and the priests would periodically row out to rebury the bones. One priest who did so at the turn of this century remarked that the old skulls all seemed to have very good teeth, a sign that the people were healthy. Today the islands are home to eider ducks, from whose nests the locals gather valuable eiderdown.

With the islands to our left, we rode on hard-packed sand, the tapping of our horses' hooves making music with the wind and the seabirds' cries. I could feel time almost stop, suspended in the wet air between sea and sky, as history clustered all around us. Close on our right rose the snow-flecked mountains of Snaefellsnes, the Snow Mountain Peninsula. Ahead loomed the Snow Mountain itself, glacier-topped Snaefellsjokull, a classic Mount Fuji-shaped stratovolcano. Jules Verne began his *Journey to the Center of the Earth* from this mountain, and New Agers now affirm it the third holiest spot on the planet, ascending it in droves on the summer solstice and bringing new riches to the fishing towns down below. Gazing at its beauty, I wondered what the two more-holy places could possibly be. Medieval Icelanders wrote of the benevolent troll, Bard, who lived in Snaefellsjokull's ice-cap and occasionally rescued storm-trapped travelers. Underneath its veil of cloud, I knew, the mountain hid twin peaks that, snow-covered, could look like a set of troll's horns. Or a pair of heavy-lidded eyes. Beneath the mountain, the golden sand was punctuated by black clusters of troll-shaped rocks.

Then suddenly we were off the sands and into another farmyard. It was Skogarnes, where, Haukur told me, my horse Elfa was raised; she was the foal of a mare called Gudridur, named for the farmwife at Skogarnes, Gudridur, who also had a daughter Elfa. (The farmers at Skogarnes delighted me as well with the name of their dog, a fat black Labrador retriever they called President Clinton.) Until the early 1900s, Skogarnes had been the site of a fishing station and a merchant's shop serving the farms all along the coast. In 1933, the wooden warehouse was dismantled and trucked inland ten miles, where it was rebuilt by the side of the new gravel road and where it still sits, as gas station, snack bar, grocery, and art gallery. The moving of the shop marked the decline of the Longufjorur, its transition from true highway to pleasure ride; after 1933, most traffic went by automobile along the inland road instead of by horseback across the sands.

We rested the horses again on a grassy hillside out of sight of the Skogarnes farmhouse. This time the schnapps made the rounds as the riders compared the soreness of their seats. (Although the tolt is not jarring, it does create a bit of friction, and chafing can be a problem.) The horses milled about us, stepping carefully between the lounging humans, who occasionally got up to chase a straggler back toward the herd.

The buzz had been growing in our ears for some time before any of the riders registered what it was (some of us were half asleep with our hats over our eyes). A plane was coming in low. It zoomed over our hillside, making us sit up and snatch at the nearest bridles. A little red and white two-seater, the craft rose and banked steeply over the sea, then turned its nose toward us and dove again. Again it turned, and now it sparked Haukur's ire. He waved his cap at it, hollering the Icelandic equivalent of *You asshole!* The other riders had mounted their horses and were circling around the spares. Again the plane passed low over us, then dipped even lower until it was skimming the mudflats. Haukur's holler suddenly turned concerned. The pilot would crash, would kill himself if he tried to land in that soft mud. There must be something wrong with the plane. Haukur thrashed his hat in the air again and began riding toward the beach. The plane lifted slightly, sailed across a wide tidal stream, and came down at last on the sandbar a quarter-mile offshore.

Haukur shook his head. There must be something wrong, he said again. The pilot must be out of gas. There was no way off that sandbar, and the tide was rising. He turned and looked over his riders, all quite experienced except for me and one young girl. We'll have to rescue him, he said. We'll have to swim.

Down he rode toward the stream, riding the cream-colored Bjartur and leading the black, and, without hesitating, urged the two horses in. The water rose above his thighs. The horses lifted their heads and bared their teeth, all but their heads and necks underwater. The loose horses and the other riders followed, but my hand horse balked and Elfa skittered farther down the shore before I could steer her in—with the result that she missed the sloping bank and was instantly swimming. My boots filled up. The current pressed hard against my right leg and tugged away at my left. I lost my stirrups. My hand horse began swimming with the stream, dragging her rein around behind my back. Elfa began turning seaward as well, her swimming a strange rolling motion. I began to panic. The water swirled across my thighs and rose into my lap. I thought, frantically, of the notebook in my belt pack, the only record of my thoughts and days, and wondered if it was already ruined.

Rationally I knew that what we were doing was quite ordinary. Horses have long been called "the bridges of Iceland," and Icelanders still will not go out of their way to stay dry crossing a bit of a brook. The Reverend Arni Thorarinsson, who had lived at Stora Hraun around the turn of the century and whose autobiography, *Hjá Vondu Folki* ("Among Bad People"), I'd been reading back at our summerhouse, spoke of crossing eighteen streams just to make his pastoral rounds. Another preacher, the Scotsman Robert Jack, who held a parish in the north of Iceland in the 1940s, had written glowingly about *sundríða*, or "swimming-riding." "I would stop Stjarni at the water's edge," he explained, "slacken the reins and see that the saddle strap was not too tight under his belly. Then I would mount, urge him into the stream, and let him swim. I myself would be submerged waist-deep in water, half standing, legs firm in the stirrups, holding on only by the mane, leaving the reins loose on his neck. To touch the reins is fatal, for then the pony will drop his head, and down the rider will go, with little chance of swimming. Stjarni would paddle with his front feet like a dog, and we could be over, saving many a weary mile of riding."

The English painter Samuel Waller wrote of a day in 1874 (I hope it was a warm day) when he crossed forty streams. He warned, "The great thing to beware of is looking at the water. You lose your head at once if you do so, as the eddies swirl around you so rapidly." If you should become unseated, he advised, "strike out for the bank at once and leave the animals to take care of themselves. To be engulfed with a horse in the water is a very complicated piece of business."

And I had two horses. It occurred to me suddenly that I was not "used to horses" at all.

The thought came as quite a shock. I looked all around, careful not to stare at the eddying water, and tried to suppress my panic. Only the young girl was still in the river with me. The girl's uncle, a thickset man on a very small horse, had turned back and was watching from the far shore, ready, I could tell, to ride to the rescue—so bailing out was no option. Worse than the cold swim in boots, or the danger of being "engulfed with a horse in the water," a dismount would bring on the heroics of a stranger. That thought, oddly, reassured me: If I wasn't ready to accept anyone's help, I must think, deep down, that I could get out of this predicament myself. I quickly took inventory and concluded I was hardly a rider. Rather than standing "firm in the stirrups," I had no stirrups. My hand horse was pulling me out to sea, tipping my balance awry with her rein tight behind my back. Determined at all costs to stay on, I had cocked my feet up to lessen the drag on my water-filled boots and was clenching my knees, my hands in a death-grip on the reins. In spite of all this, Elfa was swimming steadily, her ears back, but otherwise not noticeably upset that we weren't gaining the shore. Suddenly I knew what to do. Keeping firm hold of my hand horse, I dropped Elfa's rein, grabbed onto her mane, and relaxed my legs. Immediately, as if I'd called out in a language we both understood, Elfa's head swung toward shore. My hand horse fell behind and swam nicely along after us. Soon we had sand under our hooves. Elfa kicked up and we came splashing out onto the beach in a fine smooth tolt, balanced and at ease even with water-filled boots and no stirrups. We charged over to where the other horses waited and I gratefully slid off.

My first thought was to empty out my boots. Someone handed me a beer. I chugged it down, standing on one foot, holding two fidgeting wet horses and a boot full of water. Haukur was laughing and cupping his groin to show how high the water had reached. Slowly I made out the tale. The pilot was the boyfriend of one of our riders and had flown out to treat her to a cold drink.

Hardly had the absurdity of the situation sunk in when I realized the riders were remounting. The plane's engine was being revved up. Someone grabbed my empty bottle and I was up and off, Elfa stretching out behind Haukur's Bjartur in the incredible gait called the flying pace—fast enough that my hand horse had to gallop to keep up, yet still Bjartur outdistanced us. We eased back into a canter and let the loose horses catch us, while our little beer-plane scooted by overhead, waggled its wings, and disappeared. For what seemed to be the first time since the murder of my husband's mother, I was filled with the pure joy of life.

So I was not "used to horses"—and I desperately wanted to be.

For the rest of the ride on the sands that day I listened to my horse. Elfa was keying off Haukur, I realized, for pace and gait and pathway. I was but a lump, a bit of baggage he'd asked her to carry—and she was doing it as well, as professionally, as possible, ignoring most everything I did.

It was a hard realization to swallow. Since girlhood I'd defined myself as a horsewoman. Granted, I'd never owned a horse. Never even ridden out alone. But horses drew me in the way that cats (sneaky and distrustful) and dogs (fawning and obsequious) did not. I'd assumed that love of the beasts was the defining trait, and that all the rest, whatever it was, would follow.

When I was a child living in the Philadelphia suburbs the hunt rode nearby—though I never saw the riders except in my mind's eye, brilliant in their red coats after an imaginary fox. I'd sneak across the Hunt Club on my way to see an equally horsey friend; by the time I got up the nerve to poke into the stables, they were abandoned, the housing developments and highways clustered too thick. The name of my street seemed elegiac: Steeplechase Drive.

One autumn my Girl Scout leader agreed to give horseback-riding lessons. Her daughter, an older teen, was riding the jumper circuit. She had a seventeen-hand gray gelding that, for some reason, she untrailered on her suburban front lawn one morning, and I was there to be awestruck and envious. I don't recall the lesson horses, only watching Sandy muck out the gray's stall and wishing I could help. We advanced to the posting trot before the lessons suddenly came to an end. Next summer I volunteered to weed the leader's gardens—though I was terrified by the mourning doves, whose cooing was the call of ghosts and spirits. But even that selflessness didn't bring the lessons back. Something unspecified had gone wrong—with the horse, with the daughter. It was never discussed.

Until I began taking lessons again—at the ripe age of thirty-five, with years of weekend trail rides behind me, as well as those two six-day treks in Iceland (one ridden entirely in a chill rain)—I thought I knew how to ride. I could sit a horse. At least, I *would* sit any horse I was offered. When things seemed to go wrong, it was always the stirrups (too long) or the girth (not tight enough) or the reins (too thick), not something I was doing. I had no fear of falling off until the instructors at the equestrian school near my home repositioned me into hunt seat, which seemed, in fact, no seat at all, just a habit of hovering above your horse, your only contact a thin strip of inseam squeezing the animal's girth. I fell off a fat white pony named Marshmallow. (A few bruises, no lasting harm.) But slowly my balance improved. I had the natural build of a rider, the instructors said, long-legged and lean, but I learned, lesson by lesson, that I was too timid. What satisfied me most about riding school were the sensual pleasures, the grooming, the stroking, the slick feel of oiled leather, the muscles hardening in my wrists and arms from lifting and slinging, from gripping a hoof tight to pick it clean. I enjoyed what poet Maxine Kumin called the "large and redolent company" of horses. I bragged to my family that I was never hungry, tired, or cold in the company of a horse.

But until I rode Elfa out of the stream, I'd never really *ridden*.

Before, when I'd gone trekking in Iceland, I'd paid little attention to my mount. Those had been research trips, historical reconstructions, a way to get closer to medieval life, to see Iceland with Saga Age eyes. My mind was set on the passage of time, the pace of travel, the trials of hard weather and sore legs and rough paths. The horse was a vehicle. Pleasing, efficient, yet a means to an end. I was a courteous passenger, gentle, polite, and the horse knew the way, where to walk, when to speed up. Like the old school horses in the lesson ring, it responded to certain signals and so convinced me I was in control.

Then I rode Elfa into the stream.

I'd thought communicating with a horse was a metaphor. All the riding instruction I'd had (and no, it wasn't much) had stressed control, dominance, mastery, how to make the animal do what you wanted. But I didn't know what I wanted. Perplexed, on the edge of panic, swimming out to sea, suddenly I heard Elfa's call: *I cannot do this if you don't cooperate.* And when I'd replied, by relaxing and letting go of the reins, relinquishing control, everything had changed. A year later, taking my first lesson on one of my own Icelandic horses, I would nod in agreement when the instructor, a German from an Icelandic riding school, explained how to ride: "It's only possible if the horse says *yes* and the rider says *yes*. Then the information flow can happen."

Swimming with Elfa, I had discovered that flow. I'd never opened myself up before, never said *yes*, never joined the conversation. And now that I had, I didn't want it to stop. I'd never before felt that intense oneness with a different creature, rarely even with another human being. It was a lack in my life, and now I knew how to fill it.

On the way back to Snorrastadir that night, bumping along in the back seat of a neighbor's van, I asked Haukur if he would help me find a horse like Elfa to take home to Pennsylvania. Elfa herself, I assumed, was not for sale.

Haukur flung his arm around my shoulders and grinned. "What color do you want?"

"It makes no difference," I said. I plucked his caressing hand from my neck and held it against his knee. Choosing a horse by its color was what tyros did. I wanted him to take me seriously now. I wanted to be thought of as a horsewoman. "I want a horse with a good solid tolt," I said matter-of-factly. "I want a horse like Elfa."

"A horse like Elfa." He trapped my hand between both of his.

The district horse show would be held at the show grounds near Snorrastadir at the end of the month, he said gently. I would be his guest. He'd introduce me to every breeder in the West. One was sure to have a good horse for sale, a horse just like Elfa. He squeezed my hand tight, leaning close, his breath sweet with pipe smoke and whiskey. And on Saturday night, he said in a deep whisper, there'll be a midnight ride on the sands. "You on Elfa. Me on Bjartur. Under the midnight sun," he sighed.

It didn't happen. The week before the horse show came another heart-stopping phone call from home: My fifteen-year-old niece, on her way to Paris with her high-school French club, had died in an airplane crash. We went home to the funeral, the hissing sound of *hurry, hurry* louder still in my ears. I kept thinking of Haukur, riding the sands alone.

CHAPTER THREE

A HORSE LIKE ELFA

A year later, in late July 1997, I was back in Iceland. I'd come alone this time, traveling light. I intended to stay for a month—and to go home the owner of two Icelandic horses.

The decision had come to me in midwinter.

Some five years before, while being shown a new friend's house, I was lured by a photograph on a far wall. My host found me some fifteen minutes later, alone in a darkening room, staring at the image, transfixed. He said nothing, but stood beside me, matching my gaze until by some barely perceptible sigh or sign he understood that I'd drunk my fill. The photographer was a friend of his, and soon of mine.

It was a print of a horse bent sharply to bite at a fly. I knew what that horse was doing—itching—yet the print, with its silvery gray tones and exquisite lines, radiated nothing but peace. It had for me the sacred quality of a pieta. It restored emotions I had long suppressed, ever since my husband of two years had backed the truck up too quickly on a dark snowy night and killed my dog of twelve. It led, more or less directly, to my taking up riding lessons and letting myself become engaged with the animal world again.

Then, this winter past, feeling chill and inhuman after the emotional stress of the murders of my mother-in-law and niece (we, like many of the other families who had lost loved ones on TWA Flight 800, were then still convinced the plane had been bombed), I toured a museum exhibit in which famous people identified photos that had changed their lives. My companion, a woman I knew professionally but not well, asked me what I would have picked. I chose the horse print on my friend's wall—and having said it out loud, to a comparative stranger, I knew the decision had already been made: I was going to buy horses of my own. I was going to restore my joy in living.

There was never a question but that they would be Icelandic horses, bringing with them the wide skies and the lingering history of the land I loved. I could escape to a minor Iceland every time I went out to ride.

The two-horned glacier, Snaefellsjokull, hung above the sea the morning I left Reykjavik, heading for Snorrastadir to see Haukur. Its rocky base, which comprises most of the mountain, had taken on the same saturated hue as the blue sky and the blue bay, and the icecap seemed to hover, unattached, another cloud, only cut sharper. It winked at me through the cityscape as the bus cruised out of town. It shone again across the marshes, marshes full of horse herds.

I knew I was risking failure—spectacular failure—complete with threats to life and limb, if I ended up with a horse that was unsuitable, that was no joy at all. And the first few days of my trip did not bode well. I took a riding lesson in Reykjavik, and the horse ran away with me. I went to a stable with horses for sale, was pegged as a sucker and shown a snappish nag with an angry wound on one leg.

That convinced me, as I'd suspected all along, that I couldn't find a good horse on my own, and I was counting on Haukur and on another horseman, a man I'd never met but whom I'd been told I could trust—Einar Gislason from the northern district of Skagafjord.

I had written to Haukur in May. I wanted two horses just like his Elfa, I said, two so they wouldn't be lonely and so I could ride for miles, ponying one, on the wooded roads near my home. Would he help me find them, as he had offered to do the summer before? Could I come to Snorrastadir in July?

I had received no reply, which was not to say I wasn't welcome. I had been writing to the farm family at Helgafell, whom I'd met on my first trip to Iceland, for eleven years. I'd sent three or four long letters a year, as a way to practice my Icelandic, and they'd only ever sent me one reply—when the twins were born, Oskar and his sister, Osk, now ten years old. Yet each time I'd shown up at Helgafell, unannounced, at approximately two-year intervals, I'd been made more than welcome.

And here, I had phoned ahead.

I had written out what I would ask Haukur. I placed the call sitting alone in a friend's apartment while she took her two-year-old to the playground in the rain. I picked up the phone: May I come for a visit? *Welcome! Welcome!* Haukur answered, plus a lot more that I couldn't decipher. He sounded happy to hear from me. May I come on Wednesday morning? He repeated *Wednesday*, and the gist of it seemed positive. Will you meet the bus at the road? On Wednesday morning? (I repeated the time, just in case.) *Yes, yes*, Haukur said, and something else—I thought it was, *We'll see you then*.

I repacked my belongings from two bags into one, leaving behind my city clothes (scarf, slacks, blazer), cramming my sleeping bag into an outer pocket of my suitcase with the backpack straps, stuffing into my red Wellington boots some extra socks, my long underwear, and a telephoto lens. I would have to wear my Icelandic sweater (too bulky to pack) and carry my riding helmet (ditto). Into a small daypack I put snacks, a water bottle, my dictionary and maps, gifts for my hosts (quilted pot holders for Ingibjorg and a bottle of Johnny Walker Black for Haukur), money and gloves, my camera, my notebook, and a small red binder into which I'd collected all I could of the Icelandic language: *Essentials*—how to say "hello" to a mixed group of men and women (*Komið þið sæl*), as opposed to one of all men (*Komið þið sælir*). *Horses*—the horse (*hesturinn*), about the horse (*um hestinn*), from the horse (*frá hestinum*), to the horse (*til hestsins*). *Phrases*—it makes no difference (*Það skiptir ekki máli*). *Grammar*—the twenty-four forms of "the" and "this" and "who." *Gender rules*—how to decline masculine, feminine, and neuter nouns (if you know in advance which is which). *Verbs*—a list of sixty-five verbs with definitions and the first-person singular forms (*Ég bíð*, "I'll wait"; *Ég skemmti mér*, "I'm enjoying myself"), and another group of forty verbs, fully declined.

Finally, I packed my reading book, a novel called *The Swan*, by a modern Icelandic writer, Gudbergur Bergsson. I'd bought it in Icelandic for one hundred kronur (about a dollar fifty) at the flea market. I had intended to also buy an English translation to help me through it, but there were none at The Owl or the other used book stores, and a new copy, in paperback, cost thirty dollars. It would be sink or swim, I thought—like the rest of my trip. I started reading the book on the bus to Snorrastadir. It was the story of a city girl sent out into the country. In the first few pages, she has to catch a horse the farmer says is *mósóttur*. She's never caught a horse before. She doesn't know what color the word *mósóttur* designates. I didn't either.

Out the window, the glacier winked at me. On my way home from Iceland the summer before, I'd bought every book on horses I could find, and I'd spent the winter studying them. Yet of the eighty-four colors named in *Handbók Íslenskra Hestamanna (The Icelandic Horseman's Handbook)*, I could remember only a few: the common *rauður* (chestnut), *jarpur* (bay), and *svartur* (black), the pretty *bleikur* (dun) of Elfa, and Bjartur's *leirljós* (cream). I wondered what else I didn't know. We stopped at Borgarnes, a market town a half an hour from Haukur's farm. My throat was dry. I filled my water bottle and bought a small carton of Florida-brand orange juice at the snack bar. As the bus continued north, the glacier grew into a constant presence on my left. In the sunshine it seemed to be laughing. The bus stopped on the roadside by the Snorrastadir lane. No one was there to meet me.

I busied myself with the backpack straps. When the bus and its watching eyes had gone, I stood up and looked around. No one coming from the direction of the house. I clipped my riding helmet to a strap and shouldered my pack. It was heavy. The sun was hot. In a few steps I had to stop and take off my sweater and roll it around my hips. My helmet banged against my elbow. The lane was 1.9 kilometers long, said a sign—a bit over a mile. The houses were hidden behind a knoll. On a hillside I could see a tractor working.

A car blew past me down the lane. It didn't stop: tourists, probably, on their way to climb Eldborg. The Fire Fortress showed itself prominently now, between me and the laughing glacier.

I was still walking when the car came rattling back the other way. The woman in the passenger's seat stared at me, but still they didn't stop.

I took off my pack and rested, glad I'd remembered to fill my water bottle. I took a long drink and wondered what had gone wrong.

I'd done this before—walked down a farm lane in Iceland, carrying a pack, not knowing who I'd find at home. It's an Icelandic tradition of long standing to welcome unexpected guests. To feed them, put them up overnight, lend them a fresh horse to their destination (or, nowadays, drive them to the nearest bus route). It took nerve to be a sudden guest, but it was better than sitting by the roadside for the return bus. All you had to do was walk into the house, put down your pack, and give yourself to them. *Here I am. I have nowhere to go. I'd rather be here than anywhere else.* Your meaning, of course, was easily misconstrued, and I already felt unsure of myself around Haukur. Icelanders were reputed to be cold and reserved; that account fit me better than it did him. I knew not to take his teasing too personally. I overlooked his bearhugs and the occasional kiss on the cheek. When he introduced me to another farmer as his American girlfriend, and stood talking to the man with his arm tight around me, I smiled bravely, feeling inwardly abashed. When he rubbed my neck with what seemed like more than appropriate affection, I took his hand and held on—and here I was bringing him a bottle of good whiskey!

I shouldered my pack and walked on.

Ten paces farther I stopped again. There'd been a report in the newspaper that morning of a riding accident in Kaldardal, the Cold River Valley. The River Kalda ran beside the lane I was walking down. The rider had hit his head and was in a coma. Could it have been Haukur? I tried to shrug off the awful thought and continued my trek.

The Kalda takes a bend just after the stables at Snorrastadir, and the lane crosses it on a wooden bridge. The stables were barren, no horses in the paddock, so I kept on. As I came to the bridge I saw a man—wasn't it Haukur?—dart into the house. I waved, but he didn't see me. I was at the corner of the house itself when the man came back out, in his socks. He leaped off the porch and ran toward me.

"Nancy-*mín! Elsku* Nancy-*mín!*" he cried, giving his darling Nancy a great hug and a kiss on both cheeks. He'd forgotten all about meeting the bus. He'd been busy all morning—"Do you see that horse on the hill?"

"The black one?"

"Black! That horse is *sottrauður*—blood red. He fell into the drainage ditch and almost drowned. We had to haul him out with the tractor, stupid Petur."

"Petur?'

"Yes, the horse. He's named Petur. But give me your pack—my God she's a strong woman! Come in to dinner. *Inga!* It's Nancy."

There was another guest at the table, an old man Ingibjorg introduced as her *frændi* or kinsman, Thorfinn. He was very pale. His high-bridged beak of a nose supported heavy glasses. Haukur introduced me as a writer from America, at which he and Thorfinn launched into a discussion of the book *Independent People*, written in the 1940s by the Icelandic Nobel laureate Halldor Laxness. Haukur pushed back his plate, emptied, it seemed, instantly of breaded fish and boiled potatoes, and tamped tobacco into his pipe. In his opinion, he said, sucking on the stem, Laxness had exaggerated too much. He'd made the farmer, Bjartur (the same name as Haukur's favorite horse, I noticed), too pitiful. It was particularly ridiculous, Haukur continued, lighting his pipe and drawing a long draft, that Bjartur would go out into a snowstorm to look for a single lost sheep, leaving his pregnant wife to give birth alone.

I agreed. I had given the book to my father for Christmas, I managed to say. I wanted to say what he'd thought of it, how he'd been so mad at Bjartur for abandoning his wife, who, of course, had died in childbirth, but the words wouldn't cooperate. At home I liked nothing better than talking about books—particularly Icelandic books—but here my university English was useless. My Icelandic vocabulary, I was suddenly reminded, was little better than a child's.

The two men nodded, waiting patiently. I looked at my empty plate, took the platter of fish Ingibjorg passed to me.

The conversation went on without me.

Independent People wasn't nearly as good as *Growth of the Soil*, Haukur proclaimed, by the Norwegian Nobel Prize-winner Knut Hamsun. Hamsun got it right, Haukur said emphatically: He knew what it's like to be a farmer on marginal land. Haukur knocked out his pipe and got up from the table. He went outside. A moment later, I saw the tractor rumble past the window.

I sat at the table with Ingibjorg, who was only now beginning her meal. She was as quiet as Haukur was voluble, but it was clear, for all her quietness, that nothing escaped her. She spoke with Thorfinn in a low voice, every now and then looking up to smile at me or to pass me a platter. I couldn't tell what they were discussing.

I looked out the window at the muddy horse on the hill. This sudden loss of language had always been a backwards pleasure, part of Iceland's strange allure. I made my living with words. I was an arbiter of grammar and vocabulary, style and sense—but in Iceland I could barely make myself understood. It was freeing, as if I'd returned to some indefinite and promising childhood stage. If they liked me, as Haukur and Ingibjorg apparently did, they liked more than my communication skills, more than my ability to express myself well. It was comforting to know.

Yet being liked would not get me my horse. I worried if this year the language gap would work against me.

I had planned to stay a week at Snorrastadir before taking the bus north to Skagafjord, Iceland's main horse-breeding district, where a friend had wangled me a week's invitation at Einar Gislason's farm. While at Snorrastadir I hoped to practice my riding, to stop in on our summerhouse of the year before, and to look among the local horse farms for a horse like Elfa. I wondered how to convey all that to Ingibjorg in a way that would sound grateful and polite. I listened to her conversation a little longer without understanding and decided I'd wait and try Haukur.

After dinner, Ingibjorg showed me my room. I put on my red rubber boots and hiked down through the marshes to the black beach, naming the songbirds and sandpipers I saw. I quickly grew tired. In just a year away, I'd forgotten how hard it was to walk through tangles of birch scrub and blueberry, tussocks of grass with swamp separating them. I was afraid to cross the very wet patches, where the ground sank and trembled underfoot: I'd forgotten which grasses grew short on firmer soil and which sent their roots deep into muck. I reached the black sand shores of the bay, and turned toward the lava field that edged it to the north. Litla Hraun sat on the other side of the lava, out of sight, about an hour's walk away. I couldn't find the path.

Back at the house, Branddis, Haukur's daughter, was starting to clean the muddy horse Petur. Branddis was in her twenties, fresh-faced and freckled, with a spectacular fall of red-gold hair now tied back in a heavy braid. A younger girl, with cropped hair and fashionable makeup, was pushing Branddis's infant daughter, Ingibjorg, in a pram. Four-year-old Magnus played a splashing game with a puddle nearby. Petur, his lead rope dangling, happily grazed the rich grass beside the house while Branddis brushed him with a plastic currycomb. The mud was still wet and would not come off easily. I suggested a hose, but she said it would frighten him. She'd try a bucket. But she had hardly come out of the milkhouse with the white water bucket when he started to arch his neck and snort. His ears swiveled back and forth. She took the lead rope and set the bucket by his side. He danced away from it as far as the rope would let him, snorting and flaring his nostrils. He ignored her soft-voiced crooning. When she dipped the currycomb in the bucket, he would not let her near.

"Stupid Petur," she said, "you're so dirty."

She handed me the rope and took the bucket away again. The horse settled down to graze.

"We could try the river," I suggested.

"Yes, let's."

I had the higher boots. I led Petur into the rushing water, expecting him to balk and shy, but he clumped right in. We waded upstream as far as I dared without filling my boots, letting the swift water wash his legs and belly, then turned back to where Branddis waited in the shallows. Peter was unconcerned even when Branddis started splashing water on him with the currycomb. She splashed and rubbed until he was more or less clean, then we took him across the river at the ford, through the paddock, and up the hill to where the rest of the riding herd wandered.

On the way back we stopped in the stables. There was one big room for hay, now mostly empty since the farm had switched to storing hay in round bales, wrapped in white plastic and left outside. A smaller back room, cordoned off into different-sized metal pens, was also empty. The third room, long and narrow, had only a very thin walkway between the inside wall and a long manger; the rest of the space was divided into large tie stalls, one of which now held four chestnut horses. Branddis gave them each a handful of hay and a pat. They were Hallgerdur's horses, she said.

Hallgerdur had arrived while I was out hiking. She was a horsewoman. With her four horses, she was on a six-day trek, alone, from Reykjavik to the Dales, an area north of the mountainous Snaefellsnes peninsula. One of the horses carried her tent and other gear on a packsaddle; the other three she rode alternately.

When we got back to the house, Hallgerdur and Ingibjorg were loading a vacuum cleaner into the thirty-year-old blue Volvo that Haukur called *the best car in the world*. They were taking it across the river to the new summerhouses. Tourists had rented two of them for the night, and Ingibjorg needed to tidy up. I went along to help out. But it was difficult to find anything to do. The houses were immaculate. Built of wood in a Scandinavian style, they were light and airy and bright in the sunshine. I dabbed at the kitchen sink and gathered the used bed linens while Hallgerdur vacuumed up imaginary crumbs and kept up a high-volume conversation with Ingibjorg, scrubbing the bathroom. Between the distance and the machine noise, I couldn't parse their voices into words. I had no clue what was being said.

Later, as we sat on the porch in the sun while Ingibjorg checked everything twice over, Hallgerdur introduced herself to me in English. She had heard I wanted to buy two horses.

"I need four horses," she said. "Because I am very fat!" She laughed, a great roar.

She was a large woman, though not what I would call fat. There was too much strength to her. She stood like a wrestler, firmly planted, while her upper body moved with grace. She had a broad square face and eyes given to exaggeration, opening wide and round, winking, narrowing. She was saucy and sassy and loud, and, like Haukur, she loved to tease. She seemed older than I, yet that might have been age in experience, not years. I seemed to have dropped at least ten years since I'd arrived, since I realized I'd lost my language.

When Haukur came in for coffee that afternoon, he greeted Hallgerdur by lying on the floor and lifting his knees. At least that's how it looked. Picking the words I knew from their banter, I gathered that he'd been having trouble with his lower back and she had recommended a stretching exercise. They both clearly enjoyed the obscene overtones. Ingibjorg pursed her lips, looking at me to gauge how I was taking it. The other old man I'd seen around the farm, Bogi (I hadn't yet figured out if he was a relative or a hired hand), greeted Hallgerdur with a broad smile and a handshake (he'd ignored me), and, pushing his pipe to the side of his mouth, declaimed the first half of a poem. Hallgerdur wrinkled her forehead. She placed a finger on her lips. "Don't tell me!" she said. Her eyes wandered around as if behind them some small creature were searching the warren of her memory. *"Ah!"* she announced, and triumphantly declaimed the finishing half.

I was amazed. It was a game I'd read about in the sagas—capping verses, it was called, where one party starts a poem and the second has to give the correct lines to finish it. I'd heard the game was still played, but in ten years of visiting the country, I'd never seen it in action.

In the old tales often the two contestants were poets themselves. They created verses on the spot (and sometimes at the point of death) that were true to the unbelievably exacting and inflexible rules of old Icelandic poetry. In *The Saga of Grettir the Strong*, for instance, young Grettir came back from a trip abroad to learn that he had been declared an outlaw. He slipped away, put on a black cloak, snatched a fast horse he knew named Sodulkolla (Saddlehead), and rode off just before dawn. But some servants were up and about and saw him steal the horse. They alerted the farmer, Sveinn, a cheerful fellow, fond of making up humorous verses. Sveinn laughed and reeled off a poem in the form called *dróttkvætt*, or "king's poem," an eight-line stanza more intricate than a sonnet. The number of syllables is fixed. The rhyme scheme has to follow the right pattern, both in full rhyme (*horse* and *course*, for example) and half-rhyme (*horse* and *ford*). Certain words in each line have to alliterate (*horse* and *haven*). As one scholar noted, "When a *dróttkvætt* verse is bad, the sheer metrical accomplishment of it all still evokes a kind of admiration."

The gist of Sveinn's poem? *He played me a dirty trick.* He saddled another horse, and gave chase. At the next farm, he stopped a man named Halli. *Did you see that loafer ... riding my mount?* he asked in another intricate verse. Halli, in reply, delivered a technically superior poem that the thief had taught him: *A fellow with a black hood and a bag full of tricks was riding the mare.* A bit farther down the valley, Sveinn was stopped by a woman standing before her house. Sveinn's verse asked: *Who was that fellow?* She responded, in the words she had memorized, *It was Grettir. ... The outspoken poet intends to ride her so hard that he'll spend the night at Gilsbakki.* Says the saga author, "Sveinn pondered over the verse and said, 'It's not unlikely that I'm no match for this man, but I'm going to meet him nonetheless.'" (It's not clear if it was Grettir's reputation as a fighter or his demonstrated skill at versifying that worried the farmer.) Sveinn rode up to Gilsbakki and found his black mare in the pasture. Knocking on the door, he delivered the first four lines of a verse: *Who rode my mare? What will my payment be?* Grettir met the challenge, assuming Sveinn's own rhyme scheme and pattern of alliteration to cap the verse with four new lines: *I rode the mare ... let us be friends.* "He and Sveinn stayed there overnight and had a lot of fun out of the whole episode," the saga says. Sveinn considered the poems to be excellent compensation for the use of his mare (punishment for stealing a horse ordinarily ranged from the price of the horse to death). He and Grettir repeated their poems to their host and named the entire collection the Saddlehead Verses.

A good versifier like Grettir "stood head and shoulders above other men" throughout much of Iceland's history, writer Gudlaugur Jonsson noted in 1895. Along with the sagas, long collections of poems called rímur were Iceland's primary entertainment for centuries. Said Jonsson, "There was a time when it was thought no small distinction to be counted a good rhymer. ... Knowledgeable men who told and read stories aloud, *rímur*-reciters, and rhymers were always favored guests and welcome in every home."

I began to look at old Bogi in a different light. I had no idea what he and Hallgerdur were saying, if they were reciting *dróttkvætt* or the later *rímur*. The complicated form of these poems made them easily memorized—like a riddle, you have to say it right or it isn't funny—but those same traits made them impossible for me to understand. I couldn't even tell if the two contestants were repeating known verses (as I suspected) or making them up on the spot (who knows?). They were obviously quite skilled at whichever they were doing. Even Haukur made no pretense of taking part, as Hallgerdur flung a half-stanza back and Bogi easily reeled off its match. Ingibjorg laid out the coffee and cakes and cucumbers, Haukur and I took our seats and ate and refilled our cups before the game petered out—it seemed that Bogi had won.

Hallgerdur didn't miss a beat. "Where's that hot pot you were telling me about?" she asked Haukur.

He began to give her directions—around the lava field, down the road toward Litla Hraun, back into the lava—to the hotspring where my husband and I had taken a romantic skinny-dip one evening the summer before. Iceland has hundreds of hot-water springs, many of them harnessed to heat swimming pools or hot tubs—hot pots, as the Icelandic *heitirpottar* is usually mistranslated (although in the English-Icelandic dictionary, a "hot pot" is defined as a meat stew). In the city of Reykjavik, groundwater pumped and piped to the houses provides both hot water and heat. But the spring Hallgerdur was asking after was minor; it remained nearly unimproved. Contained by a huddle of carefully fitted stones, its steaming water formed a placid blue pool. The spillover seeped into a muddy marsh, crossed by haphazard stepping stones. Larger stones sunk in the bottom of the pool let you sit with your chin just out of water—if you could stand the heat, which increased the deeper you went, searing your toes. A small stone wall blocked the north wind.

"Let's go," Hallgerdur said, looking at me.

"Now?" Haukur asked.

"It'll be good for your back." She got up. Haukur followed her, humming a little tune.

"Aren't you coming too?" Hallgerdur asked.

I looked at the two of them, charged up and giggly as teenagers.

"Don't forget your bathing suit," Ingibjorg called from the kitchen.

Haukur laughed. "Where is it? I'll start the car," he said to Hallgerdur as Ingibjorg went into the back of the house to get his suit.

"I don't want to come," I told Hallgerdur. "It's too hot on a sunny day." I couldn't imagine the three of us, cheek to cheek, in the tiny pool where my husband and I had embraced. And where were they going to change into their suits? I didn't even ask.

Hallgerdur shrugged and followed Haukur out. In a minute the best car in the world was racing down the lane. Bogi took his pipe into the sitting room. I began helping Ingibjorg with what would become my chore as long as I stayed at Snorrastadir: stacking the dishwasher.

Supper was timed to coincide with the weather report before the eight o'clock news, and Haukur always took his plate into the sitting room and ate in his easy chair. The TV stayed on afterwards, set to the state-run channel (one of two available), and folk filtered in as we finished our meal and our chores. I curled up at the end of one sofa. Hallgerdur, her wet hair turbaned into a towel, was already snoozing on another one. Bogi favored an old stuffed chair against the wall, while the two new Scandinavian sling-type chairs with matching hassocks, in the middle of the room, were obviously for Haukur (the black leather one) and Ingibjorg (the tan). That night, when Ingibjorg went back to the kitchen to prepare the ten o'clock coffee, Haukur waved me into the tan chair.

He placed his hand over mine on the chair arm and smiled, murmuring something pleasant. It seemed to be that he was glad I had come to visit him. With the clatter of dishes and the TV in the background, I couldn't be sure. I nodded and smiled back, wondering how to broach the subject of buying horses.

"You should have come to the hotspring with us," he said. That I understood. "You have tried it before?"

"Oh yes," I answered. "Last summer."

He nodded. "And the ale-spring? Have you ever been to the Raudamel ale-spring?"

I shook my head. "No, we couldn't find it."

"Well!" His eyes shone. "Let's go!" He got up. "*Inga!* Nancy has never seen the Raudamel ale-spring. We're going to go."

"Now?" She did not look terribly surprised. The sun was just starting to slant down, and the shadows on the mountains were velvet. She looked at me quizzically.

I was game. This excursion didn't require any undressing, and I was truly curious to see the ale-spring. Raudamel was where Seal-Thorir had lived, where the mare Skalm lay down under her load. Going there might finally, somehow, give me a chance to ask Haukur about horses.

Ingibjorg shrugged and turned away, giving permission in her subtle way, and I went to put on my boots.

The fog was rolling in over the mountain tops as the blue Volvo rattled down the drive again. The glacier was already blanketed: The weather was coming from the west. Haukur turned the radio on to classical music and filled his pipe, cradling the steering wheel with his elbows while he lit it. I thought about different ways to begin the conversation, but the words wouldn't fit together in Icelandic and I kept silent, staring out the window at the fire in the sky. We drove past Eldborg, looking truly like a "Fire Fortress," shadowed black against the orange sky, and toward another, smaller crater, Gullborg, or "Gold Fortress," its lava field turned golden yellow by a rich covering of moss that sparkled under the low light. We headed for the two red sand dunes, and drove along the base of the larger one. The mountains drew close. One cliff showed a perfect formation of columnar basalt, like a series of giant organ pipes. Deep green valleys began breaking off from the hills, their heads marked with slender, tumbling waterfalls. On our other side, the red sand dune towered above us, now clearly seen to be made of chunks of lava rock. We passed it and descended a steep twisting incline into the fog. The sun dimmed and went out. The gray fog had ribbons and tendrils in it; the green grass of the valleys seemed to glow. There were no animals about—no sheep, no horses, although the land looked like rich grazing. Haukur stopped the car and we got out.

I reached for my gloves. The air was chill. By the time I looked up, he had disappeared into the mist.

But the trail was plain, a black foot-track through the grass. I followed and soon caught up with him. We crossed a narrow stream on a weathered board. A waterfall out of sight played a sorrowful tune on the wind, sucking and sighing like waves of the sea; it seemed too loud to talk over. Haukur bent down to a tiny pool in the grass, just beside the stream. It was small enough to step across, yet it was reputed (at least by Icelanders) to be the highest-volume mineral spring in the world. We crouched and peered into its clear depths. I saw bubbles rising, yellowish in the odd light. Haukur reached in a hand and cupped up a sipful. I did the same. The water was fizzy, cold and crisp, slightly sweet with a metallic aftertaste.

"It's good!" I said in surprise, breaking the long silence.

Haukur smiled. "Only here, at the spring. If you take it home, it just tastes like dirty water." Suddenly he leaped to his feet and slapped his thigh. "And I forgot the whiskey!" He looked at me with his teasing eyes and the genuine warmth of his smile, and any tension between us suddenly vanished.

I had noticed his slight embarrassment when I'd given him the Johnny Walker Black, how he'd made a point of letting Ingibjorg see him lock it away in a cabinet, and I knew he'd had no intention of bringing it to the ale-spring. I understood, finally, the nature of his jokes. It was like the game that Hallgerdur had played with Bogi: capping verses, call and response. Haukur, over the years, had finely crafted his role. When Hallgerdur was his gaming partner, he matched her raucous nature flirt for flirt, innuendo for innuendo. Here, with me and my more subdued personality, the game was tempered, gentled, the suggestive content refined, so as not to chance offending me. So that we'd both enjoy the match.

I rewarded him with a hearty laugh, and we walked back to the car, relaxed and easy with each other.

On the way home we talked of many things—the names of the mountains, the hot spring, when the farms around us had been deserted, how the hay fields there were shared by several families. I even made a little joke in Icelandic, suggesting that the best car in the world was not really *besti bíll í heimi*, but *besti bíll í heimilið*, the best car in the household. The grammar wasn't quite proper, but Haukur got it. He slapped my knee in appreciation. But we exchanged not a word about buying horses.

CHAPTER FOUR

AN EYE FOR HORSES

Before she went to bed, past midnight, Ingibjorg set out breakfast: homemade bread, sweet rolls or cakes, cheeses, jam, a lamb sausage or paté, all wrapped in plastic, encircling a full thermos of coffee. Only the milk pitcher stayed in the refrigerator. Ingibjorg laid a place for each chair at the table, no matter how many guests she had. Haukur alone had a reserved seat, at the window, marked by an ornate silver spoon with his name engraved on it.

In the morning, Ingibjorg was out before eight milking the cows, which Bogi had earlier brought in off the pasture. (He was not family, it turned out; he owned part of a farm to the south, but had worked as a hired hand for most of his life at Snorrastadir.) Haukur joined them at the milking, then crossed the yard to the three-gabled house to confer with his son-in-law, Kristjan, or Stjani, a handsome blond twenty-five-year-old with a driven and ambitious look about him. Before nine, Bogi was herding the cows back out, accompanied by the old farm dog and one of the boys visiting for summer camp. Ingibjorg and Haukur came in separately. Ingibjorg snatched a cup of coffee before starting to bake bread, and then to fix dinner, which would occupy her until noon. Haukur installed himself at the window, blocking my view of the farm's goings-on. He lingered over his coffee and a pipe, listening to the radio, turned up loud. An opera program came on after the news, and he raised the volume even higher. He particularly enjoyed the tenors.

The rain had rolled in. The weather was what I'd call foul (drizzly and gray), but Icelanders generally named fair (warm and not blowy). Suddenly Haukur switched off the broadcast and hurried outside. He caught up with Stjani, heading toward the stable. I tagged along and found Branddis there already, with a trio of horses beside Hallgerdur's four. One of them was Elfa.

The horses were not tied. The concrete floor was slimy with manure, as if they'd been there all night, and the manger was empty of hay. Branddis fetched a few handfuls, then stood at the horses' heads petting and talking to them. Haukur brought in a bucket of tools. He was going to shoe Elfa and the others, I realized. I smiled. While stacking the dishwasher the night before, I had tried to talk to Ingibjorg. Asked if Haukur could help me find good horses, she had said, "Oh yes, he has an eye for horses," and then gone on to say something I didn't understand.

I had also asked to ride Elfa again.

At fifteen, Elfa was too old for export (not to mention she wasn't for sale). Although Icelandics are long-lived—a horse named Eitill ("Knot") had just had its fortieth birthday announced in the newspaper, while one that pulled an egg cart somewhere near Copenhagen was said to have lived to be fifty-seven—none over age ten were generally exported. The change in environment was considered too tough on them.

You should buy one eight- to ten-year-old horse, I had been advised, and another younger and more expensive one, about five to seven. My informant was a friend-of-a-friend I'd had dinner with on my first day in Reykjavik. Her sister owned a horse farm in the south. She herself was well-connected with the city riding clubs, and had already put me in touch, over e-mail, with a riding instructor who was to give me a lesson the next morning.

Nicknamed "Gugga" (her given name, Gudbjorg, was a mouthful even for Icelanders), she was firm in her opinions and spoke with authority, although she was somewhat younger than I. At six feet tall, she was strongly built and angular, her short auburn hair framing an asymmetrical face. She wore a chartreuse silk shirt, tight and buttoned high, atop a black print miniskirt. She was loquacious, out-talking everyone no matter which language she chose. The restaurant, where she waitressed on other nights, was set up like an old-fashioned house. Cut-outs of antique paper dolls decorated the hutches and dry-sinks; in the parlorlike lounge, one of our company remarked, you expected to find grandmother at her knitting. Gugga had booked us a private room, and the chef, known for his inventiveness with native ingredients, sent up a large selection of appetizers: cod-roe caviar; smoked *langvía*, an oily seabird; large oysters baked in cheese and sauce. For my entrée I picked breaded flounder in a gorgonzola-cream sauce with fried bananas, a combination that surprisingly good. We ate and talked until midnight.

The older horse should be very calm and well-trained; the younger will give you the fun of seeing it improve in its training. That younger five- to seven-year-old horse would still be very green. Unlike a Thoroughbred, for instance, which can be fully trained and racing at age two, an Icelandic horse is not introduced to the saddle until it is four. For its first years it runs wild in a family herd, learning the hierarchy, learning to be a horse. It sees people only occasionally, sometimes as infrequently as twice a year, when the herd is rounded up and moved to different grazings. Even at four it is ridden only long enough to accept the idea; that summer it will be ponied by a rider on an older, steady horse so that it can begin to understand its profession. The real training in gaits and obedience begins the winter the horse turns five, when it will be brought into a stable for the first time and worked for a few minutes every day through the summer. The horse isn't considered mature enough to ride on an all-day trek until it's six or seven.

For that reason, I'd already decided both of my horses should be at least eight. Although I appreciated Gugga's opinion, I didn't really want to learn how to train a horse: I wanted a seasoned horse, one who could train me to be a better rider. Haukur's Elfa was my touchstone.

Now at Snorrastadir, watching Elfa being shod, I wondered how to quantify what appealed to me about her. Her coloring was rather plain, a milk-tea brown. She was lean and athletic, no taller than the other horses, but with a certain liveliness to her, a wariness that made her stand out. Although I knew, under saddle, she was trusty and safe, she didn't, in the barn, seem very comfortable in the company of humans.

Horseshoeing in Iceland is a two-person job. Stjani crouched next to the horse, facing its tail, and muscled up a foot. The horse squirmed and shifted, as if it wasn't used to the exercise, but Stjani held tight and refused to let the foot down. Haukur, bending toward Stjani so that their heads nearly knocked, quickly clipped the nails that held on the old shoe and tossed it clattering aside. He wiped the manure-slick hoof with his hand, then propped a thick board against his knee. Stjani held the horse's hoof against the board at a prescribed angle, while Haukur, with a two-handled knife, stroked quickly from heel to toe and into the board, paring off the excess growth of the hoof. In less than five minutes he was setting the shoe back on with six new nails.

The shoes were quite small, double- or triple-ought by American reckoning—about four and a quarter inches at their widest. Horseshoes found by archaeologists in London and dated to the mid-eleventh century were about that size; those from the time of the Viking expansion and the settlement of Iceland two centuries earlier ran smaller by five-eighths of an inch. By the fourteenth century, the London horseshoes were as big as four and three-quarters inches across: still small by modern standards, about a size 0, or ought. An Icelandic friend of mine at a picnic in America was astonished to find a horseshoe a good eight inches wide. He picked it up out of the grass and turned it in his hands, wondering at the monstrous size of the animal that had lost it. Then he realized it had no nail holes. It had been made for the game of horseshoes.

While Haukur worked, he talked to Stjani, mumbling with his mouth full of nails. Occasionally he took the nails out and spoke to the horse, once leaving his post to walk up to Elfa's neck and stroke her soothingly. Another time when she struggled, he merely barked and she stood still. When Elfa was shod, he pushed her aside and addressed the next horse in line. I walked around to where Branddis stood, petting the horses' heads. Elfa, though released, was still tense and jumpy and tried to avoid my touch, shoving against the other horses. Haukur barked again. I wandered off into the hayroom, where the tack closet stood open, a light on. I examined the different bits, finding mostly snaffles, and the cant of the various saddles, a few flat, a few deep. By the time I wandered back to the shoeing, everyone had gone.

At the house, Ingibjorg was rolling out dough and Haukur and Thorfinn, Ingibjorg's kinsman, were deep in a discussion about growing trees in Iceland, which segued somehow into an argument about where the anonymous *Sturlunga Saga* had been written, in the thirteenth century, and a mention of Halldor Laxness's theatrical works, before moving on to the ever-popular subject of genealogy, at which Thorfinn was apparently expert. I enjoyed a second breakfast and was considering getting up to make tea—Ingibjorg had shown me where to find the kettle when I'd confessed that strong coffee didn't always agree with me—when Haukur leaned over and clasped my arm. He'd made some calls, he said. He had found four horses for me: a bay gelding at Jorfi, next door; another bay gelding at Hallkelsstadahlid in the next valley; and two chestnut mares that would be coming to Snorrastadir with a trekking company in a week or so. Today, he said, he would take me to see the two horses nearby; tomorrow we would ride to Litla Hraun. I nodded, astonished to learn he'd been so busy on my behalf. I hadn't said anything since my letter last May, asking him to help me find two horses like Elfa. Suddenly the horses were found. I abandoned the thought of tea and went to put on my riding breeches.

When I got back, he and Hallgerdur the horsewoman were deep in a discussion about *Njal's Saga*, the medieval masterpiece that contains a famous "feminist" character also named Hallgerdur. Known for her hip-length hair and her "thief's eyes," this storied Hallgerdur had been wooed and wed by the handsome Gunnar of Hlidarendi, that paragon of Icelandic manhood who, according to the saga, could "jump more than his own height in full armor, and just as far backwards as forwards."

"He could swim like a seal," the book said.

"There was no sport at which anyone could even attempt to compete with him."

"There has never been his equal."

The marriage was a disaster. It ended in Gunnar's death when, his house surrounded by enemies his wife had made for him, his bowstring broke and he asked for some strands of her long hair to plait into a new one; she refused.

It was this that Haukur and Hallgerdur were discussing: why the Saga-Age Hallgerdur—an historical woman who lived and died about a thousand years ago—had refused the gift of her hair.

They chattered on too fast for me to more than snatch at the argument. I marveled again that these sagas, of esoteric, antiquarian interest at home, were so alive here, centuries after they were written. I was heading again for that hot cup of tea when Haukur gave out a great guffaw.

"*Er Gunnar á Hliðarendi, nú, hommi?!*" he asked. "Is Gunnar of Hlidarendi, now, a homosexual?"

I stopped. I looked at Hallgerdur. The answer she was arguing was *yes*. You could write a dissertation on that one, I thought— *Homosexuality in Njal's Saga*. Gunnar did have an unusually close friendship with Njal, whose manhood was in question because he couldn't grow a beard. I wished I could comprehend the details of Hallgerdur's thesis and join in the conversation, but though I'd read the saga several times and knew it inside out, my spoken Icelandic wasn't up to the task. I retreated to the kitchen, where Ingibjorg gracefully drew my attention to the fact that the dishwasher could be unstacked and the table set for dinner. With the clatter drowning out Haukur's increasing outrage, I replayed the point in English in my head and awarded the set and match to Hallgerdur.

After dinner—a strange and flavorful fish in curry sauce, again with the odd addition of bananas—Stjani came by and he and Haukur spread out a roll of building plans. A prefab structure, Finnish-made, it could house hay-balers and other heavy machines down below and twenty tourists in sleeping bags in the loft. A big kitchen, a sizeable bath— "It's a hotel," said Haukur, when I peeked over his shoulder. "It costs *millions*." Stjani wanted to build it on the hill behind the barn.

"It's more to clean," sighed Ingibjorg, but it might cut down on the cooking. Haukur had the habit of asking tour groups inside after they'd conquered Eldborg, and Ingibjorg felt obliged to offer them coffee. Maybe if they had their own kitchen? I doubted it would have any effect on Haukur's impulsive generosity.

We didn't leave for Hallkelsstadahlid (blessedly shortened to Hlid, meaning "hillside") until just before supper, to see the bay gelding for sale there.

The evening had come on rainy and dim. This time the sky had no fire in it as Haukur steered the blue Volvo back toward the ale-spring, then along the gold-mossed lava and deep into the hills. A spire standing off from the near mountain made a perfect troll's shape in the gloom. A lake lapped at the edges of the road like a long-confined sea out to reclaim its tides.

The Hlid folk were out waiting, the horse saddled, when we drove up. There was a crowd of men and one woman, my age, who held the bridle. They greeted Haukur with shouts and teasing, and he answered volubly. One man I picked out of the crowd: There was something familiar about the gray stocking cap that mingled with his own gray hair, about the quizzical look on his sharp-angled face.

"I know you," I said in Icelandic, when the teasing stopped.

The man nodded tentatively.

"You were out hunting foxes last year when I lived at Litla Hraun."

The man agreed. Now he recognized me, too. I was the elf-queen, he was the outlaw—at least that's how we must have seemed to each other, I thought, when we materialized out of the mist on the edge of the lava field, a woman alone, a man with a gun, halfway between Snorrastadir and Litla Hraun, where each of us thought to be entirely alone. He had tried to slip unseen back down the path. I had followed him boldly and greeted him in Icelandic. *Good day. What are you hunting?*

Reassured to learn I was only the odd American wife at Litla Hraun, he had promised to stop in on his way home. He showed me a new path back to the cottage. When I found him there later, however, drinking coffee with my husband and conversing in gestures while they turned the pages of a bird book, I did not tell him I had found the foxes' den.

I recalled with pleasure how, over the summer, we had watched the fox pups grow, had seen them sneak in to steal fish skins and fat from our garbage heap. We had tried to make them warier, our last two weeks, by lobbing pebbles when they let us come too near. It wouldn't do to make the hunting too easy.

The other folk were asking questions now. "You lived at Litla Hraun?" "Why did you live there?" "All summer?" "Where did you get water?"

I looked at Haukur and let him answer. I had established that I could speak Icelandic, but that was all I could do. Let them wonder, really, how much I understood.

I fiddled with my riding helmet. There was something familiar about the woman too, dark bangs over cat's eyes, a wide, high-cheekboned face; only much later did I remember seeing her picture in the Icelandic horse magazine, *Eidfaxi*, in an article titled "A privilege to live so far away."

Suddenly I realized the conversation had turned to the horse in our midst. Haukur was appraising it in complimentary tones. A second horse was quickly brought out and saddled, and the woman and one of the men rode them away from us down the drive. With the rain in my eyes, I couldn't see much beyond the fact of two horses tolting. One was a lighter bay than the other; he seemed to be the one for sale. The horses went down the hill, up the far rise, turned at the crest, and came back.

"You should buy this horse," Haukur said. "This horse is very *spes*," he said, slipping in the Anglo-slang, "special," for my benefit. "He is soft, supple—"

"Very trustworthy, very calm, very easy to catch," added the woman who had ridden him. "Do you want to try?"

I said yes, amazed that Haukur could see so much, in five minutes, in the rain. I checked the stirrups; they seemed the right length. The woman and I were about the same height. She took the horse's head and brushed his wet forelock aside to show off a white star, then held him while I mounted. When I signaled him to go, he set off at a gentle walk. I squeezed my knees harder, hoping he would speed up gradually and not suddenly bolt. Nothing. We walked on.

Behind me I heard a rise in the conversation, then hoofbeats. The woman rode up on the darker horse and handed me her whip. I had seen other Icelanders ride with one, longer than a riding crop but a bit short for a dressage whip. This one had an engraved silver cap on its handle. I took it like I had expected it, and gave the horse a tap. Immediately he picked up a nice slow tolt, as if he'd been merely waiting for me to ask. It was a confident gait: His back felt soft and rounded and comfortable beneath me, his head was high, and his neck arched. His forelock blew back past his ears, and his dark mane rippled over my hands. He seemed to be enjoying himself, glad to be about, though not in any great hurry. I must have been smiling too, for the woman looked at me and beamed. She said something I didn't catch, and suddenly we were cantering up the hill. The horse had a fine, rolling canter. At the crest, we resumed the tolt, turned, cantered up the near hill, and tolted back to the barnyard. The horse stopped easily next to its fellow, and we got off. The rain was picking up again. Someone took the two horses into the stable. Another suggested coffee, and we all dashed for the house.

In the kitchen were several grown women: Any one could have been the housewife, all seemed to be in charge. As we took seats at the table, it seemed the number of men had increased. I found myself pressed over to the end of the bench, into the corner by the window, with Haukur snug beside me and the others squeezing in until the table could hold no more. One or two of the men took their cups into the next room; the others stood in the kitchen. It was after the traditional coffee time, and the women were cooking supper. No cakes or cheeses or cucumbers made an appearance, but the woman who had ridden the horse, the youngest there, set out a bowl of chocolate-dipped cookies. They quickly disappeared.

"The price is 160,000," Haukur said to me softly. "You'll take it. You won't do better than that."

I was alarmed. It seemed the deal had already been done. I wondered how to undo it. I liked this horse—but I wouldn't even buy a book with so little consideration. I had expected to look around a few weeks, try several horses, then choose the best. "I don't have the money with me," I mumbled. "It's with my friend in Reykjavik."

"You don't need to pay her now," Haukur said. He patted my hand, then turned abruptly to the others and joined their conversation.

I added more milk to my coffee, sipped it, and looked about. With the pots and pans rattling, and ten or more people all talking at once, I couldn't even catch a word every now and then. I felt myself getting anxious, even a little angry. True, the price, 160,000 Icelandic kronur, was reasonable, but it still translated to $2,250. My friends at home thought $800 was a lot to pay for a trail horse. I got out my notebook and started jotting things down. I felt better at once, safe in my own language, and I began considering the sale.

After a moment I saw the woman watching me, the calculating look in her tilted eyes changing to a screen of politeness as I returned her gaze with a more open, childlike one.

"What is the horse's name?" I asked. It was my screen, though she did not know it, this wide-eyed ingenuousness. With my limited Icelandic, I was forced to speak like a child. And I had no eye at all for horses, I realized now: I would not recognize a good horse if I fell off one. Seeming innocent was the only protection I had. People feel awkward about bilking a child.

"Birkir. Birkir frá Hallkelsstaðahlíð" she answered, the name combining Birch Tree with the name of the breeding farm, which was standard. She motioned for me to wait a moment and extricated herself from the tight table, seeming to give a signal that made everyone else disperse, for when she came back with a large binder, only Haukur and I were left.

"And your name?" I asked,

"Sigrún," she said, and smiled. I realized we'd probably been introduced outside, in one of those exchanges that had eluded me. I wrote it down, secure now that she thought me simple—though it still chafed a bit, this new self-image. It seemed to make more difference that she, an attractive woman my own age, knew I was not actually an idiot. Yet it did not occur to me to speak to her in English.

"And your phone number?" I asked.

Haukur got up, and I realized the television had been turned on in the next room. Time for the weather report. Sigrun opened her binder and showed me Birkir's page in the farm's breeding logbook. Carefully I wrote down his registration number and the names of his sire and dam. The stallion, Fafnir fra Fagranesi (Dragon), had been fathered by a famous horse, Hrafn fra Holtsmula (Raven); when he'd died recently, I'd heard, Hrafn had been stuffed for display at one of Iceland's agricultural colleges. I pointed the name out and murmured appreciatively. Sigrun cocked her head and nodded; it impressed her that I understood the bloodlines. I grew more confident. I did know something about Icelandic horses after all.

"And how old is he?"

Instantly I lost my advantage. Sigrun smiled a knowing smile and patiently showed me how to interpret the registration number I had just written down. Birkir fra Hallkelsstadahlid was number 92137901 in the book. Thus, he was born in 1992.

I put down my pencil. "He's only five?" I had wanted a well-trained horse, an eight-year-old at least. At five, this horse was barely saddle-broke.

She nodded. "We started him early, he's so big. He's been trained for over a year."

I wondered at that. According to what I'd read, the winter a horse turns four, it might be worked for twenty minutes a day, three times a week, for six weeks to two months, then let loose for another year before continuing its education the next winter. Such a horse is considered "rideable": *That is, an experienced rider can ride it and guide it in walk, trot, and canter where he wants to go, preferably also on quiet roads and not just in a pen,* I had read. *After two months of training you want the horse to be beginning to master a clean tolt.* Some trainers, I knew, took these "started" horses on long treks in the summer, either ponying them or letting them run loose to build up their muscles and get used to interacting with the rider. Yet a horse would not be ridden any distance until it was fully mature, at six or seven. So when Sigrun said Birkir had been "trained," did she mean ridden? Or just ponied? I wasn't sure how to politely ask.

I closed my notebook.

Haukur came up, as if that were our signal. "Have you shaken hands on the deal?" he asked.

I shook my head. Birkir was not for me, I said. "He's only five." I had found the knot I needed to undo their agreement.

"But he's very well-trained, very obedient," the woman said.

"He's as good as Elfa," Haukur added, looking down at me gravely. "In a few years, he'll be better than Elfa."

I knew then that Haukur would be insulted if I failed to buy the horse, as if I didn't, after all, respect his eye—and that he would stand to lose a modicum of status among the neighbors.

The deal was back on.

"I like him very much," I rushed to add, "but I'd like to think about it, he's so young. I'm not a very good rider."

Sigrun nodded, as if indulgently.

"Can I take a look at him again?"

"Oh, yes," she smiled.

Haukur shrugged. It was time for supper, I knew. We should be home at Snorrastadir. We put on our rain jackets and boots and followed Sigrun out to the stable, Haukur calling out our thanks and good-byes to the rest of the household.

The rain was still steady, but inside the barn it was warm and brightly lit and comforting. A raised center aisle separated two large pens full of horses, each haltered and clipped to a rail. They stirred and stamped when we entered, and I looked along their orderly ranks for Birkir. Amazingly, I picked him out at once, the light bay with a star, and walked down the aisle toward him feeling as if he were already mine. Sigrun approached him from the rear, and the horses parted, leaving room for me to step into the pen and join her. We stood at his flank, looking him over, and he turned his head to watch us, his neck arced high, his ears pricked with curiosity. He had a dark, liquid, inquisitive eye, soft and friendly. Unlike Elfa, he was completely at ease around us. He did not sidle away when I reached to pat him—on the contrary, he poked his nose forward, dog-like, to the limits of his rope, as if looking for attention. I scratched behind his ears and ran my hand down his neck and along his smooth wide back. His mane and tail were thick and dark, his black stockings neat, his hooves well-shaped, his coat a glowing red. He seemed larger and sturdier than most Icelandics I'd seen, and it was clear he was in excellent health.

"He's beautiful," I said, and meant it. I was filled with desire, suddenly, to own this beast—filled with awe that it was possible to own a creature so fine, so alive—surprised that anyone would actually let me take him away.

Sigrun read my thoughts. She stroked his reddish flank and spoke softly to him. "He's very good, you'll see," she said.

"I need to call my friend in Reykjavik—he's handling my money," I said. "I'll be in touch."

I hadn't said I would buy the horse. And yet I'd given her every reason to believe I would. From the lighted doorway of the stable she watched us off.

At home, Ingibjorg, Hallgerdur, and Bogi were already at table. "We have found Nancy's gelding," Haukur announced. "Now we will look for her mare."

I smiled and ate my supper. The idea that I wanted one of each sex, instead of two geldings, say, was also Haukur's.

Eleven o'clock—twilight—was the likeliest hour to catch someone in, so at eleven that evening, in Haukur's hearing, I phoned my friend in Reykjavik to ask about my money. It was a tangled question. Thordur, a young businessman and our friend for ten years, had helped us to buy the car we took to Litla Hraun the previous year; at summer's end he had sold it. This sum, close to $4,000, I had intended to spend on my horses. I had expected it to be in our Icelandic bank account when I arrived. But there'd been a complication. The buyer had paid with government notes, with the result that, to avoid being taxed himself, Thordur had needed to reinvest the sum. When I saw him in Reykjavik at the start of my trip, I insisted he cash in the stocks and free up the funds. Now, with Haukur watching, I was checking to see if he had done it.

We conversed in a creole. Thordur, whose English was fluent, liked the fact that I would attempt Icelandic and often set himself up as my inquisitor, refusing to speak English until I was hopelessly lost. On this call, we reached hopelessness repeatedly. The problem lay in the Icelandic stock market, the workings of which he painstakingly explained. The upshot was that he couldn't cash in our stocks without taking a loss. Okay by me, I replied, I wanted the cash—any cash—but Thordur wouldn't hear of it. We argued. He held firm. He acted as though I wanted him to do something dishonest. Slowly I realized something else was troubling him. There was an odd undercurrent to our discussion. Thordur wasn't a horse person, so, to no surprise, he had little interest in the bay gelding at Hlid. But his attitude seemed inordinately negative. Finally he blurted it out, embarrassed, as if forced to make up for my stupidity by being impolitely blunt: *You must not buy a horse,* he said in English, *until you see Einar's horses in Skagafjord.* He sounded ready to back up that order by holding on to my cash, so I promptly promised that I wouldn't, of course; I'd never intended to.

I hung up the phone feeling dizzy.

I had overlooked another point of honor. It was Thordur who had engineered my week's invitation in Skagafjord, the center of Iceland's horse-breeding industry. The breeder he had contacted, Einar Gislason, had been a colleague of Thordur's father at an agricultural institute many years back. Einar was among the top breeders in the country, and it had taken some convincing before he'd agreed to host my visit. His formal invitation had been the foundation for my trip (since Haukur hadn't written me back), but I'd never taken it too seriously. Einar's was just another farm to visit, a prospect of free room and board in a part of the country that was new to me. What I'd missed was the unsaid promise: Thordur was not sending just a friend, but a sale.

Haukur came and took my hand. "That man," he said, his voice dark and protective, "do you trust him?"

"Oh yes," I answered, alarmed at the thought. Thordur was one of the most trustworthy people I knew. I couldn't explain about the car sale, the bank notes, the stock market, his distaste at taking a loss. His promise to Einar in Skagafjord. "There's some problem with the bank."

Haukur nodded and sucked on the end of his pipe.

CHAPTER FIVE

TRAVELERS' TALES

The clouds still ringed us, the horizon drawn close and soft. The mist shut out the Fire Fortress and the two red hills where the mare Skalm lay down under her load, and beside them the gap toward Hlid where the bay gelding Birkir waited; but above us the vault was a paler gray, the sky less threatening. The grass was dewed too heavily for haying. The tide was out. Haukur and I put sandwiches in our coat pockets and saddled Bjartur and Elfa for a trip to Litla Hraun.

We took the track along the River Kalda toward the sea. Hallgerdur came along behind us, racing to catch up, with four-year-old Magnus balanced before her on the saddle, but when she heard how far we were going, she waved and continued along the rocky stream course, while we turned north with the path and entered the bog.

"She's starting off fast," Haukur said of Hallgerdur. "We never do that." It was the horse he was concerned about, not his laughing grandson.

We splashed through the wet spots and cut across the sucky mud to the fine hard highway of the sands, heading for the stranded island where sea eagles had nested last year. No birds arose to scold us, and I asked Haukur about them.

He reined in to ride next to me. He'd found a dead eagle lying in the nest one day earlier this summer. He shipped it to the natural history museum in Reykjavik, where an autopsy had found a few pellets of birdshot in its breast. He shook his head. "There are bad men in Iceland, too," he said.

We rode in silence again, pondering that. The horses' hooves kept up a crisp beat on the hard-packed sand. The irreverent chant crept up on me—*Black-and-Decker-Black-and-Decker*—until I could think of nothing else but the rhythm of the four-beat gait. As I concentrated on that pulse, letting it course through me like a dance tune, I felt Elfa lighten, my better balance letting her run clear. But only for a moment: Then my pride at riding a good tolt interrupted my concentration. I fell out of step. I wobbled and bounced. Elfa stiffened, took a few bumpy steps at a trot, tossed her head angrily, and, in spite of me, regained the gait. I glanced over at Haukur to see if he'd noticed, but he was lost in the air and the sea and the sorrow of the eagles.

Once, the year before, Haukur had introduced me to a well-known riding instructor, Reynir Adalsteinsson, whose party Haukur had guided on a short tour on the sands. *Is she used to horses?* Reynir asked, speaking over my head in spite of my greeting him in Icelandic. Haukur smiled. *She's seventy percent,* he said proudly, putting his arm around my shoulders with a protective squeeze. *I've been riding all my life,* he whispered in my ear, *and I'd give myself only ninety percent.*

Still, that *seventy percent* had stung. I wasn't used to being a C student. Back home I upped my riding lessons to twice a week, eager to increase my rating to *eighty*, or at least a high *seventy-five*. But I overlooked one fact: Riding an Icelandic horse demands a different technique, not the English hunter-jumper style I was being taught. I spent nine months muscling up my lower leg (there's nothing subtle about an old school horse), nine months hovering high above the saddle, elbows in, hands low, heels down. Now I had to unlearn all that. I needed to sit deep, spread my hands up and out, loosen my hips, let my legs waggle—knees pinched in, ankles wide. *Never touch the horse with your lower leg. That's just asking for trouble,* an Icelandic riding teacher had scolded me. *A lot of Icelandics are trained with no leg at all,* explained an American who owns several. *An American rider gets on them in New York and ends up in Oklahoma.* The classic two-point seat, the mainstay of my riding classes (butt in the air, legs clamped), was worse than useless: *In that position,* warned another American, *things begin to blur.*

I had found her description true. The day after I had arrived in Reykjavik on this month-long horse-buying trip, I had taken an hour's riding lesson. I'd ridden Icelandics before, I told the instructor, but I didn't fully understand the gaits. I was hoping, in particular, to learn to shift between tolt and trot. To trot I should lean forward, the instructor said, rest one hand and my weight on the horse's mane above the withers, and "ask him to trot just like you would at home." I assumed the familiar two-point and squeezed.

The horse bolted. It had swung around the corner of the track before I knew where I was. The scenery tumbled inward. I began seeing things in the near compass with incredible clarity: the length of electrical cord loose on the grass, the break in the white rope defining the ring, the scatter of sharp edges in the gravel, the depression where water had once pooled on the track. Dimly I heard the instructor shouting, "Stop him! Make him stop! *Pull!*" It was more important to stay on. With the horse skittering on the turns like a beagle on a linoleum floor, I doubted I could do both at once. We screamed around the final turn, and I aimed right for the instructor, standing comfortably wide with her arms spread out, brandishing a long whip. The horse skidded to a stop in front of her and tried to dodge toward the barn. She grabbed the bridle, and I got off, shaking.

Once I had asked Haukur how to switch from tolt to trot, and he'd simply shaken his head. *I don't know*, he said, *you just ask*. It was as if I'd asked him how to breathe.

So now he was rocking along, riding as if he were only breathing. But his horse, the tall, cream-colored gelding he chose first of the seventy horses he owned, was neither tolting nor trotting, from what I could see. His movement was lateral, not diagonal like a trot, but instead of lifting and arching with his forehand high, as Elfa was, Bjartur stretched his legs straight in a pacelike motion, his hooves striking a syncopated two-beat instead of the tolt's even four. Was this the unwanted, in-between *lull*, the slow *skeið*, or pace, damned in English with the dismissive name of "piggy pace"? To many Icelanders it was a horrible fault. "A horse which cannot tolt is not worth much," I'd read. "Another kind of horse, which always moves at the skeid, fast or slow, is generally classified as unrideable. An animal of this kind is often known as a *trunta* or nag, a horse-breeding failure which the farmer will put down rather than sell." The rolling, pacey motion was said to be terribly uncomfortable, making the rider sway from side to side. Yet on Bjartur, Haukur looked so still he could pour tea. And I'd seen the horse keep it up for hours.

"According to one expert, a slow pace is "a gait no rider wants to be seen using." Yet the same author admits that "the tolt is difficult for the horse when used for long intervals and thus riders should only ask their horses for tolt when the ground is smooth and even." Few of Iceland's bridle paths, though ancient and well-worn, are smooth and even. Interrupted by birch brush and roots, they cross farm fields heaved and hummocked by frost, pocked and pitted with bogs. They angle up and around precipitous slopes, wind along rocky rivers, or pick their way through lava wastes.

Yet even today, when riding fast and far is only a pleasure, not a necessity, horses routinely cover thirty miles a day. On one trek organized in 1994, one thousand kilometers—six hundred miles—were ridden in two weeks, an average of over forty miles each day. Though a high-stepping four-beat tolt may be the ideal, farmers in the horse-trekking business, like Haukur, will overlook the fashion for a smooth traveling gait. *Ferðagleði á ferðaskeið* (The joy of travel at the traveling-pace), says a cartoon of a smiling, bearded farmer on a slow-pacing horse in *Hesturinn og Reiðmennskan (The Horse and the Art of Riding)*. Or, as one seventy-three-year-old rider said in a letter to *Eidfaxi* magazine, "For a troubled back, a soft tolt which is a bit closer to pace is the best massage."

Hundreds of years ago, when horse shows were unknown, Icelandic horses were bred for strength, speed, color (sometimes), and a smooth, untiring traveling gait. Today's fine distinctions between fast tolt, slow tolt, trot-tolt, pace-tolt, traveling pace, and piggy pace were unknown. A good horse was comfortable to ride all day, which meant it possessed some mid-speed gait other than a jarring, jouncing trot. In medieval Europe, such a horse was known as an ambler or a palfrey or a jennet, and would be ridden by ladies or noblemen or knights not in armor. The word "ambler" comes from the early Roman *ambulator*, or walker, while a trotting horse in these same documents is called a *cussator* or *cruciator*, a "tormentor" or "crucifier." "Palfrey" derives from the Greek *parippi* or the Celtic *paraveredus*, both meaning a horse used for long journeys. The jennet was originally a particular breed out of Spain, known for its beauty and easygoing lateral pace. In Ireland, an especially calm-gaited horse was bred for the sport of falconry. This horse—said to be safe even if the hawk you were carrying on your wrist took fright and began to bate, flapping upside down from its jesses—was called a "hobby" or "hobby horse," from the name of the small falcon popular in the sport.

When roads became widespread during the Renaissance and carriages were the noble way to travel, selective breeding for smooth-gaited riding horses declined. People bred for trotters, faster and with more stamina when under harness. Only in the roadless outposts of European culture were the smooth, lateral gaits like the tolt retained, producing, in the New World, such breeds as the Tennessee Walking Horse and the Peruvian Paso. Yet several writers maintain that horses of any breed can still be taught to tolt.

"The amount of tolt a horse has can't be measured, any more than you can measure the amount of mambo, samba, or fox-trot a human has," noted Elizabeth Haug, proprietor of the Viking Saga Ranch in California, in one of her sales flyers. "The truth is that, once you know how, you can teach any horse of any breed to tolt, just like you can teach a specific dance to any normal human being." The exercise, however, might not be worth the trouble, she acknowledged. "All horses are not equally balanced and graceful," she added.

German riding instructor Walter Feldmann is more exact. "In my opinion you can find three types of horses within every breed," he told *Eidfaxi*. "The first group consists of natural tolters, then there are trotters who can be taught to tolt, and the third group consists of trotters who cannot learn to tolt." Even among Icelandic horses, there are some with only three gaits: walk, trot, and canter; or walk, pace, and canter. These are usually culled; at the least, they are excluded from the breeding stock. According to Kristinn Hugason, until recently the Icelandic government's horse-breeding advisor, the ability to tolt is genetic and is easily improved by selective breeding: "It is part of the quality of the trait, how easy it is to breed it. Well-bred Icelandic horses should therefore be almost self-trained to tolt, though it is preferable that they trot when not ridden," as the trot is less tiring.

In Iceland, where roads are a recent improvement, horse breeding over the centuries has been influenced more by nature than by fashion. Whereas Russia boasts twenty-seven breeds of horse, at last count, and Britain, France, the United States, and Germany are each home to sixteen or more, Iceland has only the Icelandic horse. In the early 1100s, Icelanders banned the import of more horses to their island. No story tells how or why they reached that decision, but given that the lawmakers of medieval Iceland were the forty-eight chieftains, their motive was probably to keep the means of transportation concentrated in the fewest hands. The law remains on the books today, kept there by the horse-breeders' fear of foreign diseases, for which the isolated herds have built up no resistance, and by their conviction that the breed cannot be improved except from within. Cross-breeding, according to one Icelandic farmer, is "revolting," a "bottomless disgrace." "It is a unique gene bank," she continued, "being in so many ways totally different from all other horse breeds. It's developed in a very difficult land. It has survived with the Icelandic people in hunger and frost. It has died along with the Icelandic people in famine. If we lost this breed, we could never ever breed it again."

Cold winters, short summers with little grass, constant wind, frequent rain, and a rough landscape "where at any moment the ground might open under your feet," as one American rider told me, have created a hardy, agile beast. In 1783 the ashfall from a huge volcanic eruption, and the widespread famine that followed, killed off nearly three-quarters of the estimated 32,000 horses in the country. Only 3,000 of the survivors were mares. Yet the number of horses rebounded until by the late 1800s Icelanders had enough spare horses to sell 62,000 of them to England for use as draft animals in underground coal mines. Horses of small stature were preferred, of course. The author of *Hestar í Lífi Þjóðar (Horses in the Life of the Nation)* called this era of cruelty "a phase of unprecedented degradation in the story of the Icelandic horse." Nothing could be crueler than to subject these creatures of wide-open spaces to a claustrophobic life underground.

In 1840 the farmer Thorkell at Svadastadir bought a black colt from his neighbor and began to breed up a line of black horses. Svadastadir, in the Skagafjord district of northern Iceland, was a rich farm, with many acres of good pasture, and the horses flourished. Thorkell's blacks were prized as friendly, easygoing, all-purpose horses. His son Jonas wanted spirited riding horses, so he added chestnuts with blazes to the herd, since legend said that these made the best mounts. The two lines mixed, and their descendants spread throughout Skagafjord. Late in the nineteenth century the farmer Palmi fenced in the Svadastadir fields—the first Icelander to restrict his stallions. He bought back a number of Svadastadir-bred mares from his neighbors and went about scientifically improving his stock. Today, the Svadastadir line, with its branches in Saudarkrokur, Kolkuos, and Kirkjubaer (whose herd is all chestnut with blazes), is one of the most famous pedigrees in Iceland.

Palmi's ideas caught on, and in 1901 the Icelanders passed a law requiring stallions to be kept fenced so that paternity could be guaranteed. In the late 1940s, when tractors and cars replaced horsepower on most farms, breeders began exporting riding horses to Germany. Gunnar Bjarnason, the government horse-breeding adviser at the time, declared in 1951, "The heavy horse used for farming is history. Today we need more than ever before strong, willing, easy-to-ride, and most of all nicely tempered horses. This can easily go along with breeding good riding horses. ... The high-tempered, quality-gaited horses will be used for experienced riders, but the others can be versatile horses for all." Color didn't factor into the equation, despite the urging of foreign horse dealers who had argued earlier in the century that a distinctive color, like the pale dun of the Norwegian Fjord horse, would give greater identity to the breed. Only lately have a few breeders begun to select for the rarer grays, blue-grays, silver dapples, palominos, pintos, and roans. "If someone wants to sell a very fine horse which is also of a beautiful and rare color, he can do good business," said one exporter.

"It is a notorious fact," wrote R. H. C. Davis in *The Medieval Warhorse*, "that breeds can be lost much more quickly than they can be established. Breeds are maintained by ensuring that good mares are not covered by any stallion which has not been specially selected." Such is the rule now followed in Iceland. Since the 1950s, breeding horses have been judged at shows on conformation (head, shoulder and neck, back, limbs, joints, hooves, and overall proportions), as well as performance (tolt, trot, canter, pace, willingness, character, and form under saddle), with current fashion weighting the various traits. In 1986 the procedure was computerized, providing a prediction of the "breeding value" of a foal. Only stallions and mares with a certain judged score are approved for breeding—although farmers often disregard the rule. "The defects we are trying to get rid of," wrote one expert, "include various hereditary problems such as broken-windedness, having only one testicle, air-sucking, and other ailments and vices. Also we must remove a few other shortcomings from our stock, such as lack of versatility, incorrect gaits and short steps, laziness, kicking and bucking, unwillingness to leave the stable, shying away, and being difficult to catch."

"The breeding goal," explained another expert, "is to make the front of the horse as light and fine as possible, since the Icelandic horse has a rather short and thick neck compared to other horse breeds." Good legs are also stressed. "The Icelandic horse is renowned for strong and healthy legs. It is one trait breeders do not want to see disappear." (The legs are, in fact, strikingly stout and sturdy—so much so that an American farrier, reaching down to lift the hoof of one of my Icelandics for the first time, abruptly stood up and declared indignantly, "This horse's knee is swollen." Then he realized all four knees were that size, as well as the four knees of my second horse.)

In judging the performance score for an Icelandic horse, the tolt carries the most weight, followed by the pace, the expert continued. "Not all horses have pace worth showing, but it is considered good for the tolt if the horse has some pace. ... It is thought that without breeding for pace, the tolt would be lost."

"Some pace" ranges from piggy pace to traveling pace to flying pace, called the "crown" of a good riding horse. Bjartur excelled at the flying pace; this, not his idiosyncratic traveling gait, made him Haukur's favorite. To be a true pacer, a horse must reach a speed of at least 30 kilometers an hour (about 20 mph), or run a 250-meter course, under saddle, in 26 seconds. The race record for thirty years was 22.6 seconds, set by a mare named Gletta in 1946. Since then, several horses have been clocked at a few tenths of a second faster, and in 1999, at an international meet, one horse repeatedly broke the 22-second mark. Once, in the summer of 1996, when we raced along the sands with our party of city riders, Haukur had hung back, then sped Bjartur in a flying pace past all of us, making faces and wagging his tongue, the horse stretched out long and sleek beneath him, an arrow-line from its croup to its nose. Another time, when I rode with his daughter Branddis while Haukur led a different group, he had seen us resting on one of the grass-topped islands near the mouth of the Kalda (Denmark, I think this islet was named, or else England) and had raced Bjartur past us, the farm dog yipping and snapping at the horse's heels and eventually outstripping it, to Haukur's dismay.

Bjartur's spectacular flying pace and Elfa's smooth tolt were no advantage at all, however, when Haukur and I left the sands and turned toward the lava path. Two ways led from Snorrastadir to Litla Hraun, roundabout over the sands or straight through the lava. The lava path, which I'd been unable to find on my walk a few days before, was called Thraellyndisgata, a compound linking the Icelandic words for "path" or "way," "mind" or "mood," and "slave" or "thrall." When we'd lived at Litla Hraun and used the path almost daily, we'd amused ourselves making up English translations—"Bad Mood Path" was one, and "The Way of the Mind of a Slave"—and speculating on how the name had come to be. My favorite theory was that a horseman, passing at speed on the packed-sand highway, had opined that only a slave (who couldn't afford a horse), or someone with the blinkered mind of a slave, would travel by that twisted, tortuous track. Now Haukur, on fast Bjartur, was choosing that route even though the tide was low.

The path opened out between two lava stacks at the foot of a grassy bay. We got off and let the horses rest the few minutes it took Haukur to fill his pipe, light it, suck a few draughts, and knock it out against a rock. Then we entered the lava. The track was etched lightly on the black earth, sometimes just a scratch on rock as smooth as macadam and as slick to the horses' smooth-shod feet, sometimes a hoof-wide gouge into softer earth, winding or splitting around protruding stones. It skirted ancient tumbled cairns and ten-foot chasms, plunged down into birch scrub or up rubbly slopes. Twice we passed spots that had seen human improvement: chasms filled in, stones laid to make a bridge. The "paving" here was fist-sized chunks that rolled and clacked under the horses' hooves. I walked back a few days later and took photos to show my friends: No one in my riding school would have dreamed of crossing such terrain on horseback.

Suddenly, halfway along the path, Haukur stopped. "We get off and walk here," he said. "This part is bad."

I couldn't see any difference. This turn was no sharper, that hill no steeper. The path was plain to see, if perhaps narrower. In a few paces he remounted again and we rode on, Haukur with his reins long, letting Bjartur pick his own way, me quarrelling with Elfa, thinking we were going much too fast, holding her back, then having to hurry to catch up.

"Over ground that would seem elsewhere almost too bad for any horse at a foot-pace," wrote Elizabeth Jane Oswald in 1882, an Icelandic horse will go "with a gay snort at a hand-gallop. As a rule, they wish to go fast wherever the road will permit; and unless indulged in a rattling gallop now and then, can be decidedly skittish, especially if they suspect another horse of a design of going before them."

Elfa clearly suspected Bjartur of having designs, yet I also knew I should trust her instincts, for as Sabine S. Baring-Gould said of Icelandic horses in 1863, "neither persuasion nor blows will make them tread where their instinct tells them there is danger."

Oswald and Baring-Gould were among the many British gentry who went adventuring in Iceland in the nineteenth century. She was a Scottish general's daughter and descended from a duke; he, a Devonshire parson who wrote fairy tales, novels, and the hymn "Onward Christian Soldiers." "It was the literature that brought me," Oswald said, "the vivid sagas which set the men and women of the past before us as if we had known them ourselves." Baring-Gould was similarly inspired. Yet once in Iceland, they could not help but notice the horse. Until the 1940s, much of the country was inaccessible except by horseback or on foot, no matter how deep the traveler's pockets.

"An Icelandic horse is a most remarkable object," wrote Baring-Gould. "As he spins along, he holds his head toward the ground, observing it intently, so that he seldom trips, and when he sees a crack or hole in the lava, he swerves rapidly and avoids it. ...

He will climb wherever a goat can clamber, will trot over wastes of angular stone fragments, and tread fearlessly over bogs, supported only by a network of long grass."

Of these hazards, the bog seemed chief in Baring-Gould's mind. It is "a formidable affair," he wrote. "It rolls and quakes underfoot as though one were riding over an air cushion. The surface is matted with long grass, and the ponies, with wondrous instinct, select the right places for planting their feet. ... When they come to a red glistening patch or streak, they will leap, but should they consider the ground on the opposite side to be doubtful, they will track the seam up till they find a place where they can overstep it."

William Bisiker encountered a different sort of bog on his Icelandic expedition in 1902: "Hard-looking surfaces—apparently gravelly areas with a few stones in them. ... A pony comes to a halt on the edge of one of them and sniffs; its rider, a newcomer, unused to the country, urges his beast onward, but as a rule it will not go. If it does consent to move on a few paces it suddenly sinks in, and then makes a wild endeavor at recovery. After one or two experiences of this kind, the newcomer sometimes thinks it better to allow the pony to have its own way, for it seems that it knows more about the country and the nature of the ground than its rider does."

Iceland's gravelly hills of volcanic ash and scree pose other hazards. Wrote Baring-Gould:

We lost our way, and in following a sheep-track, or what we took to be such, got into a sufficiently perplexing situation. The river boiled a hundred and fifty feet below us, and we were on a ledge canted over the gulf, the rock sheered up some hundred feet above our heads, and a fall of washed shale lay in a slant on the terrace before us. ... Knotting my bridle on the pony's neck lest it should slip and entangle its feet, I crept along the slant, supporting myself on my whip, which I drove at each step into the loose soil. 'Bottle-brush,' my piebald, put his nose to the ground and advanced one foot, snuffed out a firm spot, and planted the other; then came a particularly critical slide of shale, which was wet with tricklings from the rock overhead. Bottle-brush pawed the earth away till he had scraped a hole through the rubble to the firm rock, and then fixed his hoof resolutely in it. Slowly and cautiously he advanced. Ah! The crumbling basalt gave way at once, he floundered down, was up again, the dislodged rubbish puffed into the indigo abyss, and the little flat slatey fragments of clinkstone tinkled down the slope and leaped into the water. ... When the dangerous slant was passed, my pony pushed his droll big head under my arm and rubbed it against my side, evidently expecting to have a word of praise.

D. B. McKean told a similar tale in *A Boy's Visit to Iceland* in 1921. One of his young companions, McKean wrote, "stumbled and fell and would have gone bounding from crag to crag had he not kept a firm clutch upon the bridle of his pony. ... He could not regain a footing on the path, but hung suspended in the air. ... The pony seemed at once to take in the situation and began to back carefully and slowly so as to drag the boy's feet once more onto the path. ... As soon as F— had recovered his footing, it stood quite still, all four feet gathered together on one rock, while poor F—, sick and giddy, with the bridle still in his hand, threw his arms around the pony's neck."

The gorge that separated Litla Hraun from the lava was small and grassy, not treacherous, but still Haukur dismounted to lead Bjartur down. He unhooked one side of the reins, which clip onto the bit conveniently with swivel hooks, and let the horse go, still saddled, the long straight rein dragging.

"Won't they run off?" I asked as I came up leading Elfa. Over the flats toward Stora Hraun the tide was creeping in, too high already to wade across to use the phone. It'd be a long walk home without a horse.

Haukur laughed. "Look at this grass!" he said. It was higher than the stirrups. "Why would they go anywhere else?"

He lifted the shutter off the door of my old summerhouse—it looked desolate and abandoned in the gray gloom—and we went in.

It was cold and damp, the fresh paint from last summer already peeling. I made a quick inventory. Whoever had been there last had wrapped the mattresses well in plastic and hung them from the ceiling. The pillows were stowed in the wooden sea chest. The little dry food we'd stored was still mostly there, in good shape, the plastic containers not much chewed, though the mice had been at them. Haukur climbed the old ship's ladder to poke his head into the attic and pronounced it *horrible*, just as I'd said. The original insulation had been turf, and with the roof full of holes (the patching we'd done the summer before was too little, too late), the attic had turned into a mildewed mess. The house needed a new roof to stay standing much longer, and I hoped Haukur would offer to fix it, but though he owned much of the land around us, the house, it seemed, was someone else's problem.

We sat on the two plastic chairs in the main room and unwrapped our sandwiches. I wished I could offer him coffee, but the stove was cold, the thermos was gone, it wasn't our summerhouse any longer. Out the windows the clouds hid both the far glacier and the volcano that had always seemed so close. Even the hills behind Stora Hraun were blanketed.

"I remember the first time I came to Litla Hraun," Haukur said. "I was eleven. It was 1943."

Haukur had been born at Snorrastadir, the third generation to farm there, and the family at Litla Hraun was in some way related, but I had never quite untwisted the genealogy. My friend Anna, whose mother had given us permission to live here, called Haukur her *frændi*, or "kinsman," and that was specific enough. It must have been a hard life at Litla Hraun, I thought, so cut off by the lava and the tides; we'd found it hard enough living here for just one summer—so many hours spent fetching water from the spring, collecting driftwood for the fire, crossing the marsh and driving to the crossroads or the market town for supplies, to make a phone call, to bathe or fetch our laundry.

"It was a good farm, Litla Hraun, before there were cars," Haukur said.

Suddenly I saw the place in a new way: The horse highway went past its door. The salmon river and the islands, full of birds' eggs, were a short walk at low tide. The lava path was well used back then; the children went that way to school.

"It was a better farm than Snorrastadir," Haukur said. My eyebrows arced up in surprise, and he went on. The sheep could graze here two weeks longer in the fall than at Snorrastadir, he explained—as far as I could tell, it had something to do with the prevailing winds—and you could let them out of the sheds two weeks earlier in the spring. Four weeks when you didn't need hay. "Some years," he said, "that could make all the difference."

Independent People, the Halldor Laxness book that Haukur and Bogi had been discussing, and the sagas before that, were full of tales of starvation, of the flocks dying, the cattle going dry, those years when the spring came late. People ate their horses then, all but the best.

Haukur nodded. "The first time I came to Litla Hraun, it was November, in the snow. My brother and I were gathering in the sheep. We walked over to Litla Hraun and we had a hot meal, then went back by way of Fitjar"—the grassy peninsula that stretches into the sands from the lava's edge. "I was so light-footed and strong that I ran the whole way," Haukur said. He looked hard at me. "I am much richer today for having gone to Litla Hraun that day. Something about this place makes one stop and think."

Before we left, I went to get a drink at the spring that Bishop Gudmundur had blessed in the thirteenth century, down the grassy hill and into a lava gorge, where the clear water bubbled up cold and sweet from the back of a cave. I felt strangely light-hearted and cheerful, as if I knew from Haukur's nostalgia that the Litla Hraun I remembered would always remain. He had kissed me on the cheek as we left the house and said with great gravity, *Thank you for bringing me back to Litla Hraun.*

He was holding the horses when I came up from the spring, and we retraced our steps, going slowly, getting off for the "bad" part, then tolting back over the sands, before the tide could cover them. I saw a large bird lift off a tussock, and I would have pointed it out, it could have been an eagle, but it was too far away to be sure.

All day I had wanted to ask Haukur about the bay gelding at Hlid. What had he seen in the horse? Why, exactly should I buy it? What gave it the same rank as his Elfa (who was tolting happily now that I'd relaxed and wasn't getting in her way)?

Riding home over the wet sands, I knew that those were questions I couldn't ask. I didn't know enough—about horses, about the language. It would sound critical. Impolite. I had requested Haukur's help. Now I would have to trust his eye. As we turned up the river course toward Snorrastadir, the wind brought rain, stinging our faces. Haukur shook his head, laughed, and let the horses race home.

CHAPTER SIX

THE BUSINESS OF HORSE BREEDING

"They have many bay horses," Ingibjorg said as she rolled out the dough for sweet rolls.

I was in the kitchen, sipping my morning tea, and trying to learn what to expect at Sydra-Skordugil, the farm in Skagafjord where I was due the next day. The weather was classically Icelandic: forty degrees and raining sideways. The horses stood strung out on the hill with their tails to the wind. Even Bjartur looked black.

The rain had chased Hallgerdur back to her job in the city, postponing indefinitely her long ride north. Haukur and his son-in-law were also in Reykjavik, seeing a model of the Finnish "hotel" they were thinking of setting up beside the barn. And Ingibjorg was gracefully evading my questions.

I was sure she knew a lot more about Einar Gislason.

I had been introduced to the two horsemen, Haukur in the west and Einar in the north, through completely different routes. Haukur was the "kinsman" of Anna, whom I'd met through Petur, the half-brother of Gunnar, who had studied for his doctorate at the Pennsylvania State University, where I work. Einar had been suggested to me by Thordur, who was friends with Venni, the brother of another Petur, who had also earned his doctorate at Penn State. Yet as was often the case in Iceland, Einar and Haukur had crossed paths several times.

The two had been roommates at Hvanneyri, the agricultural college in western Iceland, in the early 1950s. In an interview with the magazine *Heima Er Bezt (Home Is Best)* in 1996, Haukur reminisced about his college days. Once he and Einar had had a fierce desire for boiled eggs to go with their coffee. They hung out by the chicken coop until the man in charge came to feed the hens. One of the boys engaged him in chat, evincing great interest in the raising of fowl (I suspect the talker was Haukur). The other filched a half dozen eggs and hid them in the big sack of sawdust bedding beside the door. A little later they retrieved the eggs, and ate them, but one they overlooked. When the keeper next spread fresh bedding, he was amazed that a hen had snuck out, through a door kept carefully locked, and laid an egg in the sack. "It was the greatest theft I have ever taken part in," Haukur professed.

A few years later, while Haukur was farming with his father at Snorrastadir, Einar moved in next door at Stora Hraun—where the farm wife had done our wash and where we'd gone to use the phone the summer we lived at Litla Hraun. Two years later, Einar and his wife moved to the government's experimental farm at Hestur (which means "horse"), a long day's ride inland from Snorrastadir. It was at Hestur that Ingibjorg was working as a housekeeper when she married Haukur in 1970. Not until 1974 did Einar leave the west and move north to Sydra-Skordugil, taking over the farming from his father-in-law Sigurjon, nicknamed "Duddi."

Duddi was famous for his horse-dealing, long a popular pastime among farmers in the north. A group of farmers would meet at a roundup or on the road. "Someone suggests a trade, and each describes the qualities of his own horse," noted one chronicler. The deal is clinched with a handshake: Buyer beware. "Test rides were not part of the deal as a rule." Yet in Iceland, as early as the tenth century, the law provided some guarantee. A horse could be returned within five days if it proved to have such defects as "deafness and blindness, impaired breathing and lameness, spasms, and a balky disposition."

Duddi acquired a fine fast pacing horse one summer at the end of a series of five horse trades, once throwing in a load of smoked lumpsucker (an oily, smelly fish his wife wouldn't let in the house anyway) and once receiving a half-bottle of moonshine (his wife liked the bottle; it was empty by the time she saw it). To get the pacer, he offered half of the prize he was sure to win riding it in the local races. When he lost, the question arose: Who really owned the horse?

Another time Duddi and a group of Skagafjord men met a friend sitting forlornly by the road beside an unknown horse. The man had been drinking more than was good for him and had traded away his wife's favorite mare. The new horse wasn't bad, but he couldn't face his wife. He offered a reward to anyone who could get his wife's horse back. The Skagfirdings took up the challenge. They brushed the new horse until it shone, trimmed its mane, and rode off in search of its former owner. The horse looked fine and fiery under its new rider (who admitted later he had to work like the dickens just to keep it in gait), and the former owner casually suggested a trade. Nope. Couldn't part with this horse. Then the wife's favorite mare was put up in trade, if the newcomer would pay a little extra, since mares are more valuable than geldings. Nope. Got enough mares. The price dropped. Now it was half as much as the reward for the mare. Well, all right, said the newcomer. He flung the saddle on the mare, paid up, and rode off as fast as he could go. In the distance, he heard the other fellow curse. "What the devil! I've got my old Mosi back again!"

In giving up the farm at Hestur, I'd heard, Einar had also earned himself a nickname: Einar "Hestlausi," or Einar "Without a Horse." I was sure there must be stories about him as well.

But all Ingibjorg would tell me was the color of his horses.

I wondered if there was a hidden message here. I knew she assumed that if I seriously intended to buy Icelandic horses, I'd buy the bay gelding, Birkir, at Hlid. And, if so, that my second horse would be a mare, as Haukur had suggested, and not a bay. With so many colors to choose from, who would want two of the same? (Which was why, I supposed, I hadn't heard another word about the second bay gelding for sale nearby at the farm called Jorfi.) So was Ingibjorg now saying, ever so gently, that I wouldn't find a horse to my liking at Einar's?

According to my friend Thordur, Einar was the best horse breeder in Skagafjord, which was the best horse-breeding district in the country. But Thordur was not averse to a little hyperbole—like another Icelandic friend who insisted that the best salt in the world came from a single spot on Iceland's southwest coast—and I'd heard from other reputable sources that Sveinn Gudmundsson in the Skagafjord town of Saudarkrokur was considered "the most prominent breeder" in the district and that "horses descended from his stock dominate the Icelandic horse-breeding scene." Head of the produce department at the local co-op, Sveinn had been awarded the Knight's Cross of the Icelandic Order of the Falcon for his work in horse breeding. Einar had happened to work closely with Thordur's father while at Hestur. "I think he is the right guy," Thordur had written me. "I mean his reputation is very solid. He won't cheat you."

The next morning on the bus to Skagafjord, in between reading the dictionary and writing down such words as *sópur* (broom), *rúmföt* (bedsheets), and *leggja á borðið* (set the table) in anticipation of helping out another elderly housewife who spoke no English, I thought back to those conversations and wondered if Einar really was "the right guy." It wouldn't help to say, "I want a horse like Elfa." In Skagafjord, I'd have to explain what I had seen in Elfa that I liked. I wasn't really sure. Nor did I have the words to say it in Icelandic.

"There's a pretty view from Vatnsskard," Ingibjorg had said, when she'd decided to change the subject. "That's between Blondudalur and Svartardalur."

I thought the view all the way to Skagafjord was pretty.

The rain had passed, leaving the sky a cool washed blue. The low sun set everything in sharp relief. It's always "evening" light in Iceland, because of its high latitude. Even at midday the light has a golden glow.

From the bus, the lava looked like the sandcastles I'd made as a child, dripping bits of wet sand, drop by drop, through my tight fingers, making turrets and spires and corkscrew twists—only these castles were black. Surreally set inside these black borders, the farm fields and even an odd golf course shone a gemstone green. As we entered the highlands, the fields grew into pastures, the rocks turned white and clustered in bigger lumps. The earth, according to Norse myth, was made of the giant Ymir's body: his bones are the bare rocks, his flesh is the dirt, his teeth make caves and caverns, grass and trees grow from his hair, his eye-whites are ice caps, his brains are clouds, his blood is the sea.

These rocks were definitely giants' bones.

As we crossed the pass, I could see three separate ice caps shimmering like giants' eyes gazing up at the sky.

Coming down into Skagafjord, the land grew tamer. The lava disappeared. Densely settled and banded in many greens, a broad valley cut by braided streams and ringed by snowy mountains fell gently to a shallow bay, its mouth guarded by a straight-sided rock. Called Drangey, the island was said to be a troll's cow, turned to stone by the rays of the rising sun. The troll himself has fallen into the water, but his wife still stands, a slim rock stack to the island's east.

Drangey was the outlaw Grettir's hideout during the last few years of his life, where he was finally overcome by a posse of local farmers who'd engaged the services of a witch. *Grettir's Saga* had always disturbed me. For all its fine poetry, its lively action, its feuds and loyalties, its ghosts, trolls, and witchcraft, and the essentially noble, if ill-fated, character of the mature outlaw, I could never get past a scene early on, when Grettir was a rebellious teen. Grettir's father owned a dun-colored mare with a dark stripe, or eel, down her back. Called Kengala (the name may come from *kenna,* "to know" or *kengur,* "a bowed back"), she was "so wise about the weather" that when a storm was on its way, she would refuse to graze. "If she does this," Grettir's father told him, "you are to stable the horses, but otherwise keep them grazing up north on the ridge, once winter sets in."

Grettir hated the chores his father gave him. This one, at least, was "man's work," he felt, and things went well until the weather grew cold and snowy. "Grettir was thinly clad and not yet fully hardened," the saga says, "so he began to feel the cold bitterly, but Kengala grazed away in the most exposed places during the worst of the weather." One morning, Grettir came to the stable with a sharp knife and jumped onto her back. "There was a fierce struggle, but in the end he succeeded in cutting loose her back skin all the way to her loins"—essentially flaying off her eel stripe. When he drove the horses out to pasture that day, Kengala, not surprisingly, ran straight back to the barn.

His father told the household to get set for a blizzard. After two nights and still no sign of a storm, he went out to the stable to see Kengala for himself. Greeting his favorite mare, he ran a hand along her back and was horrified to find the skin coming away at his touch. Grettir stood there smirking. His father went out "swearing violently" and ordered Kengala to be put down.

The story is meant to shock, and the effect hasn't faded since medieval times, when these sagas were told or read aloud to a household sitting and working around the winter fire—carding wool, spinning, weaving, braiding rope, whittling. Not only was it cruel, to disfigure a man's horse was to attack his honor. When the man was your father, and the horse his favorite, the insult was enormous. Grettir had broken the code of Icelandic society, and though he eventually grew into a generous and great-hearted hero, he remains a flawed character, one the reader cannot fully trust. I could understand why the farmers of Skagafjord didn't want him on Drangey.

The bus dropped me off at the hotel in Varmahlid, ten minutes from Einar's farm. No one was there to pick me up.

A sudden shower scurried across the patio, then dried up. I tossed my pack inside and scanned the racks of travel brochures until no one was left in the parking lot. A clerk waited politely at the front desk. It was a small hotel, thirty-eight beds, I'd read in my guidebook, fifteen rooms with private bath, singles for $65 a night. I saw a blue phone sign in the café across the lobby and made for it.

The expected old lady answered the phone. "Nancy?" She inhaled a sharp breath and began talking very fast, her voice musical and liquid as if she'd laugh if she weren't so startled. "We were expecting you tomorrow!" I picked out from her stream of otherwise incomprehensible Icelandic. Then, thankfully, "I'll send someone right away!"

A few minutes later, a fine new jeep-type car came racing around the bend in the road, its several antennae whipping. A young man stepped out, silently grabbed my bag, and motioned me in.

"*Sæll,*" I said, greeting him in Icelandic. "Hello. I'm Nancy."

He turned slowly to look at me. His eyes, set wide beneath a short forehead and a cap of metallic blond hair, were slightly protuberant and so terribly blue, almost turquoise in his ruddy face, that I found it hard to meet his gaze. I thought of a comment Richard Burton, the translator of the *Arabian Nights*, had made when he visited Iceland in 1857: *A very characteristic feature of the race, whose hardness, not to say harshness, of body and mind still distinguishes it from its neighbors, is the eye, dure and cold as a pebble—the mesmerist would despair at the first sight.*

"*Takk fyrir að koma að sækja mig,*" I added. "Thank you for coming to get me."

"*Þú talar góð íslensku,*" he said finally. "You speak good Icelandic."

"I'm trying to learn," I said.

"Good. Now we don't have to mess around with English."

He swung into the gas station next door to the hotel, reeled off something unintelligible, and left me alone in the car. I wondered if I'd made a serious mistake.

The farm at Sydra-Skordugil straddled the main road between the Varmahlid crossroads and the larger town of Saudarkrokur, houses on one side, horse barn on the other, trucks and tractors and tour buses *shushing* all day in between. *Syðra* means "southern" or "lower"; the *Skörðugil* is a gill, or deep ravine, in the hills opposite the farm. Close next door was Ytra-Skordugil (Upper or Outer Skordugil), and other farms could be seen on every side, scattered like chess pieces on a green-checkered board. It was the most unrelievedly agricultural valley I'd seen in Iceland—horse pastures and hay fields and farmhouses as far as the eye could see, no craters or lava fields to interrupt the pattern, just good fertile land, the mountains pushed back to a mere backdrop, the flat river bisecting it neatly.

Strangest of all, each house was surrounded by a thicket of trees.

Trees, at least what a Pennsylvanian would think of as trees, don't grow in Iceland. In some sheltered areas, a stand of birches may reach a scraggly thirty-five feet, but most "trees" are shrubby things, huddled in cracks in the lava, or clinging close to the ground, pruned daily by wind and sea spray. In the sagas, when an outlaw is said to be "hiding in the woods," he's usually described as squirming on his belly and hoping the rustle of leaves above him won't give him away. A joke that was a great favorite with our son William when we spent the summer at Litla Hraun was: *What do you do if you're lost in an Icelandic forest?* Answer: *Stand up.* Yet here in Skagafjord, the trees made hedges. Planted too close together to assume tree-shape, they were nonetheless the healthiest, greenest, lushest, most plentiful free-standing trees I'd seen.

My driver pulled in between the two houses at Sydra-Skordugil and ushered me into the older one. He was Einar Gislason's son Elvar, I had learned, and would be my host while I stayed at Sydra-Skordugil. His house was low, concrete, white with a red roof, the trees choking it on two sides. The narrow entry, cluttered with barn boots and coveralls, opened onto a small kitchen filled with people finishing a meal. Fjola, Elvar's wife, introduced herself to me and showed me to a seat. "It was my fault," she said sweetly. "I have your letter right here"—she tapped the refrigerator door, where a photo of my house in Pennsylvania was displayed, the trees topping its roof by some thirty feet—"but I'd remembered it was tomorrow." She pouted.

Fjola was about twenty-five, the same age as Elvar, blonde, buxom, very pretty, and frank-looking, with dark eyes in a smooth, round face. She set a plate of boiled meat (lamb, I thought) and potatoes in front of me, and a glass of milk. A jar of dark rhubarb jam, used as a relish, completed the meal. The other couple at the table, who seemed older and were dressed in stylish outdoor clothes, were visiting for the day. I understood neither their names nor their relationship to my hosts, only that they had provided the fancy four-wheel-drive vehicle Elvar had used to fetch me. "Our car died," said Fjola, again with that petulant look. Also at the table was Fridrik, a tall young man in his late teens who was too shy to even look at me, but mumbled his hellos into his plate. I liked him immediately.

"It's *gluggaveður*," announced Elvar, when he had eaten, "window-weather. Let's take a ride to Holar. It's too windy to do anything else."

"But first, a look around the farm," said the visiting man.

We put on our sweaters and parkas, for the wind was still flinging occasional handfuls of rain, and went out. Across the drive was the fine new wooden house where Elvar's father and mother lived with their other sons, who were all bright blond and ruddy. Its picture window looked west toward the horse barn and the mountains behind it. Elvar and Fjola, who had moved into the old house Duddi had occupied before he died, had taken over half the responsibility for the farm. Having earned the required certificate from the agricultural college at nearby Holar, Elvar had set himself up as a horse trainer. Fjola, too, had a degree from Holar and was a competition rider and trainer.

Down the hill from the dairy barn, two large sheds exuded an obnoxious smell. Elvar headed for one. I clamped my nose and followed him in, to find cage after cage of sad-eyed pretty fox pups. I quick-stepped through, taking light, shallow breaths. The minks in the adjoining shed were not quite as bad-smelling and not nearly as forlorn-looking, but Elvar said fox skins were often easier to sell. One of Elvar's brothers, a tall, wall-eyed fellow, sat among the cages calmly fixing something; he nodded to us, but said nothing. Later I learned he was headed abroad for a degree in fur-farming; he hated horses.

Outside I drank in great draughts of air, glad for the cleansing bursts of rain. We hiked across a field to a metal trailer with a small door in its side. Inside stood a continuous row of plastic fifty-five-gallon drums cut in half lengthwise to make mangers and a heated watering trough. It was the winter shelter for the horses not in training: the mares and foals, the four-year-olds and younger. Only the riding horses were brought into the stable and shod. "They come in and out as they please," Elvar said, "and everyone gets enough."

When we came back out to the pasture, horses crowded around us, curious. Bays and browns and blacks, but some other colors too. Even one pinto. A black horse with a star caught my eye but wouldn't let me get close. A light chestnut with a white snip on her nose as well as a star was appealingly friendly. Elvar and his visitor were making a fuss over a handsome bay, when I noticed the odd fact that each horse had a number stenciled on its side.

"That?" It's a frost-mark. No, it doesn't come off." Elvar rolled his eyes.

The other man asked a question, and Elvar nodded.

"Yes, some people put it on the neck, under the mane, but it's better here, under the saddle. You see it only when you want to."

On the way to Holar, Elvar began to snore. The visitors in the front seat hushed their talk respectfully. I watched out the window. It was hard to turn away from Drangey, which looked nothing like a troll's cow there in the middle of the water but more like the stump of the great ash tree, Yggdrasil, that in Norse mythology connected the worlds of gods, dwarves, elves, trolls, giants, men, and the dead.

Elvar snorted abruptly and woke himself up. "There's Holtsmuli," he announced, as if no time had elapsed. "You know, Hrafn fra Holtsmula?"

The guests in the front seat muttered vague replies, but I, indeed, did know Hrafn (Raven). He was the famous black stallion that had just been put down, at age twenty-eight, and was supposed to be on display, stuffed, at Holar—a plan that had elicited cries of outrage from Icelandic horse-lovers in Europe (*A freak! Stuffed like a crow in a museum! I cried when I read it,* they wrote to *Eidfaxi*). I was hoping to see him. He was "beautiful and elegant," according to another *Eidfaxi* article, tall, with a long neck, high shoulders, a stiff back, short loins, slim thighs, long pasterns, and strong hooves. His offspring were superb riding horses, with "great and confident willingness," although they were not considered very "joyful." According to the recent national horse-breeding adviser, Kristinn Hugason, Hrafn was the best sire in Icelandic breeding so far.

He was also the grandfather of Birkir, the bay gelding at Hlid.

"Here's Saudarkrokur, Sveinn Gudmundsson's herd. That horse there?" Elvar pointed into a crowded paddock where the road turned away from the town. "He's by Hervar."

The stallion Hervar fra Saudarkroki is not always highly praised. "Hervar" is a hero's name, but this one was said to be cow-hocked with thin legs and feet with no "feathers," the fine brush of hair on the pasterns. "Featherless legs are of course uglier than those which aren't, but that doesn't mean they're weaker," argued one proponent. Hervar's offspring share his ugly legs. Worse, they have "coarse" heads, and their ears often point outwards. But some have been splendid riding horses, winning prize after prize. And Hervar under saddle was said to be "incredibly impressive." Elvar's father was one breeder who disregarded the ugly legs. As he wrote, "I saw Hervar first in Saudarkrokur when he was three years old. Sveinn Gudmundsson was crossing the town's square leading an elegant chestnut colt. I liked that colt instantly, his head carriage was so impressive. I praised the colt to Sveinn, I couldn't do anything else. ... I asked where the colt would be in the spring. 'No one wants to use him,' said Sveinn. I told Sveinn that I was interested."

I was reminded again that to find a good horse you needed a good eye. At three, the colt had not yet been ridden, had not even seen a saddle; there was no proof he had any talent at all, and his conformation was somewhat questionable: At least, for any horse except an Icelandic, being cow-hocked was a serious flaw.

"An English judge of horses is somewhat at fault in Iceland," wrote Sabine S. Baring-Gould, the nineteenth-century Devonshire parson. As before, he and the Scottish adventuress Elizabeth Jane Oswald were in agreement. She wrote: "All preconceived ideas of a horse's manners and powers must here be laid aside." As for being cow-hocked, a representative of the U.S. Icelandic Horse Congress once remarked, "Lots of Icelandics are cow-hocked and toed-out. Many knowledgeable people say that horses which toe out are most sure-footed. I certainly don't know if these statements are true, but I do know that there are an awful lot of great cow-hocked and toed-out Icelandic horses. I have always felt that the importance placed on straight legs is largely due to the fact that it is a trait that any idiot can recognize."

Farm after farm flashed past, and Elvar named horse after horse. When we turned into the college at Holar, he directed us past the famous cathedral, built in 1759, a simple white building next to a square-sided bell-tower of lighthouse proportions; past the aquarium and its collection of Icelandic fishes; down the hill to the stables. He opened the door and switched on the lights. It was dusty, deserted, the horses all at pasture for the summer. Not even the stuffed stallion Hrafn was there—the taxidermist had not finished the mount. We toured the shower stall and saw the medicinal boots that could be filled with cold water to treat an injured hoof. We examined the mechanism that lifted a heavy round bale of hay from the loft, trundled it over to the stalls, and cut it into portable wedges. And we saw the stalls themselves, empty now, which I measured off in boot-lengths: I was trying to decide how big to build my own barn back home.

My rubber boots, I knew, were thirty centimeters long, making the largest of the stalls three meters square, or roughly nine by nine feet. "Is this usual for one horse?" I asked. American stalls are twelve by twelve.

Elvar laughed from the middle of a stall, a high, boyish cackle. "I'd put *five* horses in here."

Back home, Fjola had spread the logbook out on the kitchen table. When the coffee was drunk and Elvar and the company had gone off, she began explaining the way things were done at Sydra-Skordugil. Her Icelandic was slow and careful, and she repeated herself until she thought I understood.

"We have forty broodmares up in the hills with our stallions," she said. "Each year we keep twenty-five foals. We start training them when they're five years old. All the mares have to have foals when they're four, then we can decide which ones are going to be broodmares, and which ones we'll sell, and which ones we'll train or keep as our own riding horses and for competitions. We'll keep between six and ten for ourselves, out of all the horses."

Broodmares, stallions, riding horses, foals—altogether, the farm had 160 horses. In the logbook, each was listed by name and number, when it was born, when it had died, whether it was sold, and at what age. A man named Reynir had bought many horses; another frequent listing was "Japan."

"I didn't know Icelanders sold horses to Japan," I said.

Fjola looked at me. "Horse *meat*," she said, trying to suppress a smile. "Japan is a good market for horse meat."

She went on, while I pretended the news hadn't thrown me. "All the foals of our four-year-old mares we slaughter, and any others that we don't sell, except for the twenty-five we want to keep."

I swallowed. "How can you decide?"

"Elvar and his father go out in the field in September. They look at them. They take the ones that aren't good enough."

"But they're so cute—"

"Yes," she said sternly, "but lambs are cute, too." She closed the book. "Don't you eat horse meat?"

I shook my head. "I've never had it," I said politely. "They don't sell it in America."

"Really?" Fjola stared at me wide-eyed. "We eat about five foals a year, the family here."

She got up from the table and began unpacking the clutter off the top of the chest freezer in the corner. The collapsible wooden bowl I'd brought as a house gift. Stacks of papers and bills and binders and magazines. A pot or two. Riding pants that needed mending. A couple of towels. A tablecloth. As each item made the jump from freezer to tabletop, I mentally piled them back on. I knew what she was doing. I didn't know what to say to stop her. Inevitably the lid was clear. She opened the freezer and took out a largish package.

"This is the best," she said. "Leg of foal. I'll fix it for you tomorrow."

Why do we not eat horses? asked Desmond Morris in his book *Horsewatching*. Because in the year 732, he reported, Pope Gregory III prohibited it.

Horses were sacred to many of the old religions of northern Europe. When Scandinavians settled Iceland in the year 870, the gods most of them worshiped rode Shining One, Fast Galloper, Silver Forelock, Strong-of-Sinew, Shaggy Fetlock, Golden Forelock, and Lightfoot. Only the mighty Thor the Thunderer went on foot across the rainbow bridge to the Well of Destiny, where the gods held court each morning beside the root of the ash tree Yggdrasil (which, incidentally, is translated by some scholars as

Odin's Horse). The gods of Day and Night drove chariots drawn by Skinfaxi (Shining Mane) and Hrimfaxi (Frosty Mane): The brightness of the sun was the glow of the day-horse's mane, while dew was the saliva dripping from Hrimfaxi's bit. The goddess Gna had a horse that could run "through the air and over the sea." Called Hoof-Flourisher, it was sired by Skinny-Sides on Breaker-of-Fences. The most famous horse was Odin's eight-legged steed, Sleipnir, who was born of the god Loki.

One day, so the story goes, a giant came knocking at the gates of Midgard (Middle Earth), which the gods had just established, and offered to build them a strong wall, guaranteed to keep out Fire Ogres and Frost Giants. All he would take in payment, he said, were the sun and the moon and the goddess Freyja for his wife. The gods debated. Loki the Trickster suggested they set the giant a time limit—one winter, an impossibly unrealistic deadline for the task. That way, winked Loki, they'd get *most* of a wall and would risk nothing. The unsuspecting giant agreed to the deadline, provided his horse could help him.

The days passed and the wall grew. The giant laid up by day the stones his horse hauled by night. When the first day of summer was only three days off, the gods realized that the giant would keep his end of the bargain. They wanted out of theirs. Whose idea was it, they argued, to ruin the sky by sending the sun and moon to Giantland? Who had promised beautiful Freyja as a giant's bride? It was Loki, everyone agreed, and he'd better come up with a trick to fix it.

That night as the giant's horse set off to haul stone, he scented a mare in season. The giant's horse raced off after her, with the giant in pursuit. All night they galloped about, and work on the wall came to a halt. The same happened for two more nights. When the giant realized he wasn't going to make the deadline, he flew into a rage and began throwing things—at which Thor stepped in and, swinging his mighty hammer, sent the giant to the realm of the dead before he could do any more damage. Some time later, Loki the Trickster bore a gray foal (the story doesn't tell if he'd been able to change out of mare's shape in the meantime). That foal was Sleipnir, the eight-legged steed, renowned as the best horse among gods and men.

Sleipnir was owned by Odin the Wise, the one-eyed god of poetry and battle, and chief of the Norse pantheon. Once, on a whim, Odin rode Sleipnir into Giantland. There a giant complimented him politely on his fine horse. I'll wager my head, Odin said, that his equal is not to be found in your land. The giant was put out. He owned a horse called Gold-mane that could step out much better, he said. Losing his temper quite suddenly, as giants were wont to do, he mounted and chased after Odin. Eight-legged Sleipnir truly was unequaled, and Odin was soon out of sight. But the giant was in such a towering rage that he galloped on until he found himself inside the gates of Asgard, right at the doors of Valhalla, the gods' great hall. Thor, the gods' protector, was not at home and, uncertain how to handle an angry giant, Odin and the other gods invited him to sit down and have a drink. The giant had nearly drunk up all the gods' good ale, and was boasting and beginning to make wild threats, when Thor came home, demanding to know who'd let a giant into Asgard. Words led to hotter words, until the giant challenged Thor to a duel. He mounted his horse and galloped back to Giantland, where his reputation took several steps up, until the day of the duel itself, when Thor proved the victor. Rushing across the battlefield surrounded by lightning and thunder, Thor flung his mighty hammer, shattering the giant's weapon and bursting his skull. The giant's horse Gold-mane was given to Thor's son (over the objections of Odin, who wanted it for himself).

Because of their close association with the gods, horses were a worthy sacrifice in ancient Scandinavia. A horse, usually white or gray or with unusual markings, would be ritually slaughtered, its blood sprinkled on the altar, the meat stewed and shared among the celebrants. Earlier cults saved the head and hide and set them up on poles to guard a grave or other holy place, but by the Saga Age, these poles had devolved into a type of natural magic. *Egil's Saga* tells of a time when the Viking hero Egil, cruising along the coast of Norway, ambushed and killed the king's son. Afterwards he went to an island, "picked up a branch of hazel and went to a certain cliff that faced the mainland. Then he took a horse head, set it up on the pole, and spoke these formal words: *Here I set up a pole of insult against King Eirik and Queen Gunnhild*—then, turning the horse head towards the mainland—*and I direct this insult against the guardian spirits of this land, so that every one of them shall go astray, neither to figure nor find their dwelling places until they have driven King Eirik and Queen Gunnhild from this country.*" A year later, King Eirik was deposed and had to flee to England.

When Iceland became Christian in the year 1000, three things were banned: worshiping the old gods in public, exposing children (a form of infanticide that involved abandoning a newborn in the wasteland or on a mountainside, there to succumb to the elements, be eaten by wild animals, or—if the gods so desired—be rescued and adopted by a passerby), and eating horsemeat. Sagas covering that time ridicule the old horse sacrifices. *The Saga of Saint Olaf* tells of the Norwegian king responsible for Christianizing much of the North. In one version, Olaf visited a poor family so benighted that they worshiped the penis of an old cart horse, wrapped in linen and kept in a chest with garlic and herbs so that it wouldn't rot. King Olaf witnessed a ceremony in which the phallus was passed from hand to hand around the circle, each person solemnly saying a verse over it. When the "idol" came to him, he threw it to the dog, who gobbled it up. "The king then cast off his disguise, and ... talked to them of the true faith."

The story blames an old woman for making the idol. When the cart horse was butchered, she had snatched the penis from the farmer's son, who was giggling and shaking it at his sister. "She said they shouldn't waste this or anything else." Her attitude survives in present-day Iceland. American anthropologist Paul Durrenberger spent the summer of 1988 working on a farm in the south. "When Halldor said we would butcher a horse the next day, I thought I had misunderstood," he reported in his book, *Icelandic Essays*. "I thought it could have been a joke; it could have been slang for something I did not understand." But the next morning, Halldor led out a mare and dropped it with two shots from a .22. "We had found horse meat in the grocery stores and had eaten it as it was somewhat cheaper than other meats, and food is terribly expensive in Iceland," Durrenberger wrote. But this was different. "I had ridden this horse before. ... I felt some qualms about the murder of a horse I had ridden, even if it had been a bad ride." He tried to stick to the task. No, he learned, they didn't need to clean the intestines. "We can get plastic sausage casings," Halldor explained. But the slabs of yellow fat—these he should save. They were good for frying *kleinur*, a kind of Icelandic doughnut.

"I felt sad about killing the horse," Durrenberger noted.

Halldor wasn't sad. "She's fat and lazy and not good for anything," he said. "She just eats grass."

"Not knowing any better," Durrenberger wrote, "and not having a farm to run, I would keep a useless horse for a pet, just to look at or just to have around."

Halldor couldn't afford such sentimentality. "He was glad to be rid of it, and they needed the meat."

At Sydra-Skordugil they also needed the meat. There were Einar and his wife and their four sons to feed, Fjola, Fridrik and the other hired hand, named Odin, the occasional visitor or relative, the American guest. Meanwhile, in the line of business, they had to dispose of fifteen unpromising foals a year, each of which would otherwise cost them four thousand dollars, according to a recent government survey, in feed and facilities and time and training before it could be sold as a riding horse at age five—if, that is, they could find a buyer for a riding horse of dubious merit in a country already burdened with an estimated 12,500 horses over the carrying capacity of its grasslands and hay fields, and if (an even bigger if) they wanted to hazard their reputation as horse breeders by selling horses that weren't of top quality. Horse breeding is still less a science than an art. Even the best mare, bred to the best stallion, can drop a foal that is awkward or unbalanced or stiff, too short in the back or too tight in the loins to offer an acceptable tolt.

Understanding all of this, I watched carefully the next day as Fjola browned the leg of foal in butter and onions and covered it with paprika before roasting it and serving it with mushroom gravy, boiled potatoes, and rhubarb jam. The meat was sweet-tasting, with hints of pork loin, or roast turkey. I praised its tenderness. Fjola beamed. She tilted her chin and gave Elvar a glance. He looked at me with the hint of a smile and passed me the platter. I took seconds.

CHAPTER SEVEN

WILLINGNESS IS ALL THAT MATTERS

A fax came from Germany in the night. It was typed in English—rather poor English. I smoothed it out on the kitchen table and tried to parse some sense into it. The house was quiet, the doors to the bedrooms still shut at almost noon, the trees blocked the view of the barns. I'd seen no one since I got up. I'd cleaned up the coffee cups littering the table (from last night? this morning?), swept the floor (the linoleum was pitted and puckered, the floor itself so uneven the dust tended to pool), played with the border collie puppy, Tumi, who was chewing the lace off a shoe, and brewed a cup of tea with a bag I'd brought from home. "Dear Breeders," the fax read. The writer was looking for a horse for her four children. Good gaits, calm and quiet. "But we are only wanting a rare color": dapple gray, silver dapple, pinto, or "black with a light mane and tail." She asked that a video be sent of any suitable horse.

It seemed a tall order—a little insulting, too. First, she implied that Icelandics were children's ponies. Second, that harping on color. Third, the request for a video—as if the breeder's word and reputation weren't enough. I pushed the letter aside, dismissing it. She should look around at home.

Germany has 40,000 Icelandic horses, half as many as in Iceland and twice as many as in all the rest of the world put together. Germans have been breeding and importing Icelandics since 1949, when nine horses (including one from this farm) were sent to an Icelander living in Bavaria to help out farmers after the war. What happened next depends on who's telling it. In the Icelandic version, according to the government horse-breeding adviser, Gunnar Bjarnason, who sent the nine horses, they "attracted so much attention that Frau Ursula Bruns, a well-known German author and horse breeder became deeply interested in the Icelandic horse." Bruns liked their independent spirit and smooth gaits; she bought two and was soon spreading interest among riding circles.

German rider Christine Schwartz tells a slightly different story: "In 1957, Ursula Bruns started a big campaign to save foals that were going to be slaughtered in Iceland. The response was incredible, but once the new owners had their horses, they didn't know what to do next. The horses were afraid of people; they had different gaits, different needs; and most of the people who had bought these foals had no previous horse experience. Ursula Bruns solved the problem by starting a magazine about the care of Icelandic horses." Both nations credit Bruns' books, *Heissgeliebte Islandpferde (Dearly Beloved Icelandic Horses)* and *Reitertraume (Riders' Dreams)*, with sparking German interest in the breed.

There was no American Ursula Bruns. At the Butterfield Stage Coach Steakhouse in Holbrooke, Arizona, in early January, I had chanced upon a cowboy poet and strolling singer who said he'd owned an Icelandic horse in the 1960s. It must have been one of the earliest in the States. He said an Icelander working out West for a few years had brought it over, but because of Iceland's ancient prohibition on importing horses, she was unable to ship it back home and had asked him to take it. Fourteen hands tall, it made him a fine cow pony. An easy keeper, it "could get fat on a rock pile," he said, but that trait did not attract much attention in the land of mustangs.

Ten years later, the man who had introduced Icelandics to Germany, Gunnar Bjarnason, met Linda Tellington-Jones, inventor of the Tellington Touch Equine Awareness Method or TTEAM, a "holistic training approach for the body, mind, and spirit of the horse." She arranged for fifteen Icelandic horses to compete in The Great American Horse Race, a New York-to-California stunt commemorating the American Bicentennial. One, a horse named Borkur (Warrior), became somewhat famous as the only horse of any breed "on the ground every day—never sick or lame." Another died en route, from drinking "poisoned water." The stunt convinced Tellington-Jones's sisters to buy and breed Icelandic horses, and their two farms in Canada remain active. But the breed failed to catch on in North America. Today, out of the estimated seven million horses of all kinds in the U.S., Icelandics tally no more than two thousand. Another thousand live in Canada.

I wondered why they were so few. "It's difficult for people here to relate to the horses," Anne Elwell told me. Elwell is the secretary and one of the founders of the U.S. Icelandic Horse Congress, the breed registry in America, set up in 1986. She has a herd of some thirty Icelandics on her farm in New York's Hudson River Valley and owns others in Germany and Iceland. "The trouble is, people here don't have a sense of their culture," Elwell said. "Horse psychics—people I otherwise raise my eyebrows at—say a lot of this stuff: 'This horse has a sense of its history, it's a part of its culture, its past.'

"And because Icelandic horses are culturally interesting," Elwell continued, "it's important to keep the culture in as you breed and raise them. Otherwise you get really boring horses."

For example, imprinting, the current fad in American horse breeding, is not practiced in Iceland; rather the opposite. Instead of handling a foal at birth—as one article in *Horse Illustrated* magazine put it, "rubbing the foal all over, using a curry and brush, touching its feet and ears, putting a finger in its mouth, putting on a halter, using a thermometer to take a rectal temperature, running clippers over its head and body, and anything else you can think of doing"—Icelanders approach a new foal most often on horseback and intervene only in the case of illness or injury. "Foals need freedom and wide-open spaces in which to grow up," Sveinn Gudmundsson of the Skagafjord town of Saudarkrokur explained in a 1994 newspaper interview. The Saudarkrokur horses are currently the top-of-the-line in Iceland, so much so that the 1998 national championship show was said to be "nearly a family show for Sveinn's horses, with a few guests," according to Sveinn's biographer. One horse of that line, Galsi, born in 1990, is one of Iceland's most valuable stallions, with a purchase price of $200,000 and a stud fee set at $2,700, no guarantees. Yet this future prize-winner, like all of Sveinn's horses, was born outdoors in the midst of a herd grazing in its summer pastures, high up in the mountains. There was no wrapping of the mare's tail against infection, no slinging her up in a hammock to assist in the delivery. Sveinn, who raises horses only as a hobby, might not have even found the foal for a day or so. "I keep an eye on our horses regularly throughout the summer," he explained to the newspaper, qualifying that *regularly* with, "It's only a two- or three-hour ride to where they graze." But he doesn't interfere, except to help move the herd in the autumn down to its winter pastures closer to town.

"This freedom, void of human interference, shapes the personality of the horse," one expert says. "The young horses grow up independent, learn how to treat their environment and become more sensible—even wiser. It is believed that horses brought up in these circumstances become more attentive and intelligent than horses brought up in narrow fields with constant interaction with humans." They become the kind of horse Sveinn cherishes—"highly spirited, bursting with life, but well disciplined," each having had to earn its place in the herd. Said Sveinn, "It's great to watch the foals when they begin to compete with each other; you'd think you were watching a race. There's nothing quite like it."

A character in Halldor Laxness's novel *The Atom Station* calls such equine competition "one of the loveliest and most magnificent events that can happen in the country. ... All at once it is as if the fire had started flowing right under these strange creatures, they charge away like a storm incarnate over scree and bogs and landslides, dipping the tips of their toes for a fractional moment into the furnace that blazes beneath their hooves, cutting across waterfalls, gulleys, and boulders, galloping steeply for a while until they stand trapped at last on some ledge high in the mountaintops."

In America there are few half-wild herds of Icelandic foals with fire under their feet. "We have predators," points out Elwell. Coyotes roam the wooded edges of her Hudson Valley farm; California and Canada, home to other breeding herds, have mountain lions; in Iceland, the only wild carnivores are minks and foxes, much too small to tackle a healthy foal. But with that caveat, Elwell and some others still manage to "keep the culture in" their horses by leaving them loose in well-fenced ten- to twenty-acre pastures and resisting the urge to play with the adorable, cuddly foals. Other American breeders are not so careful. "I saw one foal, two months old, that was so boring it was unbelievable," Elwell told me. It was kept alone with its mother in a small paddock beside the house, where it had frequent visitors. "I said to the owners, 'This foal is going to grow up to be a turnip.'" It had no spirit and, worse, no respect for humans. Elwell offered to set it straight.

A distinguished-looking woman in her fifties, Elwell walks with a slight limp from a fall on the ice some years ago. By profession she is a divorce lawyer. Her first words to me, responding to my letter asking for advice on buying Icelandics, were, *What is your agenda?* She often rides one of her three prize-winning stallions. Behind her glasses, her two eyes track on slightly different paths, making her face a challenge to read. She deliberates before she speaks, but once she gets going, she can be as brusque and opinionated as any Icelander.

Approaching the "turnip foal," she told me, "I walked out quietly into the field, and, when I was within five feet of the foal, I jumped in the air and screamed. He jumped four feet in the air and took off. I chased after him and, when he stopped, I jumped again. Within two days he was starting to act like a horse again.

"Icelandics are so inherently bonding," Elwell warned. "One of these foals will get up a few minutes after it's born and crawl into your lap. And the mare will say, 'Go ahead, take it.' You need to make them always alert to people, not quite sure what a person will do."

Sitting over a second cup of tea at Sydra-Skordugil, musing over the difference between raising horses at home and the way things were done here, I was startled when both doors to the kitchen suddenly opened at once. Fjola entered, disheveled, from the bedroom; Elvar, equally so, but smelling of fresh rain and manure and machines, came from the barns. He greeted me warmly. He'd been cleaning out the sheep shed all morning, he said, and spreading manure on the fields. Fjola poured them both a cup of coffee, glanced around at the clean kitchen, smiled at me, peeled herself an apple, lit a cigarette, and began making dinner. Elvar picked up the fax and studied it.

"Their English is very bad," I offered.

Fjola looked up from her frying. "I had no idea what they wanted." She sounded surprised to learn the fault in understanding wasn't hers. "I was going to ask you to read it."

"This—" Elvar tapped the paragraph about colors. "What do they say here?"

I searched my mind for the color words. Eighty-four colors, some three hundred descriptive terms. ... At Haukur's I had found a book with pictures of each color and had spent some days studying it. Now I could quickly come up with the Icelandic terms for dapple gray, silver dapple, and pinto. *"Apalgrár, vindóttur, brúnskjóttur,"* I said, and stopped, struggling over how to say "black with a light mane." Chestnut horses with light-colored manes were called *rauð glófexti,* so perhaps *"svart glófexti."*

Elvar unveiled his turquoise eyes. *"Svart glófexti?* Where the hell would we find a good horse in a color like that? *Svart glófexti!"* He tossed the fax onto the pile on the chest freezer and stalked out.

"Now we go riding," Elvar said after dinner.

As I went to fetch my helmet, I heard Fjola ask, "What horse will you give Nancy?"

"The little bay mare," Elvar replied.

Something in his voice made me feel disappointed—or maybe it was just the juxtaposition of "little" and "bay." Secretly, I too wanted a "rare" color, and not a horse so small people would call it a pony.

I caught up with him as he was crossing the road, the puppy, Tumi, tumbling along at my heels. It was chilly out, dreary and gray, the clouds close, curling down the mountains on a dank wind. I was wearing my heaviest riding breeches with long johns underneath, an Icelandic sweater, a rain parka, my red Wellington boots, and leather riding gloves, my helmet in its rain cover in my hand.

Elvar looked at me appraisingly—he was in a heavy one-piece coverall fitted with a leather inseam and seat for riding purposes—then the dog caught his eye. He barked a command. Tumi scampered halfway down the drive and sat there thumping his tail.

Together Elvar and I crossed the yard, its mud roiled by hoofprints and smoothed again by the broad tires of machines. Behind the stable sat a cavernous hay barn, its broad doors open wide, awaiting the year's new bales. Out front was a round pen, made of wooden poles lashed together with rope, where Elvar and the other trainers gentled the four-year-olds, horse-whisperer style. In a pen without corners, a horse never feels trapped, and so doesn't quite panic. Round and round it will run until eventually it learns to pay attention to that presence in the center, to bend when it bends, to move when it moves, to ultimately accept it as the dominant member of this new two-creature herd.

Since *The Horse Whisperer* and *The Man Who Listens to Horses* were published, the round pen has enjoyed a boost, but it is less of a novelty in Iceland than would be its opposite, the bronco-bustin' Wild West style, in which a horse is tied and whipped until its spirit is broken. "To destroy the willingness in a horse is a crazy, unforgivable act," wrote Monty Roberts in *The Man Who Listens to Horses*. An Icelander would readily agree: "Willingness is all that matters," says an Icelandic proverb describing a good horse: *Vilji er allt sem þarf.* Moreover, if the language is to be trusted, horses have never been "broken" in Iceland. The Icelandic word for the act is *temja*, a word cognate with the English "to tame." A 1925 Icelandic manual on horsemanship explains that to "temja" a young horse you should work slowly and gently with it until "step by step the horse comes to fully trust you and learns to understand and obey your orders; before you know it, he will gladly do whatever you ask of him."

Monty Roberts is admired in Iceland; trainer Magnus Larusson called working with him "an extraordinary once-in-a-lifetime experience," but Magnus commented as well that "there are many roads to Rome, and it's good to have choices." As he explained in *Eidfaxi* magazine, "Monty Roberts's method, that is, working with the horse in the round pen, is only a little part of what I do. It is only part of the beginning. People have been much too taken up with what goes on in the round pen. All that happens, as a matter of fact, is that the horse trainer gets the horse to acknowledge that he, the man, is the leader. When the horse has agreed to this, he stops fearing the man and trusts him to look out for his welfare." Continued Magnus, "It takes many years to train and condition a horse, because it takes the horse a long time to grow up and become strong. We can never speed up the training or the usefulness of a horse by means of any kind of tricks."

To tame a horse the Icelandic way does not take strength or bravado. It's not a rodeo act but a skill calling for great focus and attention, with equal parts of patience and self-control, so as not to get angry at a recalcitrant pupil, but instead offer repetition and reassurance.

Shy Fridrik, who met us now at the stable door, his hands full of bridles, struck me as one who would be very good at the task. He and Elvar conferred quietly, before wading into the herd, packed into a pen along one wall of the barn, thirty horses or more, in the space that we (or the experts at Holar) would devote to five box stalls. On the right side of the barn were several pens of varying sizes: Each held two or more horses, except for one narrow stall in which a single horse was tied. "She hurt her leg," Elvar called, when he saw me checking her. A back leg was tightly wrapped; blood showed through the dressing. "We don't want her moving."

Elvar had bridled two dark-colored horses in the middle of the herd. Slowly he waded back toward me, pulling them behind. It was like a child's slide-puzzle, the kind with one open hole: Moving one piece means all the others have to move. Elvar pressed on, forcing a path. The loose horses swirled and danced away, their backs rippling, their manes and tails blending. It was hard to tell where one horse left off and another began. They stamped and squealed, threw up their heads and bit at each other. Fridrik, further back in the herd, bent and twisted as the horses swarmed around him. I wondered how he kept his feet untrodden. He paid them no attention, his concentration fixed on getting close to the horse he'd been asked to catch. He stretched over another horse's rump and caught a tall chestnut by the chin. Holding it firmly, he wiggled his way closer until he could slip in the bit and pull the bridle over its ears. The horse immediately surrendered, making no more attempt to step away. Fridrik looped the rein over his arm and began stalking a black horse that swivelled his ears and tried to hide behind his neighbors. But he was cornered. No room for escape. Fridrik talked to him softly, and this horse, too, accepted the bridle. Then Fridrik began forcing his way to the gate. Horses dove under the reins. They slipped between the two captives. They stood firm with their rumps facing the man. *"Færa, færa,"* he said softly in Icelandic, "Away, away." He pressed until there really was no room to move. Elvar was at the gate with his two horses, and half the herd was packed in between him and Fridrik.

"Here," Elvar called to me. "Take these two."

He handed me the reins over the gate, unlocked it, and let the two horses slip past. Then, clicking the latch after them, he turned to the herd. "Move!" he shouted, and slapped the nearest neck.

The horses backed away, practically sitting on each other. Fridrik, at the end of what seemed a domino row, held firm.

"Færa!" Elvar shouted again.

Finally a horse at Fridrik's end of the herd reared up on its hind legs, turned, and clattered down to the far corner of the pen. Another horse and another followed. The logjam freed up, and suddenly Fridrik found himself at the gate. Elvar climbed over, took the reins from him, and led the two horses out. Then Fridrik turned back for one more.

He was already deep in the herd when he called out, "Where's *Gæska?*" The name was a word I didn't know.

Elvar looked up from saddling one of the dark horses. He scanned the puzzle of the herd. "She's 513," he said.

"She's not here," Fridrik said.

Elvar glanced into the stall in front of him. "Oh, here she is."

I looked in. There in the corner, hiding behind three other horses, was a dark-colored mare with "1K513" frost-marked on her back. She had her head down, her ears back, and her tail toward us, and seemed to be making herself as small as possible. Elvar caught the bridle Fridrik threw him and went into the stall. The mare never moved. She followed meekly as he led her out and slipped her rein over a hook on the wall.

"You can saddle this one," Elvar said, pointing to his saddled horse, then to the mare, to make sure I understood his Icelandic. "Pick any saddle you like."

I went into the tack room and took an old brown saddle with a deep, quilted seat. It looked soft and well broken in.

"Good," said Elvar. "That's the saddle I use when I round up the sheep."

I had watched carefully as Elvar had saddled the other two horses: no pad, the saddle set back from the withers, the girth not too tight, the crupper loose enough to slip a hand under sideways. I knew even his critical eye would not spot a mistake. But still I took my time, trying to get a feeling for the horse—undoubtedly the "little bay mare" he had picked out for me. I wasn't impressed. She was technically "bay," I knew, thanks to her black points—mane, tail, and socks—but I had been expecting the glowing red bay of Birkir at Hlid, not this dull blackish-brown color. Nor did she have Birkir's agreeable character. Though her ears tracked me as I went from side to side, settling the girth, attaching the crupper, she studiously avoided catching my eye. Birkir, in a similar situation, had gazed with curiosity, even affection, reaching out a soft nose to investigate. But neither did this horse show the spunky independence I had admired in Elfa, whose submission to Haukur's bark was clearly due to respect. She did not dance away from me, or stamp, or swish her tail. She just stood there, looking small, as if she were trying to pretend I wasn't really there, that I wasn't really going to ask anything of her.

By the time I was ready, Fridrik had saddled and mounted the black and sat waiting at the door of the barn, blocking the exit, the rein of the chestnut in one hand.

"You get on now," Elvar said to me, and came up to hold the mare's head. "Are the stirrups okay?"

I nodded. Icelanders generally thought my stirrups were too short, but I felt unsafe with them much longer. Elvar shrugged and tipped his chin at Fridrik and we started out of the barn.

We went through the paddock gate and, without waiting while Elvar stopped to fasten it, headed up a wet black track between the fields. Fridrik started out fast, and I realized there'd be none of the slow warm-up Haukur had insisted on for Elfa. It was also apparent that the "little bay mare" wanted to go still faster. She'd stepped right into a tolt, with no direction from me, her head high and almost on top of the horse in front of us. Then we heard the fast steps of Elvar's two horses behind us as he hurried to catch up. Gaeska swerved suddenly out from the pack and took the lead. I couldn't tell if she was terrified or just eager to race.

"How do you like her?" Elvar shouted as he rode up next to me.

"She likes to go fast," I said, diplomatically.

He nodded, as if that were a very good thing. I noticed his horse, also at a tolt, had no trouble passing us, even though we had the track and it was negotiating tall grass.

The pace never let up. Over a tussocky pasture to a plain of rough stones. Up a shifting slope of scree, along the narrow track on its crest, down the steep further side, across the shallow river, through the marsh, around a grassy hill, we tolted, the horses' heads high, hooves flashing, tails rippling out. There was no question here of the tolt being "difficult," of these riders only asking for the gait "when the ground is smooth and even." Uphill, downhill. Gaeska kept her clear four-beat rhythm, always urging a little more speed. I was the one who quickly grew tired, who found the tolt difficult. I bounced and swayed in the deep saddle, lost my stirrups frequently. My seat grew sore and I wriggled around to reduce the friction. But Gaeska never slowed. I didn't trust her to listen even if I'd asked. She seemed very much ill-at-ease, her ears constantly in motion, checking on me, this unknown presence on her back, checking on the other horses. She did not like to be too close to them, in fact, seemed desperate to get ahead, an urge I could check only by steering her at another horse's rump—which, of course, made her more anxious. Her personality seemed, in fact, very much like mine: willing to try, eager even, and then amazed, terrified, at the predicament I'd gotten myself into. What was I thinking, jumping on an unknown horse and keeping up with two professional riders?

At last Elvar reined up in a grassy hollow, jumped off his horse, and pulled a cigarette from his pocket. He lounged against a wet hummock, smoking, letting the horses graze with the bits in their mouths, their reins dragging on the grass. Fridrik followed suit.

I dismounted and stood looking at the horse that had just flown me here. It was the same horse I'd saddled in the stable: Not pretty. Thin and bony, mane scraggly. Her mottled brown coat patchy and dirty. She was totally unremarkable. And she seemed to know it, giving way instantly when one of the other horses coveted her patch of grass. Yet she had just run over rough ground at an amazing clip, eager for even more speed, tolting easily in spite of the unbalanced amateur on her back.

Elvar snuffed his cigarette and leaped up, slipping the butt into his pants' pocket. He went up to Gaeska and unsaddled her. "Next you'll ride Uggi," he said, meaning the chestnut.

I sighed and stretched and looked at the next prospect with as much enthusiasm as I could muster. Immediately I felt my willingness return, my try-anything spirit. Uggi was a very handsome horse. A light golden-red, almost palomino in color, with a blond mane and tail and a wide, even blaze. He was big and powerful-looking. His name meant "Stripe," or "Blaze." As Elvar brushed him off with the back of his hand, I noticed something else: "No frostmark?" I asked.

Elvar laughed. "We forgot."

It was another point in Uggi's favor—I found the frostmarks hideous, like a barcode slapped on a Picasso. Yet they were better than the marks they'd replaced. Baring-Gould, here a century ago, had ridden "a beautifully made creature" who'd been branded by "slitting his ears into ribands, which danced and quivered in the most ludicrous manner when the animal was in motion."

We mounted and rode back up the gravel hill to the track on top—though what was "riding" to Elvar seemed like hurtling to me. We were out to cover ground, to get somewhere. He wasn't showing me his horses; he was showing me what his horses could *do*.

Unhappily, beautiful Uggi was not an easy tolter. He leaned against the reins and stretched into a flat and bumpy trot. Behind me Fridrik said something I didn't catch, and Elvar angled down the hill to a flat meadow of marshy grass. He reined in to ride next to me. "Shift your weight back," he said. "Bring your hands higher. Loosen your knees." Under his guidance, I felt Uggi soften and round and pick up a smooth tolt again.

Suddenly Elvar's horse leaped to one side and cantered a few steps to a fence, bucking and twisting. Fridrik shouted and Elvar jumped off and held the horse's head, talking to it softly. I had stopped and gotten off as soon as the ruckus began, grateful that Uggi hadn't spooked too. Fridrik, who had been ponying both the spare horses, handed me their reins and walked quietly toward Elvar's mount. A snarl of barbed wire had gotten caught in its long tail and lashed it across the legs. Calmly, Fridrik untangled it and tossed it aside. Then, for no good reason, my horse, Uggi, started acting up. He kicked at his girth strap and snorted and danced about. Elvar ran over and threw the saddle off, thinking something must be stuck under it, but nothing was. He shook his head, as if to say, *There went that sale.*

"Walk him around," he said, and to Fridrik, "You ride him, and give her Heimir."

Heimir was a man's name, derived from *heim*, "home" or *heimur*, "world." He was jet black. Of all the dark horses, he was the prettiest, his coloring the most even, his mane and tail thick. When we were underway again, I found him very calm and methodical, not at all concerned with running close behind the other horses. And his tolt seemed almost as smooth as Gaeska's—or perhaps it was smoother and I was just more sensitive than when we'd started out hours before. (I was beginning to envy one of the Icelanders Baring-Gould had ridden with: "We were delayed a short while by my guide catching a sheep and ripping off its wool ... This he tied into a bundle and inserted between himself and his saddle." How nice that would have felt!) Heimir needed more encouraging than Gaeska—or at least he didn't have to be first. And unlike Uggi, when he lost tolt, he found canter: a bounce, not a bumpy trot. Yet his tolt could be very fast, I discovered suddenly, when he saw the barn and went full tilt toward it. I could only turn him, not stop.

"*Taka og losa!*" Elvar called harshly. "Give and take. You're pulling too much. *Taka og losa!* Take the reins and give them back again. That's rule number one with horses."

Elvar looked discouraged, and a little worn out. He didn't ask what I thought of this horse.

The next day when Elvar asked which horses I wanted to try again, I said only Heimir. I liked his looks, his even coloring, and his more laid-back, even lazy, character.

He raised his eyebrows. "The little bay mare, too," he told Fjola. It was her turn to ride with me.

Shy Fridrik was busy working some young horses. He'd saddled a pretty yellow dun and was mounting outside the paddock as we crossed the yard. The horse reared suddenly and backed away from us. Fridrik sat easy on it, loose and balanced, and spoke soothingly until it settled down. Then he turned to Fjola. "That was a surprise," he said. He signaled the horse and set off down the bridle path that bordered the main road just as a tour bus swooshed by. The dun horse didn't miss a beat.

We got our horses and followed him a short way, then crossed onto a long gravel lane. The wind was gusty. The horses tolted fast. Suddenly Heimir jumped and swerved and cantered out past Fjola's horse. He picked up speed. The gravel skittered under his feet. He was on the edge of running away. I was on the edge of panic: There was no sturdy riding instructor with a whip to steer into, no fence to stop a runaway, and this lane looked very long. *Taka og losa!* I heard in my mind. I stilled my fear and tried it. Gently Heimir slowed and came to a stop. I got off. Fear flew into my mouth and I began shaking.

"Are you all right?" Fjola asked, riding up. "What's the matter?"

"He was frightened. Something frightened him," I stopped. "I was frightened too." I shook my head. "A frightened horse and a frightened rider is not good."

"No," she agreed. She got off her horse.

We stood there in the lane, within sight of the house and barns. Over the hill, we could hear Elvar's tractor at the haymaking. A car went by on the main road behind us. The wind gusted again, and flapped the hood of my jacket.

"Maybe that was it," I said, relieved. "He heard my jacket flapping."

"Maybe," said Fjola. She didn't sound convinced. "He's afraid of trucks," she added. "Do you want to go back?"

I nodded.

"You can ride my horse—but he's not for sale."

This horse was also black. As we turned toward home and picked up a tolt, I felt an enormous power coming from him, combined with a grace and smoothness far beyond that of any of the other horses I'd tried. I felt like I was riding a rocketship. I stopped him and got off.

"What's the matter now? Don't you like him?" Fjola asked, her eyes wide.

I admired him very much, but I felt seriously over-horsed. I remembered the story of Otkel, a pompous fool in *Njal's Saga* who prided himself on his fine riding horses. Setting off on a journey one day, he was galloping ahead of his friends when his horse "became excited and bolted off the track." Up through his enemy's fields Otkel went, out of control, "much faster than he wished." This enemy was none other than Gunnar of Hlidarendi, the great hero who was married to the feminist Hallgerdur. Gunnar was sowing his fields, the saga says, and so was unarmed. "Otkel, who was wearing spurs, rode into him. His spur struck Gunnar's ear, making a deep gash." Gunnar demanded an apology, but at that moment

Otkel's friends rode up jeering. "That's good riding, lads," one said, and Otkel laughed along with him. It wasn't long before Otkel and his friends were dead.

"He's too much horse," I said to Fjola. "I'm afraid he'll run away with me." In today's world, the equivalent of Otkel's demise would be bolting up the road, out of control, unable to stop, and meeting, not Gunnar of Hlidarendi, but a tour bus. I took a breath. And admitted: "I had a horse in Reykjavik run away with me."

Fjola got down. "Let's walk back," she said, and headed for the barn. I knew I had seriously disappointed her.

When we had loosed Heimir, Fjola stood thinking for a moment, examining the herd.

"What about this one?" I pointed to the beautiful chestnut with the snip and star that I'd made friends with in the meadow.

"Vera? Oh no, she's a competition horse." Fjola sighed. "Well," she said tentatively, "we could try Frodi."

Another black, he skipped and danced so much we didn't even make it out of the paddock.

"Why don't you ride Gaeska again," Fjola said, bringing out the little bay mare.

We went into a new-cut hayfield, flat and fenced all around. The little mare was smooth and eager, easy at first, but as we kept turning circles in the grass, she grew more and more rattled, urged more and more speed— It was clear neither of us knew what we were supposed to be doing, here in the fenced hayfield, going round and around, and our anxieties magnified each other's. I wondered how she'd be if my hood started flapping or a truck roared past. "She's too fast," I said, when Fjola joined us. "She's afraid of everything." Or maybe it was just me that was afraid.

Back at the barn, Fjola was still quiet, untacking both our mounts. Then, "I think we'll try an experiment," she said, with a bright smile. She brought out a big bay gelding, rather fat. "This was Elvar's brother's first competition horse—he's not for sale. He's the oldest horse in the stable. I think he's twenty or twenty-one. His name is Freyfaxi."

Can't be, I thought as we walked out to the hay field. *He's not the right color.*

Freyfaxi was the most famous horse in the Icelandic Sagas. A buckskin stallion with a long black mane, he was dedicated to Freyr, the god of horses and ships, of riches and prosperity, son of the sea god Niord and brother of Freyja, goddess of love. Freyfaxi was the greatest treasure owned by the chieftain Hrafnkel. He "loved this horse so passionately," says *Hrafnkel's Saga*, "that he swore a solemn oath to kill anyone who rode the stallion without his permission."

One summer, Hrafnkel hired a neighbor's son to herd his sheep. He warned the boy, Einar, not to ride Freyfaxi; he told Einar of his binding oath. He thought the boy was a promising youth, destined for better than sheepherding, and all went well until midsummer, when Einar lost track of thirty sheep. They went missing for a week. Early one morning Einar took a bridle and saddle and went off to catch a horse to help him search for the lost sheep. "But when he came closer," the saga says, "all the mares bolted away from him, and he chased them without success. They had never been so shy before. Only Freyfaxi remained behind; he was as still as if he were anchored to the ground." Recklessly, Einar caught Freyfaxi. He rode him "from dawn to mid-evening, traveling fast and far, for this was an outstanding horse." By the time they found the lost sheep, "Freyfaxi was all running with sweat; and every hair on his body was dripping. He was covered in mud and panting with exhaustion." As soon as Einar loosed him, "he rolled over a dozen times, and then neighed loudly and started to race down the path." Freyfaxi galloped straight to the farmhouse and neighed at the door. Hrafnkel was just sitting down to supper. "It grieves me to see how you have been treated, my fosterling," he said to the stallion when he went out. "You had your wits about you when you came to me, and this shall be avenged. Go back to your herd."

The next morning Hrafnkel rode up to the sheep pens and killed Einar with a blow of his ax.

Hrafnkel raised a grave mound over Einar's body and made Einar's father a generous offer of compensation: He would provide all the milk and meat the household could use and give Einar's younger brothers and sisters a good start in life. Einar's father refused. With the backing of powerful men from another part of Iceland, he and a kinsman stripped Hrafnkel of his chieftainship. They strung him up by the heels to torture and humiliate him, then chased him out of the district. They led his beloved Freyfaxi to a steep cliff beside a waterfall. They put a bag over his head and tied a stone around his neck. Then they used poles to push him over the cliff, saying sarcastically that they were sacrificing him to his god.

Their revenge was out of bounds. They were fools to dismiss Hrafnkel's offers. They became bitter, greedy, and cruel-hearted men, hated throughout the district, while Hrafnkel steadily worked his way back to prosperity. By the story's end, he had resumed his place as chieftain and "enjoyed great prestige" before dying peacefully in his bed. But after the loss of his Freyfaxi, he never worshiped the god Freyr again.

Did Hrafnkel kill Einar out of anger? No. The saga was clear about that: He had slept on the decision. Hrafnkel was bound by his oath, constrained by his sense of honor, forced to follow through however much he might wish now to unsay his vow. The horse was doomed as soon as the boast was framed.

How I had wished I could rewrite that saga and save Freyfaxi, flying down that cliff to his awful death. Now, leading the way to the newly cut field, with Fjola walking her horse behind, I felt fond of this old gelding with the heroic name, but a little suspicious as well. A Norwegian anthropology student I knew thought that

Icelandic horse breeders "'imprint' traditional names on the foals in order to, at least symbolically, evoke the strength, ability, and endurance" of the earlier horse. In this case, it seemed a bit much to live up to.

I mounted and soon considered I might be wrong. There were no edges to this Freyfaxi, no unfinished corners. He had the grace and balance of Fjola's black horse, with some additional quality that I could only describe as "wisdom." He followed my thoughts without the least hesitation, carrying me where I willed to go as if some godly line of communication were open.

Fjola rode a young horse, only partly trained. She raced up and down the meadow, trotting, tolting, cantering, perhaps even pacing.

It made no difference. Freyfaxi ran at a pleasant, even speed, his movements as soft and smooth as a wide river's, my saddle the raft. He cantered a step when I pressed him, as if to prove that he could, should it be necessary, but we both knew it wasn't: back to the even flow, the lazy rocking. He was entirely safe, completely trustworthy; I could ride this horse from morning to mid-evening, fast and far ...

I called out to Fjola, "He's perfect."

That evening Elvar phoned around to the surrounding farms. He had an American guest, he said, who was looking for a quiet horse, a trustworthy horse, a beginner's horse—he glanced over at me with his cutting blue eyes—yes, a children's pony.

I felt a sudden lump form in my throat.

Without spirit, I had read, *the Icelandics would be just ponies. But their will to go and their energy make them Viking horses.*

And again, the Icelandic saying rang in my ears: *Vilji er allt sem þarf.* "Willingness is all that matters."

CHAPTER EIGHT

THE DAPPLE GRAY

In the morning, while the hay was wet, we drove inland to Kelduland.

The clouds had eased back, leaving the mountains with new snow on their summits. The ground grew rugged as the valley narrowed, the landscape looking more Icelandic. Quick and foamy now, the river ran gray-blue between the red walls of a deep canyon. *Isn't Skagafjord the most beautiful place in Iceland?* Elvar's mother had asked me one evening. She was a plump, pleasant woman, and an excellent cook. I was eating in her kitchen while the haying went on, Fjola having been drafted to drive a tractor. I had demurred. *I miss the lava,* I said. *It's so picturesque.* I asked, in return, if she didn't miss Stora Hraun, with its grand views of Eldborg and the great glacier Snaefellsjokull. *No,* she replied. *It was very romantic, but it was not a good farm. The lambs kept getting caught by the tide and disappearing.*

The farm of Kelduland, when we reached it, was a green patch, cracked and crumpled, wedged between sooty hills and the red river gorge. The "kelda" of its name could have been either a spring or a bog. The farmer saw us coming and rode in on his tractor.

A wizened fellow, he studiously ignored me. "A pinch of snuff?" he asked Elvar, passing a plastic horn through the car window. The Icelandic word was *neftóbak*, "nose tobacco." Elvar took some, looking unpracticed; his eyes watered, but he didn't sneeze.

The horses were wandering on the far side of a deep gully. The farmer called a girl to help and angled down the field. "You wait here at the car," Elvar said, going after them.

The horses were wary and wild. They dodged out of reach, clumped and jostled each other, broke from the herd and then circled back. It was cold; my hands in my thin riding gloves were stiff. The farmer shucked his coat and tossed it at a straggler. At that, the whole herd stampeded, rushing down and up the gully, half jumping it, slipping, clattering across the stones and into the paddock. Somehow the girl was there before they turned and whirled out again, and she deftly shut the gate.

I went over to lean on it, feeling worthless. The old man had some real beauties here, but I knew I wouldn't be riding them.

Elvar had located five "children's ponies" in all of Skagafjord. Two I'd ridden the past evening, geldings trained for Hestasport, a large horse-trekking firm nearby. The black one I thought most handsome, but nearly unrideable, jumping and jigging and pulling at the bit. The red was more sedate, but priced out of my reach and for reasons I couldn't comprehend.

At Kelduland we'd come for a black-and-white pinto. I spotted him right away and was instantly disappointed. His face was strangely marked, with a funny white mouth that made him seem to grimace. I reminded myself that I wasn't going to base my decision on color, and yet—white lips were a weakness, I'd heard. Such horses can suffer from painful sunburn in a setting where the light is more direct.

The farmer tacked him up and led him onto the road. Elvar proceeded to pull out a video camera. He filmed the man riding back and forth. The horse tolted nicely, but I thought his head was held too high.

"Now you ride," Elvar said. "Follow us down the road."

The farmer handed me his riding whip and got in to drive the car. Elvar took the passenger's seat, craned around, and aimed the camera at the horse. "Okay," he said.

Apparently he would be immortalizing my ride, too. I got on self-consciously and let the horse walk behind the car. He was sluggish, wanting to turn back to the barn.

"Okay," Elvar said again.

I tapped him with the whip, and the horse picked up a desultory tolt, skipping a beat here and there, slowing down until I tapped again. The car stopped.

"Okay, now ride back."

I turned the horse homeward, and suddenly he found his spirit. We clattered toward the barn, tolt-canter-tolt, the car driving right beside us. I pulled up at the gate and got off.

Elvar put the camera in the back seat and shook the farmer's hand. "Thank you very much," he said, "that should just about do it." He threw me a look and I got into the car. "Those Germans want a pinto," he said in explanation, as we drove away. I was beginning to think he could read my mind—how did he know I wasn't interested in the horse? But what he was reading, I learned later, was my riding ability.

A sports car stopped us at the river crossing. Elvar got out to confer with the driver, a young man handsomely dressed in riding clothes, who seemed to be trying to convince him of something. Finally Elvar leaned in through the window. "He's got this horse he wants you to try—"

"It can't hurt to try," interrupted the other man, smiling pleasantly.

I shrugged. "Sure, I'll try it."

Elvar rolled his eyes, and I knew I'd said the wrong thing. "We'll follow you," he said to his friend.

The sports car turned into the farm Ulfsstadir (Wolf's Homestead), just down the road. A big, new house sat up on a hill, freshly painted and neat, with a nice view. The young man, Ingolfur, and his wife lived downstairs, with an older family above; three tow-headed children played happily in the yard with a go-cart they'd made from boards and a baby buggy. The stables were big and clean and well organized, the shelves dusted, the tack clean, a calendar up on the wall. Ingolfur's dog had whelped on a burlap sack beneath the feed mangers: six little prick-eared pups. Even the paddock wasn't as mucky as they usually were on an Icelandic farm. Ingolfur separated a mare from the herd, and, when he'd singled her out, she stood still to be bridled. She was a beautiful color. A dapple gray with tan in the mix, black on her feet and the tips of her ears, her tail mostly blonde, her mane black with light streaks. In the books I'd thought dapples looked ugly. This one had me enthralled. I'd never seen a color so complex.

She held herself well, alert but obedient. She did try to nip when Ingolfur snugged the girth, and she shied when he mounted, but I could overlook that. The school horses at home did worse.

Elvar waved me back into the car as Ingolfur headed down the lane and onto a grassy track at the bottom. We followed and parked where the filming was best. Up and back Ingolfur rode. "Okay!" hollered Elvar, then to me, "you still want to try?"

I did. And as soon as I mounted, it seemed I had found my horse. She lifted her head and looked glad to be about. She was slow and quiet and took a light hand on the reins, the least little pull and she'd stop, but a squeeze with the legs didn't make things blur. This horse would not go fast even when I kicked her, not even when we were aimed straight for the barn. And best of all, she was pretty.

I rode again past Elvar and smiled for the camera—but he had put the camera down.

"Ride up to the house," he said, and got in the car and drove off.

I followed slowly, feeling very pleased. "I like this horse," I said when I dismounted by the barn.

"You like this horse," Elvar said.

Ingolfur gave him a wry smile.

"How much does she cost?" I asked.

"140,000," Ingolfur said.

"What was that?" I couldn't believe she was so cheap.

"He said 140,000," Elvar repeated slowly.

That clinched it. Elvar's horses were all at least 200,000 kronur, and the red trekking horse I'd ridden the night before had been 300,000. Here I could get two horses for that: Birkir, the bay gelding at Hlid, was 160,000; this dapple gray mare, 140,000. Two horses for just over four thousand dollars, almost a thousand less than I'd planned to spend. Even my husband would be pleased.

"I think I want to buy her," I said to Ingolfur. "What can you tell me about her?"

Ingolfur laughed. "Let's have coffee," he said.

Elvar frowned. "I'll need to call Fjola."

"Here." Ingolfur pulled a cell phone from his pocket. "We'll make pizza."

The pizza had pineapple on it. Ingolfur's wife, a blonde with dark eyebrows, whisked it from the microwave and poured out the coffee. Elvar took a large slice and tried to enjoy it, while Ingolfur and his wife needled him. I felt a little bad for him. He'd been my good host, and here I was choosing his competitor's horse.

I opened my notebook and wrote down what Ingolfur said. The mare's name was Glefsa (a word I couldn't translate). She was bred at Ytra-Skordugil, the farm next door to Elvar's. Her grandfather was the famous Hrafn fra Holtsmula, just like Birkir from Hlid. She was six years old.

"You'll have to decide before Wednesday," Ingolfur said. He had hired out as a guide for Hestasport and would be leaving on a long horse-trek in a few days.

"That shouldn't be a problem," I answered.

In the car, Elvar was silent, angry—or at least disappointed in me.

I looked out the window, trying out things to say. "Will you be unhappy if I buy that horse?" I asked finally.

He looked at me with his cold blue eyes. "Will you be happy if you buy that horse?"

"I think so."

"Then I'm happy if you're happy," he said, and stared fixedly at the road.

As we neared Sydra-Skordugil, however, he suddenly hit the brakes and swerved into the barnyard. "Here," he said, leaping out of the car. "We have to move those mares. You can help."

He took Gaeska and, I was surprised to see, old Freyfaxi out of a pen and saddled them.

"Start out with her, and, if she's too much horse for you," he said with an edge to his voice, "we'll switch."

I felt my jaw tighten and I got on before he could come around to hold her head. He seemed not to notice but flung himself on Freyfaxi and took off at a quick tolt. We raced down along the side of the road to the first gate and went into the pasture. It was a few acres in size, humped and tussocky, grass mixed with blueberry and small, scrawling birch bushes. Some twenty grazing horses lifted their heads to stare.

"See that horse over there?" Elvar pointed to a very light bay, almost golden in color. "That's the stallion. You're riding a mare. Keep away from him. Work around on the far side and move them toward the gate. I'll go the other way and open it." He wheeled around the herd to the left, getting speed out of old Freyfaxi that I never would have imagined was there, and I turned the other way, keeping the stallion clear in the corner of my eye.

Perhaps it was more than the *corner* of my eye, for it wasn't until we'd pushed the horses through the gate and locked it behind them that I realized Gaeska and I had been working as a team: Slow or fast, left or right, we'd simply gotten the job done. It was almost as if she were trying to convince me I was making a mistake, choosing a pretty horse over a plain one. But then, on the way back through the cut hay field, she began her old trick of picking up the pace, and I had to turn her in a circle to slow her down. Elvar looked at me like I was nuts. *"Taka og losa,"* he muttered. "Give and take."

That evening I made a list of things to do: Call Haukur and tell him to stop looking. Call Sigrun at Hlid and arrange to buy Birkir. Schedule a vet to check both my horses. Get money. From Thordur in Reykjavik? From home?

I called my husband. *Is it a horse I can ride?* Absolutely. A children's pony, I answered. He said he'd send more money if I needed it. His mother had left him a small inheritance, and it was this sort of thing we'd decided to spend it on: Something forward-looking, life-affirming. Our son's college education. A garden. Horses.

I called Thordur. *Did Einar Gislason say it was a good horse?* I paused. I weaseled. I still hadn't even met Einar. I'd heard he wasn't well. *Elvar found it for me,* I told Thordur, *Einar's son.* Thordur said he would see how the stock market was doing.

"Glefsa?" Fjola looked shocked. "It means 'Nipper.'" She was dressed in a long black chemise, her blonde hair brushed out, a gold chain enhancing her handsome cleavage. She and a girlfriend were going out to the bar; it was Saturday night.

"Why is she so much cheaper than the other horse, the red one at Hestasport?" I asked. I was sitting at the kitchen table, jotting down notes about the day's horses.

Elvar, across from me, was working on a bottle of whiskey. He seemed put out that Fjola was taking a night with the girls; he hardly looked at her in her finery. "That red horse has a very good tolt," he replied, authoritatively. "Very high leg action. He tolts very fast."

None of that seemed important to me.

I noticed Elvar had the fax from Germany spread out in front of him; the German family had fancied a dapple gray.

He looked up at me, as if again reading my thoughts. "You buy this gray horse," he said, "and you'll be sorry. In a year you'll wish you hadn't. You'll wish you could come back and buy my Gaeska." He got up to answer a knock at the door. "But it's your decision," he called over his shoulder. "You have to decide for yourself."

The visitor was his drinking buddy, Thorvaldur, from the farm of Flugumyri, Fluga's Mire, across the valley.

"Where Fluga came from, in *Landnámabók?*" I asked.

Thorvaldur smiled. "That's right. Where she died. She fell into a bog and died."

The story of Fluga was one of my favorites. "Fluga" comes from the verb *fljúga*, "to fly." According to the *Book of Settlements*, the mare had come to Iceland on a ship bringing livestock late in the Settlement Period, about 900 A.D. She was most likely from Norway, although horses were also brought from the British Isles, and one, called Kinnskaer, or White Cheek, came from Eastern Europe or Central Asia. According to the saga that mentions him, Kinnskaer was an extremely tall horse that had to be fed on grain both summer and winter. The other horses brought to Iceland would likewise have been exceptional in one way or another. Viking ships were small. Although the settlers used the deep-keeled *knarr*—not the dragon ship, the slim longship people usually associate with Vikings—their horses had to compete for space with cattle, sheep, timber, grain, weapons, jewelry, tools, clothing, rugs, tapestries, pots, and all sorts of other household goods. Since most settlers were landed farmers or petty chieftains, the quality of their stock was already high, and of these they brought only their best.

Fluga escaped while the ship that had borne her was being unloaded. Later, a man named Thorir Dove-Nose "bought the chance of finding her, and find her he did. She was an exceptionally fast horse." One day, the story goes, Thorir was riding Fluga, traveling alone on one of the two summer routes that cross the glaciated wasteland at the center of Iceland, when he was waylaid by a mysterious character named Orn, "a sorceror who used to wander from one part of the country to another." Orn bet Thorir a hundred marks of silver (a fantastic sum) that his horse was faster than Fluga. The two men rode on until they reached a flat stretch of land, laid out a course, and raced off. But, according to the story, "Orn was only half way up the course by the time Thorir met him on his way back, so great was the difference between the two horses." Orn took his loss so badly that he rode off into the mountains and was never seen again. (The story doesn't say if he paid up or not.) Fluga, for her part, was exhausted, so Thorir left her behind, switching his saddle to another one of his horses, and continued on his way.

When Thorir came back to get Fluga several weeks later, he was surprised to find a gray stallion with his mare. Where he had left Fluga was far from any farms, in a rugged part of the country with little grass. That fact, and the mystery surrounding Orn's appearance and disappearance, hints that the stallion was the sorceror himself.

Gray horses, indeed, are often magical creatures in the sagas. They are the fairy horses, sorcerors' horses, ghosts' horses; even the god Odin's eight-legged steed, Sleipnir, is gray. If I was honest with myself, I realized quite suddenly, I knew that one reason I wanted dapple-gray Glefsa was that her color recalled so many good tales.

In the *Book of Settlements*, for instance, there's the story of Audun the Stutterer and a horse that lived in a highland lake. One day, a dapple gray came racing down from the hills above Audun's farm. It scattered Audun's herd and bowled over his stallion. A big and powerful man, Audun went out and caught the newcomer. He hitched him to his sledge and spent the morning hauling hay. The work went well until after noon. Then the gray horse started stamping. By evening, he stamped so hard his hooves sank into the ground up to the fetlocks. When the sun went down, he broke the traces, raced back to the hills, and disappeared into the lake, "and that was the last anyone ever saw of him."

Such a horse in Icelandic is a *nykur*. Their color is always gray, although *grár* in Icelandic includes what we would call white. *Grár* also means rotten, malicious, or false. The false nykur can always be known by his hooves, set on backwards so that hoofprints seem to be going away when they're really coming for you. "In winter when cracks appear in the ice and cause loud booming noises," according to one folklorist, "men say that the Nykur is neighing." A water nykur can beget a foal on an ordinary mare if she strays into the water; such a foal will lie down whenever it is taken through a river or a stream. To ride a nykur can be fatal. One old Icelandic-English dictionary calls them a kind of "sea goblin" and notes that they can take on other shapes than that of a horse. In this they are like the Scottish *kelpie*, which shifts between gnome or elf and horse shapes. A kelpie waits by the water as a horse and carries to the river bottom any traveler so keen to keep his feet dry that he foolishly mounts it. In Iceland, at least the nykur waits for the magic words.

There once was a shepherd girl, one story goes, searching for some lost ewes. She was quite tired, and a long way from home, when suddenly she saw a gray horse standing by a lake. She caught it easily, knotting a string around its jaw as a bridle. Then suddenly she lost her nerve. "I don't feel like riding this horse," she said to herself. At that the horse jumped into the lake and disappeared.

Another time three boys were playing on a riverbank when they noticed a gray horse nearby. One boy bravely clambered onto its back. When the horse didn't spook, a second boy climbed on. "Let's go for a ride," they called to their brother, but he, the oldest, refused. "I don't feel like it," he said. No sooner were the words spoken, than the nykur raced into the river and the two brothers drowned.

A water nykur can be tamed by puncturing the swelling behind its left foreleg, said to be filled with wind. "He loses his former nature completely and becomes safe for use as a saddle beast," notes one turn-of-the-century authority. Yet in general, it's just best to scare them away. "Although the nykur is not dangerous if not tampered with, it is unsafe to have them around, for children and careless persons are apt to mount them, not realizing their danger."

I looked across the table at Elvar and his friend from Flugumyri filling their whiskey glasses and amused myself by wondering if there wasn't a bit of superstition behind Elvar's dislike of my chosen dapple gray. Did he think it was bewitched? That it would carry me to the bottom of the sea? Not all grays were false, even in folktales.

The Nordic hero Sigurdur the Dragon-Slayer owned a gray horse, Grani (Gray One), said to descend from Odin's Sleipnir, the best horse of gods or men. Grani carried the hero to the dragon's lair and hauled off the gold when the worm was dead. Sigurdur had "meant to drive the horse before him," the story says, "but Grani would not move a foot before Sigurdur himself mounted," in spite of his already heavy load. As told in German legends as well as the Icelandic tales, and popularized in Wagner's operas, Sigurdur the Dragon-Slayer soon became enmeshed in a fatal love triangle. Through witchcraft he forgot his first love, Brynhildur, and married Gudrun instead. Then Gudrun's brother, Gunnar, decided to court Brynhildur. He rode to her great hall, but around it burned a ring of fire. Brynhildur would marry no man but the one who would ride through the flames. Gunnar tried, but his horse refused. Sigurdur lent him his own horse, Grani, but the gray one would not stir a foot until Sigurdur himself mounted. Then "Grani at once ran forward, while the fire crackled, the earth shook, and flames darted up to the very heavens." Sigurdur pretended to be Gunnar, with the result that Brynhildur, when she found out the trick, connived her false lover's death. But before she killed herself out of remorse, she went to the stable. "In tears, I went to talk to Grani," says one old Icelandic poem. "Weeping, I asked him what had happened. Sadly then Grani let his head sink to the ground. The horse knew his master was no more."

The phone rang and Fjola picked it up. She listened for a long time, then called for me.

"Who is that old man who talks so much?" she whispered as I took the phone.

It was Haukur, calling from Snorrastadir. "I have found the perfect mare for Nancy," he had announced. It was one of the trekking horses he'd been expecting, a red mare, *glófexti*, her mane and tail so bright they looked almost white, with a white blaze and socks. She was seven years old, *thæg* and *góð*, obedient and good, a willing horse with fine trot and tolt, and only 250,000 kronur—"but for me," Haukur said, "they will sell her for 200,000. You must come right away. I'll make them leave her at Snorrastadir until you get here."

"I'll take the bus tomorrow," I told him. I said not a word about the dapple gray.

Elvar poured himself and Thorvaldur another drink. Fjola's friend had arrived while I was on the phone, and the two girls had left for town. Shy Fridrik had come in from the barn and taken Fjola's place at the table. I made some tea and slipped a spoonful of whiskey into it. Fridrik looked surprised, then did the same with his coffee. Elvar sipped and glowered.

"He has a lot of nerve," he muttered finally. *"I have found the perfect mare for Nancy!"* he mimicked, leveling his gaze at me across the table. But he spoke to Thorvaldur. "*I* have the perfect mare for Nancy right here," he declared. "My little bay mare, Gaeska."

Thorvaldur was tall and slim, with graceful gestures and a prominent nose. He gently mentioned Glefsa, the dapple gray, and I was surprised to learn that Ingolfur did not own her. He was selling her for "a fisherman," a somewhat shady sort from Thorvaldur's tone, who merely wanted to be rid of the mare and had asked Ingolfur to handle it.

Then Thorvaldur mentioned an accident on the road that afternoon: A bus had run down a bicyclist, a German tourist. Elvar shook his head. He didn't see how the man would live.

I thought of Fridrik on that half-broke yellow dun the other morning, riding along the same roadway—or myself, with Gaeska going faster and faster—and I shivered. Fridrik, for his part, was pouring more whiskey into his coffee.

Morning found the bottle empty, coffee cups and a plate of crackers alongside the glasses cluttering the table. I had set about straightening up when Elvar suddenly entered from outside. It was clear he'd stayed up drinking long after I'd gone to bed, also that he'd hardly slept.

"Hurry up," he said angrily. "There are two horses over at Hjaltastadir. We'll go now while the grass dries. Thorvaldur will drive."

Thorvaldur hadn't slept it off either, but his mood was light-hearted, almost giddy. He had a small pick-up. Elvar took the middle seat, and I hugged the door. There'd been frost in the night, although it was only the tenth of August, and the air was crisp and cold. On the way down the road, at the turn where the German tourist had been hit, Thorvaldur began singing. His voice rose, mellow and full, in a long slow tune, part sea shanty, part ballad. Elvar joined him, his singing easy and natural, the notes strong and sure. Then he broke off and giggled, glancing at me half-embarrassed.

Thorvaldur turned to me. "That's how we do things in Skagafjord," he said. "We drink, and we sing."

To reach Hjaltastadir (Hjalti's Homestead), we drove inland, crossed a bridge, and turned back toward the bay until we were exactly opposite Sydra-Skordugil, five miles of fertile, grassy land and braided river between the two farms. The two horses to try were a red and a gray, each priced reasonably. But the red was pig-headed and wanted to bolt for the barn. The gray was nicer, a gelding, and calm, but only five years old and not yet smooth in his gaits. Oddly, I didn't find him attractive. He had neither the carriage nor the subtle coloring of pretty Glefsa, and I could not think of trading her for him.

"He's very tall," I said tactfully, and the farmwife nodded, pleased, though I'd heard tall horses could be stiff and bumpy under saddle. He measured 145 centimeters, she said, about 14.2 hands, which made him a very big Icelandic, a full hand taller than the average, though not so big he'd make the record books: A horse named Flosi had his picture in the paper the week past for measuring nearly 16 hands. He was shown next to his stablemate, called Napoleon and suitably diminutive at 12.2.

On the ride home, Thorvaldur and Elvar sandwiched me between them. They said nothing about the red or the gray.

"You should buy Gaeska," Elvar said abruptly, "my little bay mare."

Thorvaldur nodded and leaned toward me. "She's a good horse." His tone was low and soothing.

"I could have sold her," Elvar said, his voice rising. "I could have sold her two months ago, for 250,000, but I knew you were coming. I saved her for you. I knew she'd be right for you. For you," he said, in an odd echo of Haukur's promise, "she'll only cost 200,000."

I managed to squeak out "Glefsa," and Elvar erupted.

"Glefsa! That horse is a *trunta*, a *lullara*—"

The words weren't having the desired effect; I stared at him, concerned but apparently not suitably shocked. He heaved a big sigh. *"Piggy pace!"* he spit the words out in English, the only English he'd spoken since I arrived. "That's what's wrong with her," he said, repeating it. "Piggy pace."

I was quiet, chastened, and he went on more calmly.

"She looked fine with Ingolfur on her. No leg action, but okay. But I could see her going right downhill as soon as you got on. In a year, she'd lose it altogether. She'd have no tolt at all.

"But Gaeska, now, she'll tolt for anyone, anytime."

"His mother rides Gaeska," Thorvaldur said quietly.

"That's right! My *mother* rides Gaeska. She's only on horseback one or two times a year, and she's ridden Gaeska. Even Einar! You met him, my brother, the one in the mink house. *He* rides Gaeska, and he *hates* horses!"

We pulled into the drive at Sydra-Skordugil. It was just before noon. The sun was high, the hay looked dry. The bus to the south wouldn't pass until ten before five.

I hadn't really *disliked* Gaeska, I thought. I just didn't find her pretty. And Elvar was my host. It was rude to go off without giving his horse another chance. "Could I ride her again before I go?" I asked.

"Whatever you want," Elvar said. He leaped from the car and rushed into the house, kicking off his boots in the entryway. "Fjola!" he shouted. He threw open the bedroom door. Fjola was sound asleep, sprawled diagonally on the bed, twined in the sheets. A bare arm and a foot stuck out. Elvar grabbed the foot. "Fjola!" he shouted.

She started up from sleep, saw me, and clutched the covers to herself. I backed away from the door just as she lit into Elvar with a full-volume stream of outrage.

A few moments later he joined me in the kitchen, looking rather meek. He checked the coffeepot, but it was empty. He poured a glass of milk instead. "Fjola will take you in a few minutes," he said. He grabbed a cracker from the plate still on the table, and went out. I busied myself straightening up.

Ten minutes later, Fjola appeared, fresh and dressed and her usual cheerful self. "Didn't you like those horses this morning?" she asked, as if nothing had happened.

"Not really," I said, "and Elvar thinks I should buy Gaeska."

"Yes," Fjola nodded. She checked the coffeepot too, out of habit, before drawing a glass of water. "She's a good horse for you."

Before we made it to the pasture where Gaeska and the rest of the riding horses had been put out to graze the night before, Thorvaldur was back with orders from Elvar: Fjola was needed, immediately, to drive the hay rake.

"I'll wake up Odin," Thorvaldur said.

Odin had arrived in the night. Like Fridrik, he'd been hired to work with the horses; but Odin was twice Fridrik's size. A huge man, ruddy and quiet, with a round face. He rubbed the sleep out of his eyes and lumbered out to the pasture. Fjola had given me two slices of bread, the horses' favorite treat, to lure Gaeska in if she was hard to catch. Odin spotted the 513 on her side, walked over to her, and put a hand on her mane. She stopped eating and stood as if her feet had grown into the ground. I gave her the bread anyway. By the time I had her saddled, Odin was gone. I was on my own.

I mounted and rode along the edge of the road to the lane where my flapping jacket had spooked black Heimir. Gaeska's gait was rough going downhill, but slow enough, and at the flat bottom she resumed her smooth tolt. We had started up toward the neighboring farm when I spotted the hay wagon approaching. There was no berm on this lane, no flat edge at all, nothing but a ditch. Its banks were very steep. The wagon rumbled nearer, loaded with a tower of well-stacked bales, Elvar driving. There was no room to pass. Nor did Elvar show any inclination to slow down. He honked the horn, and waved me off the road. Obediently, I aimed Gaeska at the ditch. She scrambled down and, when the wagon had passed, its tires at eye level, she clambered back up again. Unlike me, she did not seem upset at all.

I turned her around and we headed back.

When I'd loosed her in the field, I took a seat in the grass in the sunshine, behind a little knoll where no one could see me. The wind was light, the mountains clear against a warm blue sky. Across the fjord, the rocky headland of Thordarhofdi (Thordur's Headland) cut a blue notch in the sky. My friend Thordur had particularly wanted me to notice it, as his family (and name) come from that region. Elves live there, the story goes, in a beautiful mansion, but you can only see it when they want you to. Now, looking at those rocks and seeing only rocks, I wondered how I would break the news to Thordur that not a single horse in all of Skagafjord suited me. I wondered if he would hear—and how quickly—that his American friend was a bother and a waste of effort, couldn't tell a good horse from a nag, was not welcome anymore at Einar Gislason's.

I looked away from Thordarhofdi, discouraged, blue, to find the whole herd of horses grazing unconcernedly about me. I put out my hand and beautiful Vera, with the snip and the star, came over, looking for bread, then a dark horse wandered up. A *trippi*, I thought, dismissing her, just a green horse, unbroken. They're always the most curious. Then I saw the mark, 513, on her side. Gaeska put out her nose to be patted, and I caught my own reflection in her dark eye. Suddenly I began to cry. I couldn't love this ugly mare, with her scraggly mane and her nondescript color. But neither could I be happy with Glefsa, that pretty dapple gray, now that Elvar had named her a *trunta,* a nag.

I got up abruptly, scattering the horses, and walked back to the old house at Sydra-Skordugil. It was open, empty, everyone out at the haymaking. I packed for the trip south to Snorrastadir. I sat on the roadside and waited for the bus.

"You have to decide for yourself," Elvar had said.

But Haukur made it easy on me. He had "the perfect mare for Nancy."

CHAPTER NINE

THE PERFECT MARE

From the hill behind the bus depot at Borgarnes, the ten o'clock sunset backlit the Snaefellsnes peninsula, coloring the angular mountains a deep plum purple. The two peaks like overturned buckets, the horse's head. The troll woman who'd owned both horse and buckets when they were caught and solidified by the rising sun was now herself a spire on the far side of the pass.

The sky was fuchsia fading to cantaloupe—gaudy in this land of lava and sand and sea. Usually the hayfields' green was the only bright shade in the landscape's palette. I peeled an orange—gaudy itself—and tried again to get comfortable on my tussock. I'd been waiting for Haukur since eight-thirty. *He'll be there in a minute,* Ingibjorg had said when I called the first time, but he was still out on the tractor when I checked back an hour later. It was haymaking weather, hot and clear, and the work wouldn't stop until the last wisp was in under roof.

So I sat in a shrinking patch of sun and waited. The wind had died. The tide was out. Floating up from the mudflats came the hollow cry of a whimbrel, soothing in its sibilant repetitions. Occasionally the *whoosh* of a car or truck wafted up to me, but the traffic noise was surprisingly light. The burghers of Borgarnes had been quite smart when they'd laid out the road. Though it was the major thoroughfare, the hub of roads leading north and west out from the city of Reykjavik, its sequence of sharp-angled turns guaranteed that cars would slow down to the speed limit. Still, each whoosh brought my head up, hoping to see the "best car in the world" rounding the far hill.

Five hours since leaving Skagafjord on the five o'clock bus, I was still confused in my mind about the two horses there, the beautiful Glefsa with her piggy pace, ugly brown Gaeska who would tolt even for Elvar's mother. Confused, too, about my host: Did Elvar truly think Gaeska was right for me, or was he just a shrewd businessman? The night before, as he'd sat drinking with Thorvaldur, I'd teasingly suggested he could sell the Germans that dapple gray for 200,000 and make a profit of almost $1,000, she was so pretty. He'd nodded. *I think you're right,* he replied, quite serious. *Would you sell them a horse with piggy pace?* I'd asked Fjola the next morning when we were alone. She looked away. *We'll send them the video,* she said slowly. *If they know anything about the gaits, they'll see it. If not—*

I wondered again what I should see in Gaeska, the horse Elvar said was perfect for me.

To order my thoughts, I made up a list: *The Perfect Horse,* I titled it.

1. *easy to tolt, smooth, comfortable to ride*
2. *easy to stop, calm, not nervous, safe and trustworthy*
3. *easy to catch, friendly, sweet, obedient*
4. *a pretty color*
5. *from good breeding*
6. *not too small*
7. *not more than 180,000 Icelandic kronur (about $2,500)*
8. *well trained, older than five*

But there was more to it than could be captured by items on a list. I was after that sense of oneness I'd felt briefly with Elfa, when my near panic as we swam the stream had attuned me to her subtle communication. I wanted a horse that understood me, a horse with whom I could create a centaur, with whom I would not be baggage, but a horsewoman.

I wanted a horse like the ones in books. A horse like Shadowfax, for instance, the wizard Gandalf's fleet gray stallion in J. R. R. Tolkien's *The Lord of the Rings*. This horse, the finest bred by the Riders of Rohan, was said to "run as smoothly as a swift stream." At Gandalf's whistle, he "came striding up the slope towards them; his coat was glistening and his mane flowing in the wind of his speed. The two [other horses] followed, now far behind. As soon as Shadowfax saw Gandalf, he checked his pace and whinnied loudly; then trotting gently forward he stooped his proud head and nuzzled his great nostrils against the old man's neck." The wizard mounted and spoke to Shadowfax, "and the horse set off at a good pace, yet not beyond the measure of the others. After a while he turned suddenly, and choosing a place where the banks were lower, he waded the river, and then led them away due south into a flat land, treeless and wide. The wind went like grey waves through the endless miles of grass. There was no sign or road or track, but Shadowfax did not stay or falter. ... They came upon many hidden pools, and broad acres of sedge waving above wet and treacherous bogs; but Shadowfax found the way, and the other horses followed in his swath. ...

"You do not ride Shadowfax," the wizard explained to one of his companions, "he is willing to carry you—or not. If he is willing, that is enough. It is then his business to see that you remain on his back, unless you jump off into the air."

Tolkien was, I knew, a medieval scholar who dabbled in fantasy writing on the side. He taught the Icelandic Sagas at Oxford and started a saga-reading group with C. S. Lewis, author of the

Narnia stories. The name "Shadowfax" is derived from the Icelandic word for mane, *fax*, and the wizard's gray has more than a little of Hrafnkel's Freyfaxi in him, even though Tolkien had never been to Iceland and probably never ridden an Icelandic horse.

He most likely had, however, read travelers' tales of northern expeditions, one of which provided the second of my emblematic horses, Stjarni (Star), the horse that took Scotsman Robert Jack on his pastoral rounds through northern Iceland in the 1940s. As Jack wrote, "I had heard from experienced explorers in the far north of the terrors of snow blizzards, and it became the special funk in my mind to get lost in a violent snowstorm. It almost happened one winter's night when despite warning I was trying to hurry home before midnight instead of staying at a distant farmhouse. At first it snowed slightly, then gradually the flakes became thicker, and a hurricane of wind sprang up which in the darkness made it impossible for me to see a foot ahead. Resorting to an old trick which has saved many an Icelander in similar conditions, I loosened the reins on Stjarni's neck and let him take me. We travelled for almost three hours, ploughing through drifts and over frozen rivers. I quickly lost all sense of direction. Suddenly Stjarni stopped, and no matter how I coaxed him, he would not move. I dismounted, the pain in my almost frozen legs cutting like a white-hot knife. I ran my gloved hand down the side of Stjarni's saddle and found the sweat on his body frozen into long, pencil-sharp icicles. I moved forward and my elbow bumped against something solid. I crept forward again on my hands and knees and, looking up, saw the dim light of a lamp through the swishing snow. It was Heydalir, and Stjarni's uncanny instinct had brought me safely home."

This was my "perfect horse": A horse who would come when I whistled, who would keep on bravely through the blinding snow. A horse that was willing to carry me. A horse that would see me safely home. *It's very important to choose the right Icelandic,* I'd read in *Horse Illustrated* magazine, *because they bond. They're known for doing that, for developing a one-on-one relationship with their owner or with just a few people. The one that you decide to buy, it needs to be the one who decides that he wants to come home with you.*

It was this I was after—the bond, the one-on-one, what another writer might have called *love*. I was waiting for a horse to choose me.

The sun sank lower, moving me off my hillside above the bus stop. I took a seat by the window in the café and resumed my wait, hoping Haukur's car would soon come into view. None of the horses I'd ridden so far were "perfect," I decided, checking each against my wish-list, but Birkir, the bay gelding at Hlid, scored seven out of eight (he was only five years old). Besides, he had seemed so singular to me, in the barn that evening after our quick rainy ride, when I'd picked him out from among the whole herd, like a person should be able to pick out her own horse. And he'd looked at me, at least I wanted to believe he'd looked at me, as if the attraction were mutual; as if he did, indeed, choose me.

A woman went by outside, cat-eyed like Sigrun. Was it she, the horsewoman at Hlid? I ought to call out, tap the window, I thought, engage her in conversation about her bay gelding. Perhaps even close the deal. But I opened my notebook instead, stayed silent, not trusting coincidence, indecision the special funk in my mind.

It was near dark when Haukur fetched me at the café, eleven by the time we reached Snorrastadir. He was exhausted, almost past chatting, though highly pleased with his day's accomplishments. The round bales (several hundred of them) having all been made while I was up in the north, he'd been collecting loose hay and blowing it up into the hayloft above the cow barn. Fifteen wagon loads in one long day, each load an hour's work to gather, with Branddis driving the tractor and Haukur the hay wagon and Stjani and Bogi feeding the dumped hay by pitchfork into the big blower beside the barn. Fifteen loads with three breaks for meals (dinner, coffee, and supper)—the workday must have started before six in the morning.

Nothing was said about the perfect mare I had come at his insistence to see, and when I woke in the morning I learned she was not in the stable.

I peeled an orange for breakfast and offered Ingibjorg some. She wrinkled her nose. "We're not used to eating that sort of thing," she said.

Now that she mentioned it, I hadn't seen fruit on the table at Snorrastadir, only marmalade and the odd banana served fried and mixed into the curry sauce for the fish. Vegetables were likewise limited: cucumbers often, and hothouse tomatoes, preferably unripe and rather hard. Canned peas, served cold. Pickled red cabbage. Onions, boiled or fried. Carrots and turnips occasionally, and potatoes with every meal.

I had six oranges in the bag from the bus station. I peeled and ate every one. Haukur was back out at the haying—everyone but Ingibjorg was out at the haying. I sat at the table and pretended to read, while she went about her housework quietly and efficiently, baking, cleaning, sorting the wash.

"Sigrun called," she said suddenly, looking up from kneading bread dough. She wondered if I had decided about Birkir. A German family was interested in him. Ingibjorg had told her to wait a few more days.

"Yes," I said, surprised by my decisiveness, "I am going to buy him. I'll call her right away." But at 10:30 in the morning, it was too early to call Hlid, Ingibjorg said. It would be better to wait until after one o'clock. I hung the wash out to dry—it was a bright and breezy day, quite hot—then made a list of things to do after Birkir was mine: bank, vet check, saddles, export. In the northern city of Akureyri lived a man I hoped would handle the export procedure, Baldvin Ari Gudlaugsson, or "Baddi." He was a horse trainer and breeder in partnership with Anne Elwell, the New York lawyer who'd cured the "turnip" foal, and he occasionally sent horses to her on consignment. Perhaps I should go north again, since the "perfect mare" was not here at Snorrastadir after all, and make arrangements for him to ship Birkir to Elwell in New York. Perhaps Baddi had a perfect horse for sale himself.

I curled up for a nap and dreamed of a little bay mare that lived in my house, slept in my husband's office, and left dry lumps of manure under his writing desk.

Ingibjorg woke me with a knock.

She had made some calls. The mare Haukur had said was "perfect for Nancy" was on the last leg of a six-day trek, ending this evening at the farm of Sturla-Reykir. The trekkers couldn't leave her behind, Ingibjorg explained, because two of their horses suddenly turned up lame as they were getting ready to leave Snorrastadir that morning, and they thought they might need her today as a spare. As things turned out, she hadn't been ridden yet, and I was welcome to join the tour at their coffee break that afternoon. The wife of the trekking guide would take me there when she came with the trailer to fetch the lame horses in less than an hour.

I washed my face, blessed Ingibjorg, and put on my riding breeches.

Your *sense of life is heightened and you perceive at once the intensity of the passing moment*, wrote Icelander Sigurdur Magnusson about the experience of riding cross-country.

This promised exaltation has lured generations of travelers, those whose home lives are too predictable and tame, who seek adventure—

In early days, these intrepids often found themselves risking their lives and those of their Icelandic guides and horses.

They faced snow, "which we were obliged to cross although we heard the waters rushing beneath; and the icy crusts over which we rode were often thin and soft under the horses' feet, and of that light blue shade which is a symptom of danger," wrote Ida Pfeiffer, a Viennese adventuress, in 1852.

At lower elevations, the dangers of rotten snow were replaced by those of quicksand: "Magnus ... went head first over his horse through its forelegs sinking in suddenly. How he saved himself I don't even now quite understand, but in a trice both he and his horse were up again. His arms had been so deep in the quicksand, that it had gone up his sleeves right up to the shoulders," wrote the Danish sea captain Daniel Bruun in 1907.

Riding across the sandbanks dividing a braided river, the Icelander who was guiding Oxford don Frederick Metcalfe in 1860 stumbled into a particularly treacherous patch. "Down sank the steed into a quicksand. The water and sand rose above the mane, and its very head was under for a moment... He struck the animal with all his might on his prodigiously strong crest, at the same time clinging to the mane. The gallant beast made a marvellous spring, and in the effort both girths snapped and one of the stirrup leathers. He is riding today with only one stirrup."

Even on relatively dry land, the travelers found sudden bogs and morasses, but above all it was the rivers in those days that held the most danger. Baring-Gould, the Devonshire parson, wrote in 1863, "I rode my horse into the river ... but he reared and snorted in such manifest alarm that I was obliged to conduct him to the bank and wade through the river myself without shoes and stockings. I found now that the main cause of the horse's alarm had been a line of little hot springs, rising in the bed of the stream; these had undoubtedly scalded his feet."

Ida Pfeiffer "came to a stream with the most extraordinary channel I have ever beheld; it was broad and shelving, formed by layers of lava, and cleft through its centre to the depth of eighteen or twenty feet by a chasm. ... A wooden bridge in the middle of the river leads over this abyss, and the stranger who reaches the banks is at a loss to account for its appearance among the foam, which entirely conceals the rift in the bed of the stream, and he would be likely to mistake it for the ruins of a larger bridge. It is impossible to see the guide ride into this boisterous flood without feeling some alarm and a great repugnance to follow him. ... Our horses began to tremble, and struggled to escape when we approached the most agitated part of the torrent, where the noise was really deafening."

What was asked of the horses when fording bigger rivers was sometimes beyond their ability. Crossing such a river in 1914, Waterman Russell wrote that his guide, Johannes, "tied a cod line around the lower jaw of each horse," eight altogether, and sitting in the back of the boat, watched each swimming horse with care. "As soon as one nose plunged below the water, he gave that pony his whole attention, and with the strong cord pulled the pony's nostrils to the surface and held it there til it had blown out the water. One after another, and sometimes two at a time, they succumbed to the cold water and to the difficulty of swimming so closely together. ... It seemed we would be swept over the bar and out to sea before we could win the beach. ... The plunging and snorting ponies, the wild rush of the waters sweeping out of the estuary at low tide, the roar of the breakers just below, the countless gulls and terns circling over our heads ... the anxiety on the face of Johannes ..."

Yet to get where you were going in the Iceland of those days, you had to accept such risks. There was no other way to travel—before tunnels were dug, roads laid, rivers bridged, and jeeps and helicopters invented. The horses had to be willing and fit; their riders grabbed hold of their courage or stayed safe at home.

It's a little of this heroism, Icelanders say, they are after when they take their horses cross-country nowadays, a slight echo of their forebears' unquenchable spirit, of the necessary dependence on a beast. *When one rides through the rugged wastes of the interior,* Sigurdur Magnusson, the Icelandic writer, had continued, *the long and hazardous history of the survival of the nation becomes almost tangible.*

Today, however, civilization comes along on the treks. The car that brought me also carried cold drinks and hearty sandwich-fixings to the riders. It took away their slickers and sweaters, the day remaining cloudless, the temperature in the sixties. All other luggage had gone ahead by van to the farmhouse where bed, bath, and dinner awaited this party of a dozen Germans.

The track we followed was a mud rut along the riverbank or a marked bridle path beside a gravel road. The rivers we crossed barely wet our boots. Our greatest hazard was a series of deep drainage ditches we had to scramble down or jump.

It was disappointing. I was ready for an adventure. But instead of trusting to a dependable beast to see me safely through Iceland's treacherous countryside, I found the horse herself to be the day's chief difficulty. Gloa (Glowing) was so flashy, so beautifully marked—brilliant red, bright white—it was hard to find fault with her. The Germans cooed when they heard I might buy her, but it was clear she didn't choose me. She was immensely fat, so round-bellied I could barely straddle her, and while all that padding made for a cushiony seat, it didn't make it easy for her to tolt. Though an *eðlistöltari*, a natural tolter who didn't like to trot, at speed she preferred the canter, locking her neck and lurching along—a fine rocking lurch, as long as I didn't interfere. She'd quickly tire in the heat, I learned, and loll along at a half-hearted tolt until we were lagging at the back of the line. Suddenly she'd dash to catch up, leaving me breathless, clutching at her lovely mane, until I came to sense the pattern: She got anxious when she lost her rightful place in the herd, and nothing I did could convince her to relax.

Once Gloa made her glory dash at a stream crossing, splashing all the other riders as we passed. I half expected to end up like the unwanted mother in *Heidarviga Saga*, who tried to accompany her sons to battle on her nag "Plow Puller." *Her going along will lead to trouble that we can do without,* said one brother. *We must find a way to take care of her.* Two of the men were to act as her escorts, treating her "respectfully and pleasantly." At the ford, under pretense of fixing her saddle girth, they were to unhook it. *While you're crossing the brook, you push her off the horse and make sure she falls in. Then take the horse away with you.* This they did. The spitting-mad mother "was in no danger there," the saga politely adds. "She crawled out of the water ... not at all pleased with her venture."

Gloa had been trained by Johannes, the leader of this trek, known for turning out good all-around horses. Earlier in my trip I'd learned just how well-known he was. Before I'd gone north to Skagafjord, I'd hiked the "Bad Mood Path" from Snorrastadir over to our old summerhouse at Litla Hraun, snapping pictures of the rocky riding trail to show my equestrian friends back home the way Haukur and I had taken Bjartur and Elfa. Then, seeing it was low tide, I crossed the mudflats to drop in on our old neighbors at Stora Hraun, whose homemade bread and rhubarb jam (and washing machine and telephone) we'd so enjoyed the summer before. The large extended family there included twin sisters, fiftyish, ample and sturdy, indistinguishable until you learned that Lauga was voluble, outgoing, and impulsive, and Veiga more hard-headed, competent, and careful. Veiga was very fond of horses. She'd like to have six of them, she said, if she could afford it. Once she had owned a fine horse, jet black with a star— She started off on a story, then pursed her lips, remembering: She had sold him to Germany; they needed the money on the farm.

"There's that man over by Reykholt," said Lauga. "He's always got horses. *Alhliðahestar*, good all-around horses. That's where you should go," she said to me. "Now, what's his name?"

Veiga came up blank.

"I'll find him." Lauga picked up the phone. "Yes," she said, when the call had gone through. "The man near Reykholt who has *alhliðahestar*. No, I don't have his name. No, I can't recall that either, but it's one of the farms near Reykholt. Yes, I'll hold."

She had dialed Information.

In a few moments, the operator was back on. "Sturla-Reykir? Yes, it could be that farm." Veiga was vigorously nodding her head. "Johannes? Johannes Kristleifsson?" She looked at Veiga, smiled. "Yes, that's him. The number?"

Veiga poked me with her elbow. "We'll find you a good horse!" she said.

"Hello, Johannes?" Lauga began to describe me to the man on the phone. I began to squirm, worrying what transaction was actually taking place.

"Two mares, *rauð glófexti*, red with white manes? Coming to Snorrastadir, you say? Haukur has already called you? He has an American there who wants to see them? Well, yes, that would be Nancy."

When the two horses arrived at Snorrastadir with the German tour group, Haukur had vetted them and dismissed one, leaving only Gloa. She was seven years old, trained by Johannes of Sturla-Reykir at five and then sent back to her owner, the farmer at nearby Munadarnes. "But he didn't use her much," Johannes told me, as he drove me back to Borgarnes after our ride was over. "She got fat. I bought the use of her back." She'd been carrying tourists since April, and had already slimmed down a lot, he said.

"I've trained many horses for Munadarnes," Johannes added. "They are all quiet, easy to tame, calm. This one is four-gaited, maybe a little pace, but an *eðlistöltari*. She holds her head high. She needs low hands." He couldn't say much more about her. "I have trained thousands of horses," he explained.

Johannes dropped me off at the bus stop in Borgarnes. I called Snorrastadir and climbed the sunny hill to wait. An hour later, it was Ingibjorg coming to get me this time, driving thirty in a sixty-mile-per-hour zone, weaving down the road. "This is fun," she said brightly, when I offered to drive. "I don't get out much anymore."

I checked my seatbelt and tried to think of something else.

"Did Hallgerdur ever finish her long ride?" I asked.

Ingibjorg shook her head. "She had Haukur shoot one of her horses. He wasn't getting any better. He'd been sick all winter. She couldn't ride him." She paused and gave a deep sigh. "You know, he had to shoot my Nasi this spring." I had a picture of Ingibjorg next to that horse, Nosey, a chestnut with a snip on his nose, her gray curly head at the level of his ear, another horse looking curiously over her shoulder.

"What happened?" I asked, sorry to have turned her thoughts in that direction.

"We found him in the pasture with a broken leg. Who knows what happened." She didn't think she would ride again. She'd never have another horse like Nasi. "It's been a hard year for Haukur," she said.

The next day I called Sigrun and clinched the deal over Birkir, then told Haukur I wasn't convinced that Gloa was the perfect mare for me.

"She is very beautiful," he persuaded.

"Yes, she's beautiful," I agreed, though I actually found her a bit too gaudy, what Anne Elwell in New York called a "silk bowling jacket" of a horse. "But I'm afraid to buy a horse of that color," I continued, "a red horse with a white tail. You see, in the woods where we live in Pennsylvania, there are many deer. In the fall the hunters come to shoot them, many hunters, a million altogether in the state. The deer are sometimes this same color red, and they have white tails. I'm afraid if I buy Gloa, a hunter might make a mistake and shoot my horse instead."

Haukur considered. He sucked his pipe stem. "That would be a problem," he admitted.

I took a chance, then, and asked him about Gaeska. "There is this horse in Skagafjord that Elvar Einarsson has. She is a good tolter, an *eðlistöltari*, but she's a little fast, a little too willing. I'm not sure I can control her. Elvar wants me to buy her. He says she's a good horse for me."

"What color is she?"

"Dark bay."

Haukur considered. "The sons of Einar Gislason are very good with horses," he said eventually. "If Elvar Einarsson says this horse is good, then it's a good horse."

CHAPTER TEN

GHOSTS

"Icelandic farmers don't have a good idea of what we would do on a horse," Anne Elwell said. I had visited her farm in New York for the first time in early June, a few weeks before flying to Iceland to start my horse-buying trip. "People in Iceland are unaware of different riding traditions. They have no idea what we want."

I wasn't sure I should be included in that "we." Elwell had a competition-sized riding track on her property and three prize-winning stallions in the barn. I had a feeling I was more on the level of the California breeder who advertised "safe, happy, friendly" horses and invited her correspondents to "live your dream."

I had, in fact, hoped to visit the California herd and others in the West and up into Canada. I wanted to see how they did things, to see how the horses adapted, say, to tall trees and traffic, but the realities of time and money crept in. Scanning the horse magazines, I found Elwell's Helms Hill Farm, only five hours' drive away. I called and drove up.

She had said to come on Saturday, but we hadn't fixed a time. Nor did I have directions. I stopped in a convenience store off the Interstate and bought a county map, but I couldn't find her lane.

Her post office, though, was an easy bet, and John's Deli on the main square in town wore a phone sign on its façade. I stopped in, notebook and map in hand, and dialed. Busy. Again. Busy. I tapped my foot and fretted. Two women at a window table stared my way. I ignored them, dialed. Busy. The younger of the two brought her trash to the can on which I'd set my notebook, Elwell's name and number on the open page.

I watched her back to her table: my age, thereabouts, a lithe and forceful walk. The other woman was older, ample, her manner businesslike. I was beginning to resent their interest. The phone was still busy. I hung up and turned to go—I didn't know where, perhaps to another phone.

Before I reached the door, the younger woman called out. "You lost?"

I considered. "No, but I could use directions," I said, going to their table. "I'm looking for Helms Hill Farm."

They nodded. "That's us," said the older woman, who gave her name as Sophie Katakozinos; she, along with Elwell, was a founder of the U.S. Icelandic Horse Congress, the official breed registry.

I looked at her companion. There was something familiar about that face, the eyes wide-set and edgy, the cap of dark hair. I took a leap. "You must be Sara Conklin," I said. She looked very pleased. "I've seen your picture." Almost every article I had read about Icelandic horses in America had a picture of Conklin riding, as I learned later, one of Elwell's stallions. Conklin's farm was an hour north of Elwell's and I had ruled out visiting it to cut down on my drive. I'd no idea she and Elwell had a partnership.

I turned down their offer of coffee to go straight to the farm. Elwell was giving a lesson, Conklin said, and after that they were going out. I would have less than an hour.

Elwell was cool when I arrived, her lesson finished. "We're leaving in a few minutes," she said. "I would have called and told you not to come today, but your message said you were traveling last night."

I apologized and stood my ground. It was a trick I'd learned in Iceland, or perhaps in my years of interviewing reticent scientists at the university: be polite, take out your notebook, and refuse to leave. Elwell was showing me her barn and her prize stallions when Conklin came up.

"We can wait long enough for her to ride Ljufur," she said. Elwell shrugged. Ljufur had been sent from Iceland on consignment by Baddi. "Come on," Conklin said, and grabbed a halter. We went down to the lower pasture, to a chestnut and a silver dapple. They came up to us, then bounced away playfully to the near corner of the field before letting themselves be caught. Conklin spoke harshly, abruptly to them, and they swiveled their ears and stood still. She haltered the chestnut. He was very thin. She led him up to the sanded paddock.

But the first time I tried to mount, the saddle swung over. Conklin's face was stony; I grinned. "I'm used to a mounting block," I said.

"She's used to a mounting block," Conklin called to Elwell and her lesson, who were leaning on the fence, watching. I had read that if you mounted an Icelandic horse correctly, the saddle wouldn't slip even if it had no girth. Conklin must think I'd never seen an Icelandic in my life.

On the next try, Conklin held the stirrup and I mounted more gracefully.

"It's a shame you hadn't planned to stay over and go on a trail ride with us," Conklin said, as I sat the horse after a short round at a respectable tolt.

"I can stay," I said, "and come back tomorrow. What time?"

She thought. "Tomorrow is busy," she said, and left me to go find Elwell, who had wandered away. Alone I let the red horse tolt around the paddock, a little trot and canter slipping in, but pretty good, I thought, for not having ridden an Icelandic in a year. When she returned, she invited me to go with them that morning: they had planned to ride the Rails-to-Trails line adjacent to Conklin's farm.

In the car, towing the trailer with three horses, we got acquainted. Elwell, driving, instructed me in the history of the U.S. Icelandic Horse Congress and its relationship to FEIF, the international breed organization (its acronym comes from the German for "Federation of Friends of the Icelandic Horse"). Katakozinos, learning I was a magazine editor, wanted to know if I'd help out with the Congress's quarterly newsletter. Conklin, who was the current Congress president, finding I'd collaborated on several sites on the World Wide Web, wanted me to consult for the Congress's website. I agreed to everything and pumped them for information.

How do the horses adapt to America?

"Different horses adapt differently," Conklin said. "The white horse I'll be riding today lost her brakes on the flight over. At least, that's what Baddi says."

Added Elwell, "The change is a big shock. They regress to some earlier point in their training. If everything is sane and consistent, they come around. But if they're treated differently than they were in Iceland, they get really screwed up."

Conklin plugged in the car phone and called in a lunch order to a roadside deli. I ordered the same as she: roast beef on rye bread, dry, lettuce and tomato. She wouldn't eat the bread, she added; all she wanted was the protein. In a few miles, Elwell pulled off onto the berm, the trailer partly blocking traffic, while Conklin ran across the road to fetch our order. Then we drove on, Elwell pushing her way through the center of the small college town of New Paltz, backing the trailer in the face of honking traffic to make a hairpin turn.

The trail was flat, gravel, straight ahead beneath overhanging trees, and busy. It was Rails-to-Trails Day, and a piano blocked the bridge, forcing us to choose the other, narrower way, away from town. Elwell, stiff from her fall on the ice years ago, used a metal step ladder to mount. "I'm a great advertisement for the horses," she laughed. Her mare, Elding (Lightning), stood perfectly still.

Conklin on the white Birta-without-Brakes (her name means Bright) set the pace—a little fast, as Elwell remarked later. I rode in the middle, with Elwell last. (Katakozinos had not come to ride; she spent the hour mowing the grass at Conklin's farm.)

My mount was from a trekking company near Akureyri in northern Iceland, product of a trainer who encourages a "can-do" attitude in his horses, Elwell said. A gelding, he was six years old and cost eight thousand dollars. His name, Ljufur, meant "The Good One." He picked his head up well; his mane rippled to both sides, a lovely red. He wanted to run next to Conklin's horse and twisted and fought when I asked him to hang back, but he did it. Elwell rode beside me for a space and gave me pointers: "It's all in the hips," she said. "Make the hips as loose and relaxed as possible. Open the hips. Your legs should be totally relaxed. Your feet should be wiggling with the motion of the horse." Another American had told me it was all in the seat-bones, those pointy protuberances at the bottom of the pelvis. They should move to the motion of the horse. Make love to your saddle, she had said.

Now "The Good One" and I slipped from smooth tolt to lurching trot and back again, unable to find each other's rhythm. It was a hot day, and sticky. Bicyclists and runners stopped for us to pass. People walking dogs stepped off into the woods: Riders have the right-of-way on this trail, Elwell said, "because we're the most dangerous."

Three weeks later I went back to New York to see two more horses Baddi had sent over. The mare, Skotta (a name given a horse with an unusual tail), was a beautiful bay pinto with a black-and-white mane and tail. She was wary and pert in the field just like Elfa but willing to make friends when I cooed to her in Icelandic and blew into her nostrils. I patted her face and held it against mine. Conklin, coming through the pasture, remarked teasingly, "There's some serious bonding going on here," but I knew she was pleased. She wanted these horses to find good homes. The dark bay gelding, Straumur (Stream), was quite tall and calm and so easy to approach he seemed a little turnip-like. He merely glanced and went back to his grazing. He didn't attract me, but to be polite I said I'd try him too. We loaded them both into the trailer, with Elwell's old mare, Elding, and a horse for Conklin to ride, Elwell's black stallion Sindri (Cinders). A German girl, Amelie, who had come to help train Elwell's horses, made the foursome.

Yet after driving a half-hour to a nearby state park, Elwell felt ill in the heat and decided to rest in the shade while we rode. Later, a driver, seeing a woman stretched out on the ground beneath a horse, stopped to check if she was alive. Conklin, too, was concerned about her, and we rode without a minute to lose, this time on a hill-and-dale woodland path, not a flat gravel track. We swerved around trees and darted up slopes, tolting swiftly through high grass while deer jumped out on both sides. Straumur kept up nicely with the stallion, his gaits cushiony and smooth, balanced and relaxed, much easier to ride than the trotty Ljufur. I would have bought him on the spot if he'd been a little more personable—and if he hadn't cost nine thousand dollars. But Skotta, whom I loved at first sight, disappointed me. Bright and flashy under Amelie's practiced hands, when we switched horses at the crossroads Skotta would only trot for me. I soon grew frustrated. We rode back to Elwell in low spirits: We all knew the sale was off.

I would go for a horse whose feeling you really like, Elwell had said once, when we were discussing how to choose the right Icelandic.

Go for chemistry, said Conklin. *It took me a long time to figure out chemistry with horses.*

"You take off their shoes—that's about it," Baddi said, when, in northern Iceland a month later, I asked him about export procedures.

He had his own shoes off and was lounging on the sofa after a hot shower and a supper of lasagna with rice and potatoes, the curtains closed against the evening light and candles lit in dishes around the room creating an intimate atmosphere. His wife, Inga, he said, liked candles, and the dark. She finished in the kitchen and brought out coffee and a bowl of butter toffees. She was eight months pregnant with their first child. A suitcase sat against one wall, its lid propped open—Baddi was leaving for New York, to visit Anne Elwell, first thing in the morning. Occasionally while we talked, he would get up to add something to it. His riding boots. A pressed white shirt. Another baby catalog. He would be bringing back a baby buggy from New York, Inga said.

Yes, he had horses for sale. Family horses, seven to eight years old, pretty ones, 130,000 to 150,000 kronur—but no time to show them to me. "I have good connections," he said. "This farmer tells me this horse is like this, I don't even have to look at it. I know what he means. I can find a hundred horses with just five or six phone calls. I have horses on video, too, but—" He shrugged. "The VCR is broken." He was younger than I, slim and straight, with a dancer's awareness of his bones, blond, his mat of hair cut close on the sides, amused blue eyes behind round wire-frames, the laugh-lines cut deep. He'd lived in America, spoke idiomatic English in a low, mellow voice with just enough accent to sound interesting. He was polite and cordial, but I knew he wasn't interested in me, either as a friend or as a sale. He'd seen me ride earlier in the day and knew I wasn't in his—or even Elwell's—class.

I had known that all along.

I had his picture on a calendar, riding a dark horse, hands high, face fierce in eager concentration. It had hung over my desk the month of March. Most of April as well.

Still, I had not been prepared for how magnetic he was. I stared at his bare feet, roaming over the white sofa, and tried to be professional, to conduct an interview, to write down what he said.

"Don't buy a five-year-old. Five is too young. They change too much, some of them." Birkir, the bay gelding at Hlid, was five, as I'd just told him. I hadn't paid for him yet or arranged for the vet check, though I'd told Sigrun I wanted him and I considered him mine. I supposed I could still change my mind.

"Six is the youngest I'll send to America," he went on. "I like them to be eight or nine or even ten, really full-grown, well-trained horses that can teach the rider. A horse like that—the horse you're looking for—a lot of people are looking for. A breeder can sell a horse like that easily to Europe."

I told him about Gaeska and asked what he thought. "Dark bay is a bad color to buy," he said. "It's a hard color to sell in the U.S. or Germany, if you decide when you get her home you can't ride her. I rarely send dark bays. Only if it's an exceptional horse, like Straumur— He's sold, by the way, but Skotta and Ljufur are still for sale."

He went on when I didn't respond. He would be glad to handle exporting my horses for me, whichever ones I decided to buy. I just needed to call Inga with their registration numbers and the names of the farms. He would tell Diddi and get both horses sent to Anne Elwell's with another three horses she wanted brought over.

I had thought he and Diddi—Sigurbjorn Bardarson, another famous rider and trainer—were competitors (Baddi's card said "Training, Sale, Export") but apparently they found it more efficient to cooperate, especially in the still-tiny American market.

"It might be a while. Later this fall, but before Christmas," Baddi promised. Horses were air-freighted in cartons of four to New York, and the more cartons that came over on the same flight, the cheaper the fees and expenses. He got out a letter from Elwell calculating the total cost: airfare, quarantine, broker's fees, export fees, vet fees, transport to Reykjavik—about nineteen hundred dollars each. "But you can just pay Anne when they come," he said.

It had been raining fitfully when I'd arrived on the bus from Snorrastadir. Baddi had driven me through Akureyri, a pretty waterside town one fjord east of Skagafjord, its winding streets curving up to an old botanical garden, a protected spot where trees grew tall enough to assume tree shape, to branch out and become robust, even to give shade—which was needed here occasionally in the summer months, the north of Iceland counterintuitively being warmer than the south, due to the effects of the ocean currents. Akureyri was Iceland's second largest city, and, like Reykjavik, it had stables on the edge of town, training rings and tracks, and well-kept bridle paths leading out into the hills.

We'd stopped to see Baddi's brand-new block of stables before supper. The stalls were all empty, the horses let loose for the summer. Baddi demonstrated the automatic waterers, unlocked the tack room, calculated how much hay he could stack in the corner, showed where he was going to set up his table and coffeepot. "To be a professional trainer," he said, "you have to live in town. You need facilities. Training tracks. A riding club to take care of clearing the snow.

"Besides, here in town you're always under pressure to do well. The club opens at nine o'clock and we all have breakfast together. We have coffee together in the afternoons. We talk about breeding and training together. You have a hundred stables here, you're always riding with someone. When you have trouble, you talk about it. If you need help shoeing, there are people all around you. Here, being with horses has a lot to do with being with other people."

He smiled engagingly. "Would you like to go for a ride?"

In a paddock across the road were four horses. Baddi chose two: For himself, Hrafntinna (literally Raven-peak, but also the word for obsidian), a black mare who'd won a regional competition that year. "She may be the highest-ranked mare in the country at the moment," he said. For me, a red mare from the same farm, called As in Skagafjord. "How do you like to ride?" Baddi asked, as he saddled them up. "Do you want to go fast?"

The rain was slowly soaking through my riding breeches. "No," I said, "I like what Anne calls a sedate ride."

He nodded, a little disappointed. "My wife," he said, "she rode with me once. I thought, if she was going to be my wife, she ought to be able to ride well. So I put her on a first-class horse. She had a bad accident."

He held the red while I mounted, delighted with that information. As soon as she stepped out, I knew the sensation: another rocketship like Fjola's black. I steered her at Hrafntinna's tail and we went down the gravel track at a fast tolt.

"Hrafntinna is very spirited," Baddi shouted over his shoulder. "She's always telling me something: 'I don't like this, I don't like that!' I like that in a horse. She's a powerful girl."

I had already fallen into a trot and could not find the balance to pull the horse back to tolt. Rather than run into Hrafntinna (which Icelandics will permit, I knew, without kicking, even if another horse has its nose in their tail), we jogged on around. When she was even with the black, the red horse slowed to a tolt on her own. Baddi smiled. "Your horse won't do much more than she does now," he said. "She's only five, but she won't get more spirit as she gets older." He said it as if it were a shame.

Little by little, the horses began speeding up. I was feeling quite out of control; Baddi was obviously enjoying himself. Then I saw him look over at my feet and immediately slow Hrafntinna to a walk. The red horse followed suit a few paces later, and I adjusted myself: My toes had slid all the way through the stirrups, dangerous (if you fall off, you'll be dragged) and the sign of a real amateur.

Around the next corner was a small wooden bridge. My horse had already stepped onto it when Hrafntinna stopped, snorted, wheeled, and refused to go forward. Behind us, over a small rise, we could hear shouts and hoofbeats, and suddenly two riders and a small herd of loose horses rushed down over the hill heading for the stables, a border collie nipping at their heels. I began to envision a mad race for home. I wondered if I would stay on this time. But Baddi was calm. He circled Hrafntinna a time or two, then slowly began walking away from the bridge. "I think we'll turn back here," he said casually.

As we drew near the stable, I asked if I could just get off and watch him ride.

He looked at me suspiciously, as if I wanted to do something perverse.

"Just show me her gaits. I've never seen such a high-ranked mare," I said, though it really wasn't the horse I wanted to look at.

He shrugged. "Okay."

I got off and held the red, while he and Hrafntinna flew back and forth in front of me, tolt, trot, fast tolt, canter, pace, his back straight and hands high, hardly moving as the horse changed shape beneath him, from taut and compact to loose and fluid, an arc or an arrow, the calendar page come to life. I wished I could ride like that, with such grace and confidence, but I knew it would never be so. It was like watching Baryshnikov, or the man on the flying trapeze. Nothing could be sexier than this man riding that black horse in the rain.

"She has even more leg action with bell-boots on," he said as he came to a stop in front of me.

I couldn't imagine improving upon perfection. I remembered reading once in *The Art of Horsemanship* by Xenophon: *It is upon horses of this kind that gods and heroes are painted riding, and men who are able to manage them skilfully are regarded as deserving of admiration.*

When he'd unsaddled the horses, Baddi suddenly recalled he'd meant to switch the red horse to a different pasture. "I should have ridden her," he said. "Well, no matter. You drive down to meet me. The keys are in the car." He shut the gate behind Hrafntinna and took off running down the gravel track, a light, leaping run, the red mare trotting head-high beside him, the misty rain casting a curtain about them, the backdrop a grass-green hill and an old sharp-gabled church, painted red with a white picket fence. I framed it in my mind as another calendar shot to hang above my desk.

Still soaked from our short ride, we switched on the heater in the car and drove out to the farm. Anne Elwell owned some part of it, and Baddi wanted to show me her new foals.

"I hope you're not afraid of ghosts," he said with a teasing smile.

"Do you have ghosts on your farm?" I asked, with real interest. I had regained my equilibrium somewhat now that he was off the horse, but I was still grateful to have a neutral topic to talk about, particularly one in which I'd done some reading. I knew, for instance, that a folklorist had once calculated there were five hundred known ghosts in Iceland.

"Oh yes. It's a very old farm," Baddi answered. "There are undoubtedly ghosts there." He turned serious. "My family is very spiritual," he explained. "My wife Inga's grandmother was one of the most famous healers in Iceland. Inga herself, when she was ten, was bothered by seeing ghosts—or spirits, you could call them.

One especially, an old man with a beard, terrified her. Her parents found her curled up and screaming in her room, and they asked her grandmother to heal her. She did. Now Inga only feels things, she doesn't see them.

"I haven't fixed up the old house on the farm because of it. She wouldn't want to live there."

In their flat in Akureyri, Inga had a corner devoted to her grandmother: her treadle sewing machine, her silver teapot, a photo of the old woman as a girl. She'd kept a house at Arnarstapi, the fishing village at the foot of the two-horned glacier, Snaefellsjokull, the third most holy spot on the planet. "She would go there to commune with her fellow spiritualists," Inga had explained.

Such a concept, I knew, dated from the Saga Age, when women with links to the spiritual world were both revered and feared. Although many were simply healers, rich in herbal lore, or fine midwives, their gifts surrounded them with a certain aura. In *Eirik the Red's Saga*, for instance, when a wise woman named Thorbjorg is invited to a chieftain's house, a special seat is made for her, with a cushion of hen's feathers. Her costume is rich and exotic, notably her "black lambskin hood lined with white cat's fur" and her catskin gloves "with the white fur inside." After a younger woman sings a set of special songs, Thorbjorg claims to see spirits in the room, charmed by the singing. "Now many things stand revealed to me which before were hidden," she said. The famine will soon end; the weather will improve; and the girl who had sung the songs will "start a great and eminent family line"—all prophecies that come true in the saga.

Spiritualists today are accorded similar respect by many Icelanders, but in the early days following the conversion to Christianity, wise women were suspect and often portrayed as witches. In *Eyrbyggja Saga*, one such seer was said to have turned her son into a distaff (used for spinning wool), then into a goat, then a pig, to hide him from his enemies. Her neighbor, who saw through these disguises and seized the boy for hanging, was accused of having bewitched another young man and ridden him as a night hag. According to later folklore, such witchcraft involved a bridle made from the skin and bones of a dead man. "This was possessed of such magic power that the youth suffered the pastor's wife to mount him, and set off at once with her on his back. ... Over fell and dale he flew; over rocks and rubble, and whatever lay in his path."

Only the best witches could make a horse of a human; others made do with the bones—leg bone, jawbone, or shoulder—of a horse, or even of a human corpse. Often these witches, as in this story, were the wives of Christian pastors, some of whom (particularly after the Reformation reached Iceland) became noted for their own sorcery, used mainly to rid the countryside of evil trolls. One minister, Sira Halfdan of Fell, asked his young nephew, Bjorn, if "he dared ride a willing horse that could go as well over the sea as on land." Bjorn was not afraid. "The pastor now led forth a bay foal with a dark stripe and told him to ride to the island of Grimsey" to deliver a challenge to a troll. "Bjorn mounted the foal and rode away, and they passed so low over the water to Grimsey that he got both his feet wet. He carried out his errand as instructed and returned home safe and sound. But when he had dismounted, he discovered that his steed was the hip-bone of a man. The pastor asked him how he had liked his mount, but he had little to say in its favour and remarked that clearly it had not been corn-fed."

Now Baddi turned up the long lane to Efri-Raudilaekur, Higher Red Brook. The place was sadly dilapidated, the gate a tangle of barbed wire and string. Baddi had bought it only recently; it was long since the farm had been worked. On the maps it was named in parentheses, meaning "abandoned," just like Litla Hraun. Heaps of old stones marked the site of vanished outbuildings: hay barn, cowshed, sheepcote, stable. A cluster of army-surplus Quonset huts, barrel-shaped metal igloos, were being used for hay storage and the horses' winter shelter. In the misty rain, the house looked decidedly haunted: dark eyes of windows, emptiness within. I could see why Inga wouldn't like it.

"I have about seventy horses here now," Baddi said. "One stallion is giving foals with earth colors—dun, blue dun, yellow dun, et cetera. Another one gives thirty percent palominos. The color is extra, of course, but it's very nice."

We parked in the muddy yard and walked down the hill to the nearest pasture. Below us a tour bus rattled by on its way west. A dozen or more mares and foals grazed the rich grass, drenched and shy, sidling away as we drew near. Baddi pointed out Elwell's horses. "And that one," he indicated a black mare, "another Hrafntinna, also very highly rated. We found her here one day, pregnant, on her back with her feet in the air. We nursed her for two weeks and finally operated. There was a twist in her colon"—a result of severe colic. "The foal survived, though it's very small. It's a son of Galsi." Galsi was the splendid dark horse Baddi rode for the calendar photo, at one point the most expensive stallion in Iceland, a horse bred by Sveinn Gudmundsson in Skagafjord.

Foals need freedom and wide-open spaces in which to grow up, I remembered Sveinn had told the newspaper in 1994, when he'd been designated Breeder of the Year. *The issue then arises as to why horses in Skagafjord have done so well over the past decades. Personally, I'm not sure this is due to better or more intensive breeding,* Sveinn said, *but rather because many of them are reared in highland pastures.*

For centuries, Icelanders have made hay in the lowlands and herded their animals into the hills for summer grazing. Medieval farms all had a shieling, a summer cabin in the highlands, where the womenfolk and a few men would work, watching the flocks and herds, milking the cows and ewes, making cheese and butter to chill in the streams or to freeze by burying it in the snowfields against the coming of winter.

As the days grew short again, the animals would be brought back down to the farmstead, the sheep and cows to be sheltered in barns, the horses—all but a few saddle horses—left out in all weather, tails turned to the wind, their thick coats and goatlike beards a capable blanket against the snow. Some would be fed hay, if the cows and sheep didn't need it, or, strange as it sounds, a barrel of salt herring. Their age was—and still is—reckoned in winters: not five years old, but five winters old. A horse that survives a particularly brutal winter earns the name *klakahross*, the prefix meaning "ice cube." A horse routinely left on its own is an *útigangshross*, a word that in recent times has also come to connote "street person" or "homeless person."

Yet sometimes, as winter approached and the farmer rode out to round up his herds and move them closer to the farm, the horses couldn't be found. *Eyrbyggja Saga* tells what could happen then. The farmer Thorbjorn the Stout queried a local seer, one who "had second sight and was very clever at investigating thefts." The seer said that the horses hadn't strayed very far, which Thorbjorn interpreted to mean that his neighbors had stolen them. "Thorbjorn set off with eleven men." In the ensuing exchange, insults led to fighting. The women of the household broke up the fight by throwing clothes on the men's swords and knives, but after Thorbjorn left, a woman's severed hand was found on the grass. The maimed woman's husband rode after Thorbjorn and killed him and many of his companions, starting a wide-ranging feud. The next autumn Thorbjorn's horses were found dead up in the mountains. His stallion had been driven away by another stallion, "and then the whole herd had been snowed under."

Even when the herds were wintering in the home pastures, the weather could be dangerous. Young horses, especially, were often fetched indoors on a bad night, sometimes at great risk to their owners. One folktale tells of a workman on a widow's farm who, sitting out a severe blizzard, began to worry about a yearling of which he was fond. Bravely, he went out into the storm. After some difficulty, he found the herd, tails to the wind, the snow blankets thick on their backs. He haltered the colt and began leading it home. The way seemed longer than he remembered. He stopped, uncertain which way to turn. It occurred to him that if he could see the ground underneath the snow, he might recognize it. He lay down and began to dig. He dug and dug until his arm was in snow up to the shoulder. Finally he grabbed up a handful of gravel and knew immediately where he was by the kind of rock he'd found. Reoriented, both he and the horse made it safely home.

Today Skagafjord is one of the few places in Iceland where horse farmers still have access to their old summer pastures in the highlands, and even there the rules are growing more restrictive. *Heavy grazing on the sensitive vegetation of the uplands has led to soil erosion and deterioration of natural grasslands*, noted one news report, *and conservation groups call for a total ban on grazing in the highlands. Farmers are still allowed, however, to use some areas ... in accordance with the regulations of the State Land Reclamation Centre and other governmental bodies.* Farmers in other districts limit the highlands to sheep-grazing, hoping to preserve the delicate taste of mountain-raised lamb. They have moved their horses out of the common hills to the abandoned farms like Efri-Raudalaekur that now pepper the countryside, as fewer and fewer young people follow the old ways.

"The old man died here," Baddi explained, unlocking the farmhouse. The entry was scrubbed and neat, the wooden floor clean, the lights working; the kitchen was fitted with a few necessities.

The rest of the downstairs rooms were crammed with old machine parts and engine pieces.

"He lived upstairs, in the loft," Baddi said.

We went up the narrow steps, ducked our heads. The long room, unfinished, was too low to stand up in. It was lit by a triangular window in the far gable end. A narrow bed and a table with a two-burner Primus stove were the sum total of the furnishings.

In size and shape the room was like the loft in the turf houses Icelanders lived in until wood and concrete spread through the countryside earlier in this century. There was a reconstructed turf house in a historical park near Sydra-Skordugil. Fjola and Elvar had taken me there for coffee one afternoon and we had gorged ourselves, free, on fried breads and sweet cakes, all baked by Elvar's mother, who supplies the concession. From the back, the turf house looked like a line of haystacks, the sod layers laid up in a careful herringbone pattern. From the front it was more houselike: a series of painted gables, each with a window and often a door, leading into various rooms; some (like the cowshed and the pantry) were connected on the inside, while others (the smithy and toolshed) were not. The parlor had a polished table, a china hutch, and carpeted floors. The kitchen had a large cast-iron pot hanging from a hook over an open hearth, and lidded tubs in which sour milk would have been stored. Narrow steps led up to a sleeping loft, low-ceilinged but bright, the wood floors and paneling scrubbed yellow, a line of short beds along each wall. The whole family would retire there, along with their guests. Another loft, smaller and darker, would have been for the children, and perhaps the old grandmother who snored.

Early travelers had been horrified by turf houses. By the smell and the occupants' habit of undressing and sleeping all together in one room. *Without exception the most disgusting holes that can be imagined*, opined Ida Pfeiffer. Those I'd seen reminded me delightfully of hobbit holes, another of J. R. R. Tolkien's Iceland-inspired inventions: *Not a nasty, dirty, wet hole, filled with the ends of worms and an oozy smell, nor yet a dry, bare, sandy hole with nothing in it to sit down on or to eat: it was a hobbit-hole, and that means comfort.* Bjartur, the farmer in Halldor Laxness's book *Independent People*, reluctantly replaces his old turf house with the latest in turn-of-the-century architecture. He soon grows to despise the new wood-frame dwelling: *It was the worst house in the world and unbelievably cold. ... The walls of the room sweated with damp and were covered with a veneer of ice during frosty weather. The windows never thawed, the wind blew straight through the house, upstairs there was snow lying on the floors and swirling about in the air.* A turf house, on the other hand, was nothing if not snug. Seen from the side, a turf house would seem just a hill, grassier than most, perhaps, only a tiny window intimating the human presence. It blended so beautifully that cows and sheep and even horses occasionally forgot it was their master's abode. The saga chieftain Snorri Godi, the pragmatical trickster who was my favorite, once took advantage of that fact to get revenge for his father-in-law's murder: *Snorri and his men dismounted behind the farm buildings. He told one of his men to climb up on the right-hand wall of the house, since he knew Thorsteinn's bed was on that side, and pull up the grass on the roof evenly and steadily as if he were a horse grazing. The man did so. Thorsteinn woke up and called to the boy, saying he hadn't driven the horses far enough away last night, and for him to go and drive them off. The boy mumbled something and went back to sleep. Thorsteinn kept hearing something on the roof. He called the boy again, but nothing happened, so Thorsteinn got up to see what was going on and went outside in his underwear. When he got outdoors he saw nothing at first, so he began to walk around the buildings. Snorri and three of his men killed him before he could say a word.*

"They found him up here," Baddi said, as we went back down the steps and the house at Efri-Raudilaekur slowly proved itself to be wood and concrete, not turf. He switched off the kitchen light. "The neighbors came to check on him. Nobody had seen him for a while."

CHAPTER ELEVEN

WELL MOUNTED

After a breakfast of cornflakes and orange juice, Inga took Baddi to the airport. I pulled a half-dozen books off their shelves to kill time until she came back to drive me downtown.

Picture books showed old photos of postmen, their square boxes slung two to a horse, each tail tied to the halter of the horse behind it in a long wandering train. Horses carried hay stacked as high again as themselves. They swam behind a boat, baring their teeth. On the beach they hauled out driftwood, great trees logged in Sweden or Siberia that had escaped at a river mouth and floated for weeks at sea. A farmer rode out of the highlands with a lamb across his saddle and a dog hitching a ride up behind. A horse hovered in a sling, high above a docked ship, destined for dark days in an English coal mine.

In a book of horse names, I looked up *Gaeska*. I found only *Gáski* (masculine), "playfulness," or *Gáska* (feminine), "a playful, wanton mare." Playful was okay, I thought. (I ignored the "wanton" part.) Playful was better than Nipper, the dapple gray's name, though it didn't have the draw of Freyfaxi or Fluga.

Two hundred thousand is too much for that horse, Baddi had said when I'd asked him about Elvar's little bay mare.

The scorecard from a regional horseshow held a few weeks earlier was lying on Baddi's desk. Elvar had outscored him in the tolt, I saw; in the four-gait competition (walk, trot, canter, and tolt), they'd ranked quite close.

For two hundred to two-fifty you should be able to get an excellent six- to nine-year-old mare with a well-balanced tolt, Baddi had said.

I wasn't sure there was a contradiction here: Gaeska was six. She had a good tolt. It annoyed me that he would discount her, apparently because of her color.

The sons of Einar Gislason are very good with horses, I remembered Haukur acknowledging. *If Elvar Einarsson says this horse is good, then it's a good horse.*

Still I wondered. Was Gaeska a good horse for me?

I thought of what Elvar had said when I'd decided to buy the dapple gray: In a year you'll wish you hadn't. *In a year you'll be a better rider. You'll wish you had bought my Gaeska.*

Now I wished his prediction would come true: I wanted so much to become a better rider, to feel in control going at Gaeska's speed, to have at least a whisper of Baddi's reckless confidence.

I'd also like my Icelandic acquaintances to think well of me—and Icelanders have long judged a person by the horse she rides.

I thought of Otkel, overhorsed and out-of-control in *Njal's Saga*, having displayed his lack of horse-sense since about 1300. Or a man named Arni, a laughingstock since 1636, when a poet wrote about his horse: *Skjoni has skinny legs and a docked tail; the nag is belly-slim, hip-shrunken like a tyke; survives—just—with few teeth. If hay doesn't fail that mount, decrepit Arni will make one more outing to market.*

Hrafnkel with the noble Freyfaxi; Thorir Dove-Nose and speedy Fluga; Seal-Thorir and his mare Skalm, who carried her burden so dependably; Grettir's father and the weatherwise Kengala; jovial Sveinn and his Sodulkolla, of whom the verses were written; Bjorn with Hvitingur and his two white colts; Sigurdur the Dragon-Slayer and his Grani, who ran through the ring of fire—in all the Icelandic stories I loved, the horse, the fine horse, was the emblem of the owner's reputation and his honor, a key to his character, whether practical, adventurous, aristocratic, or good-natured—and to his fate.

Nowhere is this connection between man and horse better expressed than in a saga set on the west coast near our summerhouse, another saga I'd read in the lee of a lava wall on those lonely, sunny days at Litla Hraun. *Viglundar's Saga* tells of a conflict between the sons of two close friends, Holmkell of Foss and his neighbor Thorgrimur, and the entire plot is revealed, early on, by the description of the opponents' horses. "The brothers owned a stallion," the saga says of Holmkell's sons, "that was brown in color. He was savage. He put to flight every horse that he fought against. He had 'war teeth' so long that no other horse's teeth were like them." Viglundur, Thorgrimur's son, also had a stallion, a yellow dun in color, "the best and fairest of horses." He was very fond of the horse, but for his honor's sake Viglundur accepted the challenge to match it against the savage Brunn (Brown).

Horse fights were common in early Iceland, from the Saga Age to as late as 1623 (although they were officially banned in 1592). Two stallions were brought into a circle of men, with one or more mares in season staked nearby to excite them, and then goaded against each other with cattle prods or sticks. The goading often escalated into fistfights and violence, for the fight was not really a match between horses, but a leveling of men. The Foss brothers had at first demanded that Viglundur give them his horse outright, to acknowledge their superiority. When Viglundur refused, they challenged him to a horse fight to prove who was better.

It took the two brothers together to lead the savage Brunn into the ring, where he stood "looking fearsome." Then Viglundur loosed his beautiful yellow-dun. "He reared up with both forefeet and brought them down on Brunn's nose so that all of his 'war teeth' flew out." He bit Brunn so badly the horse fell down dead. His owners jumped for their weapons.

The feud begun at this horse fight would last for many years, scrolling into quite a long saga. But, as any practiced saga-reader could predict, Viglundur of the "best and fairest of horses" would ultimately triumph: Only a hero is perceptive enough to have a stallion that is beautiful, a good riding horse, and a fierce fighter. The brothers from Foss must fail in the end, since they could not see that Brunn's mean-spiritedness covered up a lack of true ability. They had no real eye for horses.

Even today it's something that Icelanders value—not the owning of a fine horse, exactly, but the skill, the eye, it takes to recognize one. Haukur of Snorrastadir himself, speaking with a reporter for an Icelandic magazine in 1996, said, "I remember many of the people I lived among here in the countryside, but I remember best those who were well mounted. Julius Jonsson of Hitarnes on his Toppur, for instance, is unforgettable. When I was a child, and Julius was said to be coming, I would sit at the window and wait, wanting to see him come riding over the sands and into the farmyard."

And, of course, there is the reverse effect. As Halldor Laxness wrote in *Independent People*: "Gvendur of Summerhouses was on everyone's lips that spring, in the first place because he had decided to go to America, in the second place because he had decided not to go to America. In the third place he had bought himself a horse; it was a racehorse and he had bought it from someone living in a distant parish for an enormous sum of money. Many people laughed. ... Some people said the lad must be a half-wit. Others said his horse was no more than an average horse, even that it was getting on in years. What a dunderhead! Prior to this, no one had noticed that Gvendur of Summerhouses so much as existed; now, with startling suddenness, he was everywhere notorious as an idiot and a dunderhead. ... Horse dealers stopped him on the main road, poked at the horse's teeth, made a fool of the owner when he had ridden away, and made up their minds to foist an even worse horse on him as soon as they had swindled him out of his present one."

I wondered what the horse dealers would say about me.

Birkir of Hlid was round, but not fat; his rump had a satisfying fleshiness to it. His back was wide, rather short, but smooth and flat, hardly the hint of a spine, and that colored with a line of darker burnish than his red bay coat. His neck was as thick as a stallion's and also short—he was the "old-style" Icelandic horse, chunky and rugged; in him the breeders failed in their official goal *to make the front of the horse as light and fine as possible*, which was probably why he was so cheap—but he arced that stout neck proudly. His head was quite large, as well, his eyes soft, his nostrils wide. His feet and his tail and the tips of his small, pert ears were black. His mane frizzed, thick, an explosion of hair, black with faded highlights and a few white hairs; his forelock blew straight back when he ran to reveal that palm-print star. In all, he was a beautiful beast.

By nature he was patient, phlegmatic, slow to anger, and gluttonous. Not the sensitive type, his attention tended to wander. Yet he had a stubborn temper. He would not give in to force. He insisted that his opinions be acknowledged. But he was gracious in victory, noble even. He took no advantage. He settled in to graze and declined to add, *I told you so*. Defeated, rebuked, he would pout and act sulky, but he held no grudge, and soon his native good temper would return. He was a caricature male, I decided: lazy, selfish, vain, and easily wooed, willing to give his last ounce for a little love, an old-fashioned gentleman turned out in his best Sunday suit.

I had taken him on a solitary ride before I went north to meet Baddi. It was a hot day at Hlid. The girls of the farm were out on the hillside in their bras and panties, sunbathing, their plump limbs already pink, their magazines crumpled and spotted with tanning oil. Sigrun was not at home, but she'd deputized one of her housemates to fetch me the tack. The girl slipped on a shirt and jeans. Branddis, Haukur's daughter, had brought me over from Snorrastadir, and we three walked up to the pasture to bridle Birkir. The gate was a single strand of twine between two ends of an electric fence. The horses stood or lay about the sunny hill—they had no concept of shade, and so did not seek it. They gathered in sociable knots. In one group I saw with surprise a dark horse with a bright blond mane—*svart glófexti?* Birkir was lying beside another bay horse, dozing. He got up clumsily at our approach and stoically took the bit, then let me lead him down to the barn. Branddis watched as I saddled him, interrupting her conversation with the girl to make polite suggestions. "A little farther back, I think," she said, about the saddle, then, "Are your stirrups long enough?" Satisfied, she wished me a good ride and turned to go home. The girl nodded and walked back up the sunbathing hill. Birkir and I were alone.

We were alone: just me and my first horse. He arced his head around and looked at me. I found myself reflected in his eye.

I took a deep breath and mounted. With a little urging, he agreed to go down the gravel lane at a plodding walk. There was no one to impress. *We always start out slow*, I remembered Haukur saying. I had the heat as an excuse. We walked most of the hour, just a few moments of tolt—fine, balanced, and cushiony—but when he broke out of the gait, I acquiesced. It was really too hot. Icelanders had an aversion to making a horse sweat, I knew. A farmwife with horses for rent had once upbraided her French guests for that, she told me, while holding onto my reins. *I don't like to see my horses treated like that*, she warned. It was bad form. Unnecessary.

We walked past a working tractor. Birkir ignored it. A snipe flushed at our feet. He paid it no mind. When we rested by the lake, he grazed between my feet, twining grass around the bit, his dark eye exploring me. We rode along the lakeside and had turned off the lane onto a grassy track when suddenly he jumped and snorted, wheeled, ran four steps up a mound, and stopped. I'd heard the rattle of wire. I dismounted and led him cautiously to explore. A coil of fencing lay hidden in the grass, and he'd stepped on it; luckily, his hoof hadn't caught. We stood side by side, our hearts beating, and calmed each other.

If I had ridden him first with a trekking group or fast across rough terrain, I might have dismissed him as too slow, too timid, a children's pony. He did not seem to have speed in him. But now he was mine: None of that mattered. *He will be as good as Elfa*, Haukur had said, and I trusted Haukur's eye.

What exactly was it I'd liked about Elfa? I remembered the sun and the silvery sea, the sound of hoofbeats on the sand, our surreal swim to "save" the plane that had brought us beer.

An hour into our ride that day, Haukur had asked me what I thought of his horses.

"They're wonderful," I said.

"Which one do you like best?"

We had just switched horses. I hadn't ridden the red one long.

"Elfa," I answered, with only a slight hesitation.

He nodded and smiled. "She is my best," he said. "I have never had another Elfa."

It was this that I'd liked about her: simply that I'd known enough to know she was good.

But now, having ridden many more Icelandic horses, nearly all of them "good" in one way or another—pretty, well-gaited, quiet, willing—I realized the thing I'd liked best about Elfa was how easy she was to ride. She had said yes the moment I'd mounted, and whether it was for love of Haukur or professional pride, she was willing to carry me. Like Gandalf's gray Shadowfax, she made it her business to see that I remained on her back—unless I jumped off into the air.

It seemed the same with Birkir. As soon as we'd turned out of the barnyard and down the lane alone, I knew he'd said yes. He and I were riding together. We were two halves of a centaur, if only at a walk.

We went slowly down to the end of the lane and looked toward the sea: the two blue lakes, the gold-mossed field of fractured lava, the red "sand dunes" where the mare Skalm lay down under her load, Eldborg like a queen's crown or a god's smithy, the Horse, the Buckets, the glacier swathed in cloud, invisible but still a presence. "Like a great museum filled with all of nature's many works of art," an Icelandic writer had said of this view from Hlid. We started down the hill toward one of the lakes, but Birkir balked and was unwilling to go. He didn't know that country down there. He couldn't guarantee my safety. So we stood there a moment, while I took in the view. Then we turned back.

"Where did you go?" asked the sunbathing girl.

"Down the lane."

"And you were gone that long?"

"It's a hot day," I said, and smiled.

I hadn't always been so cautious on an Icelandic horse. I've rarely fallen off any kind of horse, and it was the last thing on my mind, riding an Icelandic. I nodded at the report in *News from Iceland*: "The first acquaintance with an Iceland horse never evokes feelings of hesitation or even fear as can happen with full-sized horses. ... The horses are patient, easy-going, obedient, and weather-proof, making a first tour on horseback a thrill rather than a trial." I felt exactly as did E. J. Oswald, writing in 1872: "They are the easiest animals to ride that can be imagined. Their small size and smooth amble makes riding them seem like acquiring four active indefatigable legs of your own."

True, even a person with "active indefatigable legs" can fall—if he's drunk, say, or half-asleep.

I knew Haukur of Snorrastadir to fall, once, off his cream-colored Bjartur. My father and nephew had come to visit us at Litla Hraun for two weeks when we lived there in 1996, and one rainy afternoon we'd driven down to Snorrastadir to see about a short ride. We had just pulled in when we saw the riders rushing toward us down the banks of the River Kalda. Haukur swept up to the stoop where we waited, leaped off Bjartur, and, in a show of exuberance, gave me not only the usual bearhug but a sloppy kiss, while I remarked in alarm over the bloody gash above Bjartur's eye.

"It looks worse on a white horse than it really is," said the young man who'd taken Bjartur's bridle.

Then I looked at Haukur. He was covered in sand all up one side, from his knee to his ear. There was sand in his ear. He was more than a bit tipsy. When I introduced him to my father, he excused himself briefly, dashed into the house, and returned with a half-bottle of Johnnie Walker Black, which he ceremoniously passed around.

"What happened?" I asked the young man with Bjartur.

"He was at the flying pace," the young man said, and shrugged.

"And he fell off," I said, disapprovingly, letting out a soft *hummph* of scorn.

Haukur looked at me and grinned. He reached into his coat pocket and pulled out an empty flask-sized whiskey bottle. "But I didn't put a dent in my hip flask!" he crowed.

We all laughed, I loudest of all, for I remembered the day he was referring to. It was when I'd ridden Elfa with him on the sands, after our troupe of crack riders had left us, heading north, over the mountains, across the fjord on a ferry, to ride on to the westernmost point of Europe. After a night's sleep at Snorrastadir and a long car-ride back to where our horses were pastured, Haukur and I had met a new party of travelers led by a tour guide named Helga Helgadottir.

These were not crack riders. They did not "advance at a noble rate" over the sands. Instead, on their rented horses, they plodded along, sitting hunched and sacklike and as uncomfortable as one can look on such a smooth-gaited beast. They'd been on their way some time already before they met Haukur on the sands, and although he tried to pick up the pace, they would have none of it. Time and again we circled back to wait. Can you see them? Haukur would ask whenever we put a high dune or a spit of rock between us.

Concerned about the fast-rising tide, Haukur had turned inland, keeping close to shore. The path here was rocky and boggy, but at least there was no risk of being stranded two miles out. Often, looking over our shoulders, we saw half our riders off their mounts, leading them up a hill or around a little bit of a bog. Haukur shook his head in amazement. Yet even with all their caution, a large older man in the party repeatedly fell off, once landing so hard on his metal hip flask that he put a dent in it. As we watched him gingerly feel his limbs, the pony standing quietly beside him, I had turned to Haukur and softly asked, "How do you fall off an Icelandic horse?"

He had smiled, and cocked a finger at his temple in the universal symbol for *nuts*.

I had laughed.

Then the lesson horse ran away with me.

I had intended to take several lessons, that first week of my horse-buying trip, before going to visit Haukur. I had a nice place to stay in Reykjavik. My friend's friend, Gugga, was well-connected in the horse world and had found me an English-speaking instructor. The horse was a pretty white gelding named Kindill—Candle.

We had done a nice few rounds at a tolt when I'd signalled him to trot, exactly as the instructor had told me to—and he'd bolted. Around and around the oval track. Skittering on the turns. His neck stretched flat.

"What happened?" the instructor demanded. She was a large, middle-aged woman, older than I had expected, shorter than I, and round in a way that implied strength and physicality rather than fat, her cropped blonde hair framing a wide face and an imposing stare. "Why didn't you stop him?"

I hadn't a clue what she was talking about. Preparing for this trip, trying to make myself into a savvy buyer, I'd read everything I could about Icelandic horses, and time and again I'd heard Americans warn about the horse "with no brakes." In Kindill, I'd found him. I suddenly understood the problem.

"He wouldn't stop," I said, beginning to get angry. This was not a horse for a newcomer.

But the instructor was angrier than I. "You didn't pull," she exclaimed, leveling me a hard-eyed stare.

"I think I did," I said, retreating. Blame aside, I was simply thankful to be upright on the ground. I thought she should be happy about that too, but her expression, rather than relieved, was only cross.

"Here, take the rein," she said as we stood beside the heaving horse. She took hold of the other end in front of the bit. "Show me how you pulled."

I tugged.

"That's not pulling," said the instructor. She gave a yank that threw me off balance into the horse's side. "This is pulling."

"Oh," I said, as I collected myself. Now I was confused. A jerk like that would have sent the little horse sprawling.

"Another thing," she demanded before I could frame the question, "did you touch him with your leg?"

My busy mind tried to process that one. Her English was quite good, but when talking to any Icelander, I'd learned to think twice before I jumped to answer what seemed a nonsensical question. She had told me to ask for the trot as I would have on my school horse at home, which required a shift of weight, a shortening of the reins, and a rhythmic squeeze with the lower leg. What word could she be mistranslating as "touch"?

"I might have," I wavered.

"Well, that's your problem, then," she relaxed. "Never touch an Icelandic horse with your leg. That's just asking for trouble. Now, we'll try again."

She held the horse's head and motioned for me to remount. All those old saws about getting right back on after you've been thrown (and I'd even stayed on!) ran through my head and I shamefacedly scrabbled back on. Kindill stood calm and attentive, although still heaving, and as we picked up a nice, slow tolt, I finally relaxed.

No leg, I told myself, and wondered how else I could have stayed on.

At the end of the first lap, the instructor shouted, "Now try to find trot."

I shivered but did as I was told. I placed one hand on Kindill's neck and shortened the reins. I shifted my weight forward. I held my legs out as far as I could manage—and the white horse took off. Around and around at top speed again while everything blurred and tumbled in.

Of course I clapped my legs against his sides. I would have thrown my arms around his neck if I hadn't been too afraid of dropping the reins. I clenched every muscle from my toes to my teeth. We screamed around three turns and aimed hard for the instructor with the long whip extending her arm.

As we walked back to the barn, abandoning the lesson, I wondered how to avoid another runaway as I looked for a horse to buy. "What kind of horse is Kindill?" I asked. I was alarmed at the shakiness in my voice; I found I was close to tears.

In my reading I'd come across whole herds of horse words—*gæðingur, alhliðahestur, keppnishestur*—Icelandic horses were either "A-group" or "B-group" and the relative rankings were hard to keep straight without having an actual horse in mind. Kindill must be a *keppnishestur*, a competition horse, a fiery, unpredictable racer best ridden by experts.

"Kindill?" asked the instructor, as if the question were obvious, "he's just a *reiðhestur*, a riding horse."

I groped about for another way to save face. "He's rather *viljugur*, isn't he?" I asked. That word, viljugur, was another one I found hard to understand. On the surface it seemed to be "willing," both in the sense of "willing to please" and "willing to go," or eager, and it was generally a good thing. Yet sometimes the Icelandic seemed to carry a trace of negativity, as if *viljugur* might accommodate "willful," even pigheaded.

"*Viljugur?*" the instructor asked. She had turned her imposing stare on me again, and I saw in her eyes exasperation and, to my chagrin, a good helping of pity. "He's owned by my niece. She's twelve years old. She's never had any trouble with him."

The first horse she rode ran away with her.

My Reykjavik friends were concerned. I exaggerated the lesson. I tried to make it sound funny. I laughed at myself, letting that little horse run away, I, who had ridden big horses, Thoroughbreds even.

My friends remained sincerely concerned. They noticed I had not signed up for another session.

And I knew my bravado sounded false. I'd been shaken deeply. Having two tragic deaths in a family—a murder one summer, a plane crash the next—makes you feel intensely vulnerable, and I wasn't immune to a chill of superstition: *Third time takes all.* Would I be the next to bring grief to my loved ones? Didn't I owe it to them not to take any risks?

A few days after that disastrous lesson, we drove down to Gugga's sister's farm in the southern district of Skeid (loosely, Racetrack), where the sale of a fine stallion had paid for the new Scandinavian-style wooden house. Gugga and her sister, Stefania, put their heads together as they stepped into the barn. I stood out in the spitting rain, stamping the chill out of my feet and wishing I didn't understand Icelandic.

The first horse she rode ran away with her, Stefania called out to her husband, Bjorn, already wading into the herd. She motioned him away from the horse he'd been heading for and toward another, a chestnut mare with a star half-hidden by her forelock. Of all the horses Stefania had for sale, she was the only one the sisters thought I could ride. They loosed her in the paddock and let the dogs chase her about. She ran rippling like an athlete, turning and tossing her head. Her sides heaved. She was the summertime color of a white-tailed deer. Her name was Dogg (Dew).

Then we saddled up and started down the lane, the rain misty about us, five or six together. I stayed well in the pack. I wiggled my feet in the stirrups, adjusted my reins. Dogg had a bumpy trot. I could not find the balance that would make her tolt. My leg position felt all wrong, though it was what Gugga had recommended: pinch in the knee, turn the toe in, not out; let the lower leg dangle as far from the horse's sides as you could, the foot loose and wobbly in the stirrup.

The farm dog rushed us, barking, tail high, and I did not realize until it yelped that I had ridden right over it. I turned in the saddle to see it slink away, unharmed.

Behind me, Stefania laughed. "See how calm she is?"

We rode down the gravel lane and across the highway, here gravel too, and just a bit wider than the lane. Like most of the country roads, it had a well-worn bridle path on its berm. After an hour, we stopped to rest. I lay on my raincoat in the damp grass and felt the mare's chewing next to my ear. Bjorn sat to my right, Stefania and Gugga on my left. Bjorn was a small man, shorter than Gugga, quick-eyed, with a shaggy Beatles' haircut updated with a '90s rat-tail. Stefania shared Gugga's ranginess, but in a smaller, softer version: her dark curly hair made her look more Irish. All three had prominent front teeth, squared and tilted in toward each other. They talked about me over my head, unaware of how much Icelandic I could follow. Stefania noted that I had mounted properly, at which I was pleased; Gugga, that I sat like a passenger, not a rider. I knew it was true. I'd been taught to direct a horse entirely with my lower leg: here my legs were worse than useless, and I had no idea what to replace them with. Bjorn had a dark and burring voice. I found him hard to understand, but his tone was dismissive. He'd not been impressed. I looked up at the mare grazing nicely at my side and found her small and thin and undistinguished. I hadn't been impressed either.

The first horse she rode ran away with her.

Gugga stepped into the clubhouse and faced the cluster of men, good ol' boys we would call them in America, lounging on the benches, smoking, drinking coffee, watching the tube. We'd come to a resort on the outskirts of Reykjavik, where Gugga said they sometimes had horses for sale.

The rain was a drizzle that day, and the horse rental had not been busy. From the proprietor's tone of voice, answering Gugga, I knew he had just glimpsed a way to turn a profit for the day. He had just the horse for me: calm, between eight and ten years old, a natural tolter. As he joked and sparred with Gugga, I heard prices bandied about. I could understand only a little of what they said—too fast, too glib, too many people talking at once—but it was enough to make me feel like the goose who'd stumbled into the fox's den. He had a foxy sort of look about him, too, very handsome, with a fine head of curly hair and a keen-edged smile. He barked an order over his shoulder and the youngest man slipped out; soon a girl came up leading three horses.

She was heavily made up and pretty, like the other girls I'd seen selling saddles in the tack shops Gugga had taken me to that morning; they had looked out of place among all that sleek and functional black leather in their platform shoes and polyester midriff tops, their blonde hair clipped and held close to their heads with dime-store barrettes. This girl, at least, was wearing a quilted riding coverall and boots. She worked quietly around the horses, tacking up, while the proprietor and Gugga and the younger man chatted. He would have to charge Gugga full price to ride with me, I heard the proprietor say. How much was that? she asked, and when she heard, she declined. It was too high for me, too, and I'd seen enough already to know I wasn't going to buy the horse. I tried to tell Gugga that, but she misunderstood.

"The first horse she rode ran away with her," she repeated to the proprietor.

He nodded sympathetically.

But it wasn't that, or the high price of the ride. I had been watching the girl tack up the horse for sale, another red mare with a star, and I didn't like what I saw. Although the mare stood without being tied, her ears were plastered back, her head held low. Worse, every time the girl approached her on her left side, she shied, and I could see a deep, wrinkled scar on her back leg, just above the hock.

I repeated to Gugga that I didn't want to ride her, but she shook her head as if she couldn't make sense of me—I was speaking English—and said I'd have to deal with the proprietor directly.

I stared until I had his attention, then said slowly and innocently, in English, "What is wrong with her leg?"

His English was, as I had suspected, better than my Icelandic. "That? Oh, just an old sore. It doesn't bother her anymore." He strode over to her and leaned down to pick up her hoof. The mare shuddered violently and yanked her leg out of his hand, her head snaking back at the same instant to snap at him. It was behavior I'd never seen in an Icelandic.

The proprietor acted as if his own clumsiness had made her shy. "There, there, girl," he cooed, patting her. "Last time a really big fat man rode her," he said over his shoulder. "She's just a little worn out. Here, see how good she is—"

He muttered something to the young man, who quickly mounted her—but not before I saw her paw the ground and shake her head. He took off at a fast clip, and even I could tell that her tolt was very nice. *Black-and-Decker-Black-and-Decker* sounded crisp on the gravel drive. I couldn't see any lameness, and yet I knew I hadn't much of an eye.

"You like her?" the proprietor asked.

"I'm not sure," I said, at the same time as Gugga answered, in English, "Oh yes, she is looking very good."

The proprietor called something over his shoulder to the girl, and I saw her take one of the spare horses away. She returned with a different one at about the same time the young man rode back on the red mare.

"You'll try this one first," the proprietor said to me in English, waving at the new horse, a fat chestnut with a blaze. "He is the favorite of the Russian ambassador," he added, and laughed. "He will be very disappointed when he hears I've sold his favorite horse to America!"

Then he turned to Gugga, whispering in Icelandic, *He won't run away with her!*

The girl held the Russian ambassador's favorite horse for me to mount, and I capitulated. She mounted the third horse herself, a dark brown, and we headed up a gravel track into the hills. The drizzle had ended, the clouds lingered low. There was nothing to see, so I concentrated on the riding: feet, seat, balance, hands.

The Russian ambassador's favorite certainly wouldn't run away with me. Although his gait was rolling and smooth, I found myself thumping him (so much for *never touch an Icelandic horse with your leg*) to keep up. At the top of the first rise, I asked to switch. The girl took the Russian ambassador's horse, the young man rode hers, and I tried the sale horse. She was very nice, tolting easily and quickly. We turned onto a narrow, muddy path and I pulled ahead of my chaperones, her surefooted speed a delight. Turning back I could see the girl thumping the ambassador's horse's sides, her feet cocked up to catch him in the belly, the stirrups dangling unused below them.

"Would you like to try this one?" the young man asked, in English.

I agreed, but after a few paces at an ungoverned trot, I wanted to switch back.

"Yes," he agreed, taking the dark horse again. "You can't ride this horse."

We caught up with the girl on the ambassador's horse halfway back. The horse was standing by the side of the track, grazing; the girl, mounted, was talking on a small cellular phone. She slipped it into her pocket as we rode up, and we went back down the hill at a fast pace—even the ambassador's horse keeping up, now that he was facing the home pastures.

The proprietor met us in the paddock, laughing and all but rubbing his hands, seeing me ride up smiling.

"She has a wonderful tolt," I gushed, very pleased with my ride. I took out my notebook and had him write his name and phone number in it. I heard Gugga tell him I was going to Skagafjord; that I didn't like red horses (I had refused her sister's horse with that excuse). The price, he said, was 180,000, about $2,500.

"How old is she?" I asked.

"She is seven," he said, apparently forgetting that an hour earlier she was between eight and ten.

"And what is her name?" I asked, pencil poised to write it down.

He stopped. His smile faded. "What is her name?" he looked over at the girl, unsaddling the horses. She avoided his eye.

"We got her from—" He named a farm. "Well, we'll just call and ask. Who's got the phone?"

No one replied. The young man was in the tack room, out of earshot. The girl, as if she hadn't heard, led the horses into the nearby paddock.

I thanked her mentally, put my notebook away. I didn't need to ask about the horse's breeding. Doubtless he wouldn't know. I shook his hand and asked him politely what I owed him for the ride.

"Owe me? Oh you don't owe me anything. We're trying to sell you a horse!" he laughed jovially again, but the pleasantness had gone out of his eyes.

I acted surprised and thanked him profusely, promising to call. But I didn't even glance at him or his horse as I went back to the car. I didn't want to be the sucker he thought I was.

CHAPTER TWELVE

GIVE AND TAKE

When young Sigurdur the Dragon-Slayer was given the choice of any horse in the king's herd, he didn't know how to decide. Walking in the forest, pondering, he chanced upon an old man with a long beard. "Where are you going?" asked the stranger.

"I am going to choose a horse," Sigurdur answered. "Can you give me any advice?"

"We should drive the horses into the river," the stranger said. When they did so, all the horses immediately swam back to shore except for one young gray stallion, a very large and handsome horse which had never been ridden. That was the horse Sigurdur chose. He named it Grani. "This horse is descended from Sleipnir, Odin's eight-legged steed," the stranger said. "He must be raised carefully, because he will become better than any other horse." Then the old man disappeared, for he was the god Odin himself.

Baddi's wife Inga dropped me off in downtown Akureyri under a cobalt blue sky. After an annoying visit to the bank—Thordur had decided not to cash in my stocks; I'd have to get my husband to wire money before I had enough to pay for Birkir at Hlid, not to mention a second horse—I hiked up the hill to the botanical garden, cursing the hot sun. The temperature was topping seventy, extraordinary for Iceland, while I was dressed for the usual forty degrees and raining. I flung myself onto a concrete bench in the first patch of real shade I'd seen in the country, beneath a splendid old rowan tree, and slipped off my boots to let my swollen feet breathe.

I wished a stranger would come by and tell me how to choose a horse.

Perhaps I wouldn't listen if he did. Who would know Odin from any other bearded farmer, even if he came in his classic disguise, with his broad-brimmed hat and walking stick, a bent-over old man with one eye? He might be a German tourist.

You have to decide for yourself, Elvar had said, and I knew it was the best advice I'd received from anyone since I'd arrived in Iceland, horses on my agenda.

Of course I trusted Haukur's eye, but Haukur's "perfect mare for Nancy" hadn't seemed perfect to me. She was lazy and herd-bound and pigheaded and fat, her flashy looks only a distraction to me.

But neither was I sure about Elvar's Gaeska, who seemed to fit the other extreme: scrawny and independent and over-willing and plain, always asking for something—I wasn't sure what. If Birkir was the caricature male, she was the female: flighty, oversensitive, trying too hard to please—and resentful when her efforts went unappreciated.

I mulled over my other options.

It was disappointing to think that Baddi had a small herd of family horses for sale, seven to eight years old, pretty ones, he said, but I couldn't even see them. Should I wait until he came back from New York? Have him send me the videos, then buy a horse through the mail? I knew I had not impressed him. He didn't think much of my riding skill. And I remembered Fjola talking about the

Germans and the dapple gray: *If they know anything about the gaits, they'll see it. If not—*

All I would see would be the color. So mail order was out.

But my plane didn't depart for another seven days. Perhaps I should go south. There was that one chestnut mare at Gugga's sister's farm, Dogg, the only horse in their stable they thought I could ride. I had found her too trotty, but now I wasn't sure. And she was very well-bred, with famous stallions on both sides.

And there were other horses I hadn't yet seen.

A relative of Haukur's—the son-in-law of his half-brother—had heard I wanted a horse. He had a nice one for sale, he told me one day over coffee at Snorrastadir: a five-year-old gelding trained already for two years. (He must mean two seasons, like Birkir, I thought.) Very gentle. The man's wife and his old father had ridden him. His son rode him bareback. His name was Vinur, Friend. He was pastured quite near to Gugga's sister's farm. I took down the man's name and said I might call.

And there were horsepeople in Reykjavik I hadn't yet queried: Hulda, the marketing director of the Icelandic Horse Breeder's Association, with whom I'd corresponded over e-mail; Gunnar, the uncle of a friend, who years ago had arranged my first ride on an Icelandic horse; and Diddi, the famous rider and trainer who handled most exports to America.

As I sat there in the rowan's shade, pondering what to do, where to go next, a poem I liked came to mind, one I'd clipped from the daily paper on an earlier trip to Iceland and tacked up above my desk. Now, suddenly, it gained a new meaning. It went, in my poor translation:

> *A horse in hobbles*
> *hops through the hummocks,*
> *tasting the sharp tang of life.*
> *Hops and watches,*

> *a horse in a quandary,*
> *vigor in his mane, fire in his breath.*
> *His hoof in the hobble,*
> *the heathlands lure,*
> *the bright-colored lichens*
> *so lovely to run through.*

Now I was that horse in hobbles, unable to break free of indecision, seeing the lovely future—myself as horsewoman—but unable to reach it.

I remembered the day at Sydra-Skordugil when I had first ridden Gaeska. Late in the afternoon, after our ride, we had driven down to tour the old turf house and to enjoy the free treats—fried flatbread with smoked salmon, thin sugared pancakes rolled around jam, cream cakes and hot chocolate—that Elvar's mother made for the concession stand there. Stuffed and sugar-high, we had been driving home through bursts of rain when a full rainbow arced out over all of Skagafjord. The pot of gold looked to be seated right in the barn at Sydra-Skordugil.

Elvar pressed down the accelerator. Giggling and shouting, we raced the rainbow, trying to reach home while the pot of gold was still there. Of course it evaded us. The rainbow's end was always just ahead. Always just out of reach.

Elvar pulled into the barnyard and I jumped out, camera in hand. Now the sun was painting the old house a clean white; the rainbow cleared the clump of trees and came down in the horse pasture. Behind me I heard a shout and, the rainbow picture taken, I swung around to see Elvar riding a bay horse, bareback, pushing the rest of the herd in a swirl of color through the funnel of the gate. Down the highway they raced, while Fjola stopped traffic and Fridrek stood at the pasture gate to turn the herd. A sinuous river of broad backs and arched necks, flashing manes and floating tails, their hoofbeats loud on the macadam, they swept onto the grass and disappeared out of sight, heading straight for the rainbow's end, Elvar racing after them, at one with his horse, both of them full of spirit and bursting with life.

I hadn't told Haukur about the disastrous lesson, about the white horse that had run away with me.

I'd said nothing to Fjola or Elvar until my flapping jacket frightened black Heimir.

So I knew neither Birkir nor Gaeska had been chosen as a good horse for a *traumatized rider*, a good horse for a *fraidy-cat*, a good horse to palm off *on a sucker*. They had been chosen as good horses for me.

But which *me*?

Haukur had known me as a wife and mother, dutiful and patient, an assistant on my husband's book project, a lover of literature. He had ridden the Longufjorur with me, had assessed my skill-level at seventy percent. He knew what would please me, since I'd liked his Elfa, he had a good eye, and it seemed Birkir and I were, in fact, well-matched: Gentlemanly Birkir satisfied the *me* that liked pampering, that needed reassurance, that was respectable and well-bred and restrained.

Elvar had had to guess. What kind of horse would she ride, a woman 37 years old, a wife and mother, traveling alone by bus in an exotic country, relying on kindness for her room and board, horse dealing in a language she barely understood? Such a woman must be independent, exciting, confident. She must be something of an adventuress.

I'd written him a long letter before I'd come, in Icelandic checked and edited by a friend. I'd described the kind of riding I'd done, the sort of horse I thought would suit. I had tried to be honest, but in fact I was creating that adventuress. *I am not a very good horsewoman*, I'd said, and then softened it by adding, *I take lessons twice a week*, that is, I was learning fast. I said, *I want horses to ride on trails through the woods. Sometimes my nine-year-old son will come with me* (wishful thinking, as he'd shown no interest at all), *so I want to buy horses that are calm and friendly.* (For my son, you see; he's the one who needs reassurance.) *I want willing horses that would rather tolt than trot* ("willing," I said, not safe and slow); *horses that are soft* (I wasn't exactly sure what this meant, but it was a word Haukur had often used—*mjúkur*—and it made me sound more expert) *and well-trained. I'd also like a horse that is five-gaited* (I was remembering Elfa at the flying pace, racing Bjartur on the sands, remembering the joy I had felt at her speed—no fear at going too fast here, no fear of a runaway.) *Finally, I'd like horses that are tall and beautiful, but the color doesn't matter*—at least, that's what I'd said. And with this shopping list in hand and the picture I'd created in his head—a picture of the *me* I wanted to be—Elvar's first choice had been Gaeska, the little bay mare.

I had ridden her more often than any other horse.

I had dreamed about her.

I had held her up as the standard against which to measure Haukur's "perfect mare for Nancy."

I had been miffed when Baddi suggested she might be overpriced.

So why had I decided against her?

She wasn't *tall and beautiful*. Not exactly *hip-shrunken like a tyke*, but she was thin. Small. Her mane was scraggly. And her color was the dull dark brown of mud mottled with dust.

How ironic that I'm hung up on how ugly Gaeska is, how she really is no color at all, I'd written in my notebook, waiting in Borgarnes for the bus north to meet Baddi. Ironic because all along I had been saying *the color doesn't matter*. Dabblers and dilettantes chose a horse by its color, not horsewomen. I'd read exactly that in one of my Icelandic books, Sigurdur Magnusson's *Fákar*. "Among experts," he wrote, "it is taken for truth that a good horse has no color. Color is only mentioned after all other characteristics and qualities have been taken into account."

I knew it to be true. When I was about twelve I'd been browsing in the school library one day when a title caught my eye: *The Superlative Horse*. It was the word *superlative* that had stopped me. *Super-Lative*, I had thought, wondering what "lative" meant. I checked the book out.

Twenty-five years later, I bought a copy at a used book sale. It was a folktale from China, the story of Han Kan, a poor boy picked by the Chief Groom, Po Lo, to be his successor. Po Lo's master, a duke, prized nothing above good horses; he agreed to let the boy try. Han Kan was sent off to search all of China for a suitable horse to add to the duke's stables. He returned and announced his choice: a dun-colored mare from a small village in the province of Honan. A few weeks later the horse arrived, in the care of an undergroom.

Duke Mu scowled. "Fool!" he shouted at the groom. "That is not the horse. I sent you to Honan to get a dun-colored mare. You have brought back a black stallion."

The groom paled. "It is the horse the boy chose. The dealer swore it."

The duke was furious. "Po Lo," said the Duke, "you have advised me badly. The boy ... has no eye at all. He can neither distinguish a horse's color, nor can he tell a mare from a stallion."

Po Lo raised an eyebrow. "May I see the horse?" he asked. ... Po Lo studied the horse for a long time. Then he sighed deeply. "There is no comparison between me and Han Kan," he said at last. "He is worth ten thousand of me put together."

"Dear Po Lo," cried the Duke, "have you lost your good sense? Is that horse a dun-colored mare?"

"Ah, that," said Po Lo. "Does it matter?"

Of all the duke's thousands of horses, Po Lo asked, which are better, the mares or the stallions? Which are better, the dark or the light?

"Why," said the Duke, "it depends on the horse." ...

"Certainly," said Po Lo. "The excellence of a horse does not reside in its color or sex or breed or build. Excellence is a matter of the heart and spirit of a horse. It is this that Han Kan keeps in mind. ... He looks at the things he ought to look at and ignores those that do not matter."

When put to the test, the black stallion outran the best horse in the duke's stable, and Han Kan was named the next Chief Groom.

When I looked at the things I ought to, I knew that the best horse I'd been offered in Iceland was Elvar's little bay mare.

And yet I had fixated on her color.

It was more than ironic. It was cowardly.

With a horse I had hoped to come to life again, to learn to open myself to pain and to passion, to take pleasure in the world once more, to put myself to the test. How much easier it was to keep within my shell, to take no chances, to close off the extremes.

Haukur had let me. He'd taken the decision out of my hands, made my childishness—which I'd thought a mere screen, a necessity induced by my poor Icelandic—into reality. Like a watchful father, he'd found me a "safe, happy, friendly" horse, a beauty, to be sure, but not one that would make me well-mounted, nor one that would prove I had a good eye.

You have to decide for yourself, Elvar had said, and it was this I was resisting: deciding how far my ambition as a horsewoman would reach.

I had not told Elvar I disliked Gaeska's color. I'd been afraid he would blow up at me, that he'd dismiss me for a fool—that he'd class me with the German family who had asked for a dapple gray or *svart glófexti*, the family it was not unethical to deceive, sending tapes of that pretty horse with the piggy pace. It had seemed a wiser course, and less degrading, to beg off as a horsewoman. Surely it was a compliment to Elvar that his little bay mare was too much horse for me. And for the *me* that had been stunned by murder and violent death, for the *me* traumatized by the runaway lesson horse, for the *me* that wanted a "safe, happy, friendly" horse, it was true.

But the rest of me felt it like a slap, an insult, a challenge, when he had aimed his turquoise glare my way and picked up the phone to find a beginner's horse—a children's pony. I did not want to be the person he was describing, the person he had taken to Keldu-land.

So now I wondered: What was I afraid of? The horse? Or myself—the self I'd seen reflected in Gaeska's eye?

Another poem I was fond of, this by an American named Chase Twichell, seemed to put the matter succinctly:

I've never seen a soul detached from its gender,
but I'd like to. I'd like to see my own that way,
free of its female tethers. Maybe it would be like
riding a horse. The rider's the human one,
but everyone looks at the horse.

It was this I wanted from my perfect horse. To snap free of my personal tethers, the well-bred, retiring, female tethers, among which, if it must be said, was the fear of going too fast, the fear of losing control, the fear of giving in to any sort of passion.

A few lines in Icelandic flashed through my mind: *There are stormwinds and freedom in the blowing mane*—the beginning of that poem that ended, *One man alone is only a half, with others he's more than himself, but a rider on horseback is king for a while. Uncrowned, he holds riches and power.* You could not get the freedom, the riches, without the storm.

Elvar was right. I would regret not buying his little bay mare. I would regret letting my fear of leaving my safe place keep me from becoming a true horsewoman, from being well mounted.

I walked down to the bus station and placed a call to Sydra-Skordugil.

The sun had been shining in Akureyri, but by the time the bus came down over the heath and entered Skagafjord, the valley was filled with fog.

Fjola met me at the hotel. "Are you going to buy Gaeska?" she asked.

I shrugged. On the bus ride, indecision had again wormed its way in. I'd been worrying about her running away with me, going too fast. I was wondering, did she say yes—that is, was she the horse that wanted to come home with me? *Did she choose me?*

Elvar was in the kitchen drinking coffee. The hay was all in. "So, you're going to buy Gaeska?" It was only half a question. *And if you're not, why are you back?* he seemed to be asking.

"I thought I'd let her decide," I said, setting down my bag.

Elvar grinned. "Let's go for a ride."

The fog had dimension to it, and weight. As we walked out to the barn, the mist pressed in around us, pushed us together, two companions cut off from the world. The mountains, the fjord, even the hay fields had vanished. The wooden house where Elvar's parents lived had receded halfway to Elfland, leaving only a flat edge and a corner to hold its spot. The barn was a blotch of watery red.

We stopped at the paved road and listened before crossing.

Inside, the horses were hushed and calm. Elvar took Gaeska out of a stall, and another horse, also a dark bay. He saddled them quickly, saying nothing, respecting the fog, the only sounds the creak of leather, the clink of a girth buckle, the horses' soft breath. We mounted in the barn and rode around to the hay field, newly cut. I couldn't see the far fence.

"*Taka og losa,*" Elvar said softly. "Take the reins and give them back again. Give and take. Use the reins to talk to her, tell her what you want to do. She is always listening."

We rode to the corner of the field by the gate. Elvar stopped and got off. "Now you ride alone. Down to the fence and back."

"You'll wait here? I can't see the fence."

He nodded. There was a bit of Haukur in him, I could see now, the same confidence, the same control and industry and amusement at others' insecurities. The same depths of anger and passion. They even looked somewhat alike, ruddy, fair, and brilliant-eyed, their hands hard and large, their faces roughened by the weather. The fog had laid a film of diamonds on Elvar's bright hair. He bent his head to hide a smile, dug in his pocket for a cigarette. "I'll wait right here," he said. "Down to the fence and back."

Taka og losa, I thought, give and take.

Gaeska turned away from the other horse easily, and we walked along the fence, a grassy swath, nice and flat. We picked up a tolt while still in Elvar's sight, and I was surprised I had to urge her to go faster. *Taka og losa,* I slowed her to a stop. A hint, like tossing a thought, and we were going forward again. Now faster, now slower, a smooth and easy four-beat gait, like dancing, her footfalls so gentle on the grass, and suddenly the fence loomed, ending the field, and I knew that Gaeska had said *yes*. We stopped, and I sat resting, thinking still thoughts, letting the fog fill us with silence. It was a moment to linger over, knowing the horse was mine, knowing that Elvar wondered, and Fjola, and Haukur. It had a guilty sweetness, that knowledge, and I almost laughed. Gaeska replied with a little half-turn, and I followed it up, a lean and a thought, and we were headed back. It seemed a time to sing, or fly, so I gave her more rein and she clipped fast down the grass to where Elvar waited, leaning against his horse, legs crossed, smoking.

"I saw Nancy coming out of the fog with a smile on her face, and I knew I had sold a horse," he would tell Fjola later that evening.

Now he stubbed out his smoke on his shoe. "We will teach you to go fast," he said. "We will teach you the flying pace."

I had not known until then that Gaeska was five-gaited.

He mounted his horse. "Do what I do."

We set off at a tolt, faster and faster, the ever-competitive Gaeska keeping neck-and-neck with the other horse. At the field's end, we turned and headed back, a fast tolt and faster—

"When I say *now*, give her the reins." Elvar rode with his eyes on Gaeska's stride.

"Now!"

A round leap of canter, then the arrow shot from the bow: the horse long, low, and straight, stretched out beneath me, cutting through the soft fog with powerful strides.

"You've got it!" Elvar shouted. He was next to me still, his horse also flying. "To-to, To-to, To-to— Do you feel it? Do you like it?"

I turned to answer, to tell him it was marvelous, and suddenly we were cantering again. Cantering, then galloping, racing the wind. Elvar's horse dropped behind us.

"Taka og losa! Taka og losa!" I heard him cry, again and again, panic tingeing his voice as he saw Gaeska running away with me, the sale ruined, me likely to fall off and blame him for my injuries.

I laughed. *"Allt í lagi!"* I called. "It's okay!" Gaeska wasn't running away with me, we were running away *together*.

I saw the fence looming and took the reins, gave them back, took them again. Gaeska slowed to a tolt and Elvar caught up. He said nothing, and we tolted to the fence and then stopped.

I was giddy with the ride and could only laugh. He looked at me, surprised, and shook his head and smiled, a relaxed and welcoming smile, as if to say, *I knew you had it in you.*

As slowly as the horses let us, jazzed up as they were, we rode back through the fog to the barn. At the paddock gate I asked Elvar to ride Gaeska, so I could see how she looked with a good rider astride. He was glad to. He took her the length of the paddock and tolted slowly back: Her neck arced high and her legs curved and struck, curved and struck, like a merry-go-round steed. Suddenly, the little bay mare was pretty. *It is upon horses of this kind that gods and heroes are painted riding,* I thought again.

He got off, and we both patted her.

"Feel that?" Elvar took my hand and placed it on the bridge of her nose. Where the bone should have been flat, there was a hard bump. "She's had it since she was born. She landed on a stone, I think. I'll always know her by it."

He rubbed her forehead, stroked her neck. "I raised this horse myself. I tamed her. I trained her. I let my mother ride her." He looked away.

"She's got eight millimeter shoes on now," he said quickly. "If she had ten or twelve millimeters on the front, she'd lift her feet higher, show more leg action. I'd put ten on the front and eight on the back, if I were you."

He walked the horses back to the barn and busied himself putting away the tack.

After dinner, Fjola opened her logbook. "We should do this in English, I think," she said. She spoke much better English than I did Icelandic. I was amazed she'd put up with me so long. She ran through the procedure for the vet check: the physical, the tests for lameness, the x-rays. "If everything's okay, you pay the vet. If something's wrong, we pay—and you don't buy the horse." She'd arrange an appointment for the next day. I fought down the terrible thought: What if Gaeska doesn't pass?

Fjola explained her pedigree: Gaeska was better bred than I expected. She descended from Einar Gislason's first stallion and from the original mare of Sveinn Gudmundsson in Saudarkrokur, breeder of the hairless-legged Hervar and the beautiful Galsi that Baddi rode on the calendar page. Another well-known stallion, Thattur fra Kirkjubae, appeared twice in her lineage. This horse came from the famous chestnut-with-blazes herd of southeastern Iceland, a line that traces back a hundred years to the good chestnut riding horses Jonas had mixed with his father's all-purpose blacks at the farm of Svadastadir in Skagafjord, the first farm in Iceland to fence in its fields and practice controlled horse breeding.

According to the computer-calculated prediction of her breeding qualities, Gaeska should give good foals, Fjola said. "Her scores are well balanced. None under 100, and none over 120." Under 100 was inferior; the best horses scored in the 130s. "She had one foal already when she was four years old," Fjola said, "like all of our mares do. It makes it easier for them to have foals later. You could now wait until she is eight years old without any problems. A mare has a foal at four, is trained at five, is ridden in competition for three years, and then is put out to be a brood mare. It happens all the time."

The square on the page for *name of foal* was blank. "What did you call the foal?" I asked, pointing to it.

"We didn't. We ate it." Fjola smiled. "It was a male. They're harder to sell. There wasn't anything wrong with it," she added. "Elvar and his father, they slaughter almost all the foals from four-year-olds every September. You know, you should take some horsemeat home so your family can try it."

"I don't think it's allowed," I said. "But I am taking home two horses, so—"

Fjola laughed. "Yes, that's the best way."

I decided to change the subject. "I looked up *Gaeska* in the book of horse names, *Hrimfaxi*, when I was in Akureyri. It means 'playfulness,' doesn't it?"

"Oh, no. You were spelling it wrong. Her name is *Gæska*." She wrote it out, using the ash, the Icelandic letter that looks like *a* and *e* pressed together. "It means 'kindness.'"

Kindness. I thought of Elvar, hung over, ranting at me not to buy that dapple gray mare with the awful piggy pace. Of Fjola, patiently lending me her own fine mount when the black Heimir (and I) took fright at my flapping jacket, then just as patiently trying me on Freyfaxi to see what kind of horse I thought I could ride. Of Elvar, pressing my palm against the bump on Gaeska's nose, of the fond way he stroked her, saying goodbye. Of the look on his face when I rode out of the fog, smiling, and he knew that I knew a good horse when I'd found one.

Kindness. A lovely name for a horse.

At dusk the night before I left Skagafjord, I went out for a walk. The fog was breaking up and the sky held a soft light. The horses were in the cut hayfield, where Gaeska had shown me her flying pace. I snuck in under the fence.

Hallgerdur, the stout woman who had ridden to Snorrastadir with four horses and had left behind orders for one to be shot—she had done this one night, a dark night like this one, of fog and rain. She had gone out to *be a horse among horses at night,* she had told me.

Now I was a horsewoman myself. I wanted to see what she saw that night.

The horses were half-hidden by fog. They appeared and vanished, moving slowly among the swirls of mist, grazing in loose bunches strung out along the fence line.

I walked into the field, and they sensed me. Heads lifted. They regrouped. A few snorted, some danced away, others dismissed me and went back to grazing. I looked among the dark horses, but there were too many. I couldn't find Gaeska. I couldn't see a small dark mare with 1K513 on her side.

But Vera, beautiful Vera with the snip and the star, she was the leader. She had not scored well on the computer evaluations, Fjola told me. Elvar and his father said she was a good horse anyway. She was *frekur*: feisty, independent. Her name, *Vera*, meant "truth." She took a step toward me.

Suddenly all the horses were with her, pulled tight into a herd, manes flaring, legs prancing. Vera led them toward me, a collection of beauty, their colors muted in the fog, their breathing loud in the quiet. It was a little unnerving. I backed toward the fence, then remembered it was electric. It ran beside a ditch. I couldn't get under it, so I stood my ground.

Vera pushed her nose at me, bumped at my jacket. She knocked my arm, wanting something. I patted her absentmindedly, looking past her for Gaeska, but all the frontrunners were red. I took a step to pass through them, and suddenly the whole herd jumped. They spun around and sped away down the pasture, racing themselves, their fear, the wind, a thundering stampede, their colors blurring and blending until they were no color at all, and then silence—they must have reached the far end of the field.

The fog closed behind them, and I was left in the dim light alone. Yet not wholly alone: Somewhere, just out of sight, was my horse.

EPILOGUE

GETTING UNDER THE HORSE

"What a beautiful color!" a woman exclaimed as I saddled up Gaeska.

We were at a riding clinic at Anne Elwell's farm in New York. It was September, a few weeks after my horses had been flown to America. They had come months before I'd expected them, only a few days after I myself had returned, and Anne had arranged to board them until I found a place closer to home. This clinic would be our first ride. I chose to take the lessons on Gaeska, not Birkir.

"She's a perfectly lovely mare," Anne said. "Why did you tell me she was ugly?"

I looked from the two women to my horse in amazement.

I had thought Gaeska was small, but when I saw my horses together for the first time, I found she was every bit as tall as "big" Birkir: measured, both were 13.1 hands. She was thin, true, but muscular and athletic-looking in a way he was not. Her color, which in rainy Skagafjord I had thought a dull mottled brown, proved, after a shampoo, to be rich with mahogany highlights, the black points—mane, tail, socks, nose—bright and crisp. I rubbed her nose and remembered the little flaw Elvar had pointed out, the knob of bone below her eyes.

"It's just this," I said to Anne, lying to cover my confusion, "this bump on her nose."

Anne touched it. "That is odd," she agreed. "But I wouldn't call her ugly because of it."

I was anxious about riding her in a ring. Would she be too hot, too fast, as at first I'd found her? Was it only the fog and the flat hay field that had made us compatible on that determining ride? I asked the trainer, a small German woman named Dani Gehmacher, to ride her first. She circled the ring, taking Gaeska through her gaits: walk, tolt, trot, canter— "May I pace her?" Dani shouted.

"Of course," I answered, and Dani released Gaeska into a fast flying pace.

As they tore around the oval track, Dani motionless, her bright blonde hair floating, dark Gaeska stretched out and skimming over the ground, I saw in my mind's eye Baddi on the calendar page, and I knew it was this union that I desired.

"It is important to be part of the horse," Dani explained, as we sat our horses in the ring that afternoon. "It is only possible if the horse says yes and the rider says yes. You must be open, trusting in each other. If you block the information flow, if you tighten and hold on, you won't be able to ride. Everything tight makes the horse nervous. Grabbing the reins, curling, holding on with your legs— these things are not helpful.

"You must get under the horse.

"Close your eyes," she said. "Walk your horse on a loose rein. Imagine that you are the one walking. Then rise up through the horse until only your upper body is through it—like a centaur. Feel how your four legs are going.

"Then think about going faster. Think about something coming from behind and picking you both up and carrying you away. That's how you ride an Icelandic horse."

ACKNOWLEDGMENTS

Many Icelanders contributed to the writing of this book. In particular I would like to thank:

    Haukur Sveinbjörnsson and Ingibjörg Jónsdóttir of Snorrastaðir

    Elvar Einarsson and Fjóla Viktorsdóttir of Sýðra-Skörðugil

    Þórður Grétarsson and his parents, Grétar and Guðný

    Sigrún Ólafsdóttir of Hallkelsstadahlið

    Hjörtur Hinriksson and the family at Helgafell

    Sólveig Gunnarsdóttir, Gunnar Gunnarson, and their family

    Ástfríður Sigurðardóttir

    Guðbjörg Sigurðardóttir

    Anna Gyða Gylfadóttir

    Pétur Baldvínsson

Also essential were the early support of The American-Scandinavian Foundation and the assistance of Hallfreðar Örn Eiríksson of the Stofnun Árna Magnússonar, Reykjavík, and P. M. Mitchell and Patrick J. Stevens of the Fiske Icelandic Collection at Cornell University.

"Hestur" by Emma Hansen used with permission. Translation by Nancy Marie Brown.

"Horse" by Chase Twichell originally appeared in *The Snow Watcher*, published by Ontario Review Press. Reprinted with permission.

BIBLIOGRAPHY

Horses, General and Icelandic

Arnórsson, Kári. *The Icelandic Horse: A Breed Apart*. Reykjavík: Iceland Review, 1997.

Bjarnarson, Gunnar. *Ættbók og Saga: Íslenska hestsins á 20. öld*. Volume II. Reykjavík: no date.

Budiansky, Stephen. *The Nature of Horses*. New York: Free Press, 1997.

Danielsson, D. and E. E. Saemundsen. *Hestar*. Reykjavík: Félagsprentsmiðjan, 1925; reprinted Reykjavík: Létur, 1982.

Davis, R. H. C. *The Medieval Warhorse*. London: Thames and Hudson, 1989.

Einarsson, Jens. "On weak legs with ears pointed outwards." *Eiðfaxi International*, 4:1997.

-----. "Margir leiðir liggja til Rómar." *Eiðfaxi*, January 1999.

Elwell, Anne. "The story of Hrafn 737." *The Icelandic Horse Quarterly*, Spring 1998.

Gissurarson, Ívar, et al. *Hestur í Lífi Þjóðar*. Reykjavík: Max Indermaur, 1986.

Guðlaugsdóttir, Arnheiður. "Hollt að eiga sér draum," *Heima Er Bezt*, July/August 1996.

Hansen, Emma. "Hestur." *Lesbók Morgunblaðsins*, 7 March 1992.

Haraldsdóttir, Ásdis. "A privilege to live so far away." *Eiðfaxi International*, 1:1997.

Haug, Elizabeth. "Dancing your way to toelt." *Viking Saga Ranch Newsletter*, Summer 1996.

Hoeppner, Gabrielle. "The first 30 days." *Horse Illustrated*, March 1994.

Imus, Brenda. *Heavenly Gaits: The Complete Guide to Gaited Riding Horses*. New York: CrossOver Publications, 1996.

Jóhannson, Albert. *Handbók Íslenskra Hestamanna*. Reykjavík: Örn og Örlygur, 1991.

Jónsson, Rafn. "Should I use my mare for breeding?" *Eiðfaxi International*, 2:1996.

Kissane, Michael. "The rider is king for a while." *News from Iceland*, December 1989.

Kumin, Maxine. *In Deep: Country Essays*. Boston: Beacon Press, 1987.

Magnússon, Sigurður. *Fákar: Íslenski hesturinn í blíðu og stríðu*. Reykjavík: Bókaforlagið Saga, 1978.

-----. "The soul in the saddle." *Iceland Review*, 2:1988.

Merrill, Jean. *The Superlative Horse: A Tale of Ancient China*. New York: William R. Scott, 1961.

Morris, Desmond. *Horsewatching*. New York: Crown, 1989.

Ólafsdóttir, Sólveig. "Why do horses tolt?" *Eiðfaxi International*, 3: 1996.

Roberts, Monty. *The Man Who Listens to Horses*. New York: Random House, 1997.

Rostock, Andrea-Katharina, and Walter Feldmann. *Hesturinn og Reiðmennskan*. Reykjavík: Ástund Bókavirkið, 1990.

Schwartz, Christine. *The Icelandic Horse in North America*. British Columbia: self-published, 1987.
-----. *The Joy of Icelandics*. British Columbia: self-published, 1992.
-----. *Icelandic Friends*. British Columbia: self-published, 1995.
-----. *More Joy of Icelandics*. British Columbia: self-published, 1997.
Sigmundsson, Sigurður. "Let's pay more attention to colours!" *Eiðfaxi International*, 2:1997.
Sigþórsdóttir, Jóhanna. *The Icelandic Horse in the Home Country*. Reykjavík: Iceland Review, 1996.
Sigurjónsson, Sigurgeir, Ragnar Tómasson, and Kristín Þórkelsdóttir. *Hestar: Vetur, Sumar, Vor, og Haust*. Reykjavík: YSJA, 1985.
Siino, Betsy Sikoro. "Horse of the gods." *Horse Illustrated*, December 1994.
Sponenberg, D. P., and B. V. Beaver. *Horse Color*. College Station: Texas A&M University, 1983; reprinted Breakthrough, 1996.
Sveinsson, Hjalti Jón. "Where the horse still reigns supreme." *News from Iceland*, October 1988.
-----. "Forty years at the top." *News from Iceland*, March 1994.
-----. "Various moves were made to stop me." *News from Iceland*, April 1994.
Þórkelsson, Friðþjólfur, and Sigurður A. Magnússon. *The Natural Colours of the Iceland Horse*. Reykjavík: Mál og Menning, 1997.
Twichell, Chase. "Horse." In *The Snow Watcher*. Princeton: Ontario Review Press, 1998.
Xenophon. "On Horsemanship." In *Xenophon's Minor Works*, edited by J. S. Watson. London: Henry G. Bohn, 1957.

Icelandic Literature and Folklore

Anonymous. *Bárðar saga Snæfellsáss*. In *Snæfellinga Sögur*, edited by Guðni Jónsson. Íslendinga Sögur, Volume III. Reykjavík: Íslendingasagnaútgáfan, 1953.
-----. *Bjarnar saga Hítdælakappa*. In *Snæfellinga Sögur*, edited by Guðni Jónsson. Íslendinga Sögur, Volume III. Reykjavík: Íslendingasagnaútgáfan, 1953.
-----. *Book of Settlements (Landnámabók)*. Translated by Hermann Pálsson and Paul Edwards. Manitoba: University of Manitoba Press, 1972.
-----. *Egil's Saga*. Translated by Hermann Pálsson and Paul Edwards. New York and London: Penguin Books, 1976.
-----. *Eirik's Saga*. In *The Vinland Sagas*, translated by Magnús Magnússon and Hermann Pálsson. London: Penguin Books, 1965.
-----. *Eyrbyggja Saga*. Translated by Hermann Pálsson and Paul Edwards. Toronto: University of Toronto Press, 1973.
-----. *Grettir's Saga*. Translated by Denton Fox and Hermann Pálsson. Toronto: University of Toronto Press, 1974.
-----. *Heidarviga Saga*. Translated by W. Bryant Bachman, Jr., and Guðmundur Erlingsson. Lanham, Md.: University Press of America, 1995.
-----. *Hrafnkel's Saga*. Translated by Hermann Pálsson. New York and London: Penguin Books, 1980.

-----. *Njal's Saga*. Translated by Magnús Magnússon and Hermann Pálsson. New York and London: Penguin Books, 1960.
-----. *The Saga of the Volsungs*. Translated by Jesse L. Byock. Berkeley: University of California Press, 1990.
-----. *Viglundur Saga*. In *Snæfellinga Sögur*, edited by Guðni Jónsson. Íslendinga Sögur, Volume III. Reykjavík: Íslendingasagnaútgáfan, 1953.
-----. "The Völsi Story." In *Forty Old Icelandic Tales*, translated by W. Bryant Bachmann, Jr. Lanham, Md.: University Press of America, 1992.
Bergsson, Guðberger. *Svanurinn*. Reykjavík: Forlagið, 1991.
Booss, Claire, ed. *Scandinavian Folk and Fairy Tales*. New York: Avenel, 1984.
Boucher, Alan. *Ghosts, Witchcraft, and the Other World: Icelandic Folktales I*. Reykjavík: Iceland Review, 1977.
-----. *Elves, Trolls, and Elemental Beings: Icelandic Folktales II*. Reykjavík: Iceland Review, 1977.
Byock, Jesse L. *Medieval Iceland: Society, Sagas, and Power*. Los Angeles: University of California Press, 1988.
Cleasby, Richard, and Guðbrandur Vigfússon with William Craigie. *An Icelandic-English Dictionary*. Oxford: Clarendon Press, 1874; reprinted 1969.
Davíðsson, Ólafur. *Íslenzkar Þjóðsögur*. Reykjavík: Ísafoldarprentsmiðja, 1895.
Frank, Roberta. *Old Norse Court Poetry*. Ithaca: Cornell University Press, 1978.
Gordon, E. V. *An Introduction to Old Norse*. Oxford: Oxford University Press, 1927; reprinted 1981.
Hallberg, Peter. *The Icelandic Saga*. Lincoln: University of Nebraska Press, 1962.
Hamsun, Knut. *Growth of the Soil*. Translated by W. Worster. New York: Knopf, 1921; reprinted 1980.
Jóhannessen, Matthías. "A brightly burning light." *Iceland Review*, 1: 1987.
Johnson, Gillian. "Looking for the hidden folk." *The Iceland Reporter*, January 1996.
Larson, Laurence M. *The Earliest Norwegian Laws*. New York: Columbia University Press, 1935.
Laxness, Halldór. *The Atom Station*. Translated by Magnús Magnússon. London: Methuan and Co., 1961.
-----. *Independent People*. Translated by J. A. Thompson. New York: Knopf, 1946.
Miller, William Ian. *Bloodtaking and Peacemaking: Feud, Law, and Society in Saga Iceland*. Chicago: University of Chicago Press, 1990.
Munch, Peter Andreas. *Norse Mythology: Legends of Gods and Heroes*. London: Oxford University Press, 1926.
Samsonarson, Jón. "The Icelandic horse-epigram." In *Sagnaskemmtun: Studies in Honour of Hermann Pálsson*. Köln: Hermann Böhlaus, 1986.
Simpson, Jacqueline. *Icelandic Folktales and Legends*. Berkeley: University of California Press, 1972.
Stefánsson, Vilhjálmur. "Icelandic beast and bird lore." *Journal of American Folklore*, 19:1906.
Sturluson, Snorri. *Edda*. Translated by Anthony Faulkes. London: Everyman, 1987; reprinted 1995.

-----. *The Prose Edda*. Translated by Jean I. Young. Cambridge: Bowes & Bowes, 1954; reprinted Berkeley: University of California Press, 1966.
Terry, Patricia, trans. *Poems of the Vikings*. New York: Bobbs Merrill, 1969.
Tolkien, J. R. R. *The Hobbit*. Boston: Houghton Mifflin, 1966.
-----. *The Lord of the Rings*, Volume II. New York: Ballantine Books, 1965.

Histories and Travelers' Tales

Baring-Gould, Sabine S. *Iceland: Its Scenes and Sagas*. London: Smith, Elder, and Son, 1863.
Bisiker, William. *Across Iceland*. London: Edward Arnold, 1902.
Boucher, Alan. *The Iceland Traveller*. Reykjavík: Iceland Review, 1989.
Bruun, Daniel. *Iceland: Routes Over the Highlands*. Copenhagen and Reykjavík: Gyldendal, 1907.
Burton, Richard. *Ultima Thule*. London and Edinburgh: W. P. Nimmo, 1875.
Durrenberger, E. Paul. *Icelandic Essays: Explorations in the Anthropology of Modern Life*. Iowa City and San Francisco: Rudi Publishing, 1995.
Fergus, Charles. *Summer at Little Lava: A Season on the Edge of the World*. New York: Farrar, Straus and Giroux, 1997.
Henderson, Ebenezer. *Iceland*. Edinburgh: Oliphant, Waugh, and Innes, 1818.
Jack, Robert. *Arctic Living*. Toronto: Ryerson Press, 1955.
Jónsson, Guðlaugur. *Árbók 1970: Hnappadalssýsla*. Reykjavík: Ferðafélag Islands, 1970.
Kárason, Þórdur, Kristján Guðbjartsson, and Leifur Kr. Jóhannesson. *Byggðir Snæfellsness*. Reykjavík: 1977.
Lock, Warnford. *The Home of the Eddas*. London: S. Low, Marston, Searle, and Rivington, 1879.
McKean, D. B. *A Boy's Visit to Iceland*. Boston: D. Estes, 1921.
Metcalfe, Frederick. *An Oxonian in Iceland*. London: Longman, Green, Longman, and Roberts, 1861.
Oswald, Elizabeth Jane. *By Fell and Fjord*. Edinburgh and London: W. Blackwood, 1882.
Pfeiffer, Ida. *A Journey to Iceland, and Travels in Sweden and Norway*. Translated by Charlotte Fenimore Cooper. New York: G. P. Putnam, 1852.
Russell, Waterman. *Iceland: Horseback Tours in Saga Land*. Boston: R. G. Badger, 1914.
Sveinbjörnsson, Haukur, and Bjarni Alexandersson. "Löngufjörur." In *Áfangar: Ferðabók hestamanna*, Volume II. Reykjavík: 1986.
Þórdarson, Þórbergur. "Hjá Vondu Fólki." In *Ævisaga Árna Prófasts Þórarinssonar* II. Reykjavík: Mál og Menning, 1977.
Waller, S. E. *Six Weeks in the Saddle: A Painter's Journey in Iceland*. London: Macmillan and Co., 1874.

ABOUT THE AUTHOR

Nancy Marie Brown is the author of *Song of the Vikings: Snorri and the Making of Norse Myths* (Palgrave MacMillan 2012), *The Abacus and the Cross: The Story of the Pope Who Brought the Light of Science to the Dark Ages* (Basic Books 2010), *The Far Traveler: Voyages of a Viking Woman* (Harcourt 2007), and *Mendel in the Kitchen: A Scientist's View of Genetically Modified Food*, coauthored with Nina V. Fedoroff (Joseph Henry Press 2004). *A Good Horse Has No Color*, originally published by Stackpole Books in 2001, was her first book. From 1981 to 2003 she was a writer and editor for Pennsylvania State University. She now lives on a farm in northeastern Vermont with her husband, the writer Charles Fergus, their four Icelandic horses, and their Icelandic sheepdog. Visit her online at http://nancymariebrown.com

Made in the USA
Middletown, DE
22 October 2023